Praise for *Flagging Anxiety*

'I have seen at first-hand how Dr Barry's approach to the treatment of all kinds of anxiety really works. His book holds the key to easing the mental torture of those who have endured a lifelong struggle with the symptoms of acute and chronic anxiety. A unique book by a unique doctor.'
     –Dr Muiris Houston, *Irish Times* columnist and health analyst

'*Flagging Anxiety & Panic* is an engaging, accessible and very human approach to understanding and tackling different forms of anxiety . . . Perhaps the most exciting part of the book is the case studies, which give real-life examples of how anxiety can affect an individual and the way in which a therapist may start to tackle some of these problems . . . I think that everyone can get something from this book – those affected by anxiety, but also mental-health professionals and scientists working in the area.'
     –Prof. Catherine Harmer, cognitive neuroscience, Oxford University

'*Flagging Anxiety & Panic* is not a book for your doctor's shelf – it is a book for YOU. If you've ever experienced anxiety, stress or panic attacks – all of which are on the increase in our more stressful lives – then please, read this book . . . you will learn how you can reshape your mind and your brain so that not only will you understand where your panic, anxiety or OCD come from, but will learn techniques to deal with them forever . . . And if you don't need this book, you may have someone in your life who does – and believe me, you reading it too could be a vital change for your whole family.'
     –Cathy Kelly, author and UNICEF ambassador

'The indefatigable Dr Harry has done it again. For anyone seriously troubled by anxiety related disorders this book will inform, motivate and provide sound guidance toward lasting relief. The work of a master clinician and the envy of many, he writes with real understanding of how patients need to have complex concepts presented in simple human terms. With work and effort, people with problematic anxiety will really benefit by reading and applying his advice.'
     –Dr Justin Brophy, consultant psychiatrist

'Anxiety is a normal reaction. It only becomes a problem when it is severe and persistent. Yet many of us can become crippled by anxiety and terrifying panic attacks. Anxiety has arguably become the most prevalent mental-health problem of our time. In *Flagging Anxiety & Panic*, Dr Harry Barry simply and effectively explains the causes of, and provides solutions for, anxious minds. With his familiar insight, intellect and empathy, Barry teaches us how to "reshape" our minds and brains using cognitive behaviour therapy (CBT) and mindfulness practice. This is a magnificent addition to Barry's Flagging series of books. It is both simple and erudite, intelligent and effective, a must-read for all of us – health professionals, teachers, legislators, parents and all people – who aspire to good mental health.'

–Carol Hunt, *Sunday Independent*

'Many self-help books provide information about symptoms and illnesses but do not reach the final step – finding a solution. Dr Harry Barry's does. Using stories from real people, he explains and embeds within them the tools for managing and controlling abnormal fear, anxiety and panic. *Flagging Anxiety & Panic* will be an excellent resource for those battling these distressing symptoms.'

–Prof. Patricia Casey, psychiatry, University College Dublin

'I found [*Flagging Anxiety & Panic*] to be both inspiring and educational. In this book, Dr Barry explains in detail what causes anxiety and what anxiety actually is. The book gives a clear and detailed understanding of the common causes of anxiety, also everyday stresses that we often ignore and many ways and examples of improving our mental health. I've no doubt that this book will give more confidence and self-belief to many who suffer in silence and will enable them to make really positive changes in their lives. It certainly reinforced my belief that sometimes life can but tough, but more importantly life can be great as well.'

–Alan Quinlan, former Irish rugby international player

'*Flagging Anxiety & Panic* . . . is a practical and comprehensive roadmap to understanding and ultimately overcoming the debilitating emotion of excessive anxiety in all its forms . . . [It] is suitable for a wide-ranging audience, lay and professional alike, who struggle with or struggle to understand anxiety. Dr Barry's warm, wise personal tips and methodical explanations have universal application in a world where many struggle to control their own over-anxious behaviour. The [book] systematically guides the reader through a review of the neuroscientific basis of anxiety, to evidence-based techniques that can reshape the anxious mind and brain, including case studies and clinical dialogues to show how others have successfully mastered all kinds of anxious and phobic behaviours. The language employed in this book is remarkably jargon-free and effortless in its clarity, engaging the reader and broadening the scope of this guide to a less fractious and complicated life. This book will be a source of inspiration as well as a comfort to many who experience the turmoil of excessive anxiety in all its forms, and is to be highly recommended for all who wish to overcome, through the power of knowledge, these strongest of human emotions.'

–Dr Declan Lyons, consultant psychiatrist

'Every day I meet women who have been suffering from anxiety for years, and have no idea why. From my own training before this book, I had some understanding. Now, having read it, I have the whole picture – I get it. Well done Harry, I know this will help so many families out there.'

–Lisa Fitzpatrick, stylist, media guru and author of *Diet SOS*

'For years, mental-health professionals have struggled to marry neuroscience and psychotherapy into a unified theory of understanding mental health. We have progressed some way towards achieving this in depression. Now, at last, Harry has achieved this goal in relation to anxiety and panic. This book has the capacity to help countless sufferers to both understand and manage these conditions.'

–Enda Murphy, CBT psychotherapist and author

'This book is an excellent reference point for any health-care worker or individual who deals with or suffers from anxiety and panic. It digests the subject into bite-size pieces and will have appeal for patients and clinicians, offering practical and optimistic solutions to what can seem a hugely complex issue . . . Anxiety, panic depression and other mental health issues appear to be on the increase in society as a whole . . . This book is a great resource to demystify the subject and offers great insight and hope for recovery.'

–Occupational Health Nurses Association of Ireland

'Reading *Flagging Anxiety & Panic* will empower you with in-depth knowledge of how the brain and body react to anxiety and panic, providing up-to-date research, case descriptions and positive solutions to challenge these disorders. [Dr Barry's] insight into the power of our emotional brain (particularly the amygdala, which he describes as 'the gunslinger of our stress system') and its importance in anxiety and panic heralds an exciting new approach to treating these conditions. This book is exceptionally well written and accessible to all readers.'

–Maria Carmody, NCPII, Irish College of Humanities & Applied Sciences

'*Flagging Anxiety & Panic* gives us the belief and confidence that we are all capable of positive change and presents us with the skills needed to begin recoding our brains and reconfiguring our thinking. Of crucial importance, [it] really succeeds in delivering a unique insight into detailed case studies of doctor-patient relationships, sharing how both can work collaboratively on practical solutions to anxiety, stress and fear. Every practitioner, friend or family member should read these. I hope that in doing so, those suffering from an excessively anxious existence will be met with greater understanding, acceptance and compassion in their quest for a more peaceful mind.'

–Paul Kelly, founder and CEO of Console

'Dr Harry Barry is a GP who truly understands the shame and suffering that accompanies an anxiety disorder. He is also one of the few doctors who sees how inadequate the standard treatment for anxiety is today. In *Flagging Anxiety & Panic,* he presents people with simple but very effective solutions to break free from anxiety and panic.'

–Barry McDonagh, bestselling author of *Panic Away* and *Dare*

FLAGGING ANXIETY AND PANIC

First published in 2016 by
Liberties Press
140 Terenure Road North | Terenure | Dublin 6W
T: +353 (1) 405 5701 | www.libertiespress.com | E: info@libertiespress.com

Trade enquiries to Gill
Hume Avenue | Park West | Dublin 12
T: +353 (1) 500 9534 | F: +353 (1) 500 9595 | E: sales@gillmacmillan.ie

Distributed in the United Kingdom by
Turnaround Publisher Services
Unit 3 | Olympia Trading Estate | Coburg Road | London N22 6TZ
T: +44 (0) 20 8829 3000 | E: orders@turnaround-uk.com

Distributed in the United States by
Casemate-IPM | 1950 Lawrence Road | Havertown, PA 19083
T: +1 (610) 853-9131 | E: casemate@casematepublishers.com

Copyright © Harry Barry, 2016
The authors have asserted their moral rights.

ISBN: 978-1-910742-32-7
2 4 6 8 10 9 7 5 3 1

A CIP record for this title is available from the British Library.

Cover design by Liberties Press
Internal design by Liberties Press

FLAGGING ANXIETY AND PANIC

How to Reshape Your Anxious Mind and Brain

Dr Harry Barry

This book is dedicated to all those who live in the hidden shadowy world of anxiety – may it act as a beacon to lead them into the light.

Contents

Part Three: Reshaping the Anxious Brain

Acknowledgements

I would like to start by thanking Seán O'Keeffe, publisher of Liberties Press, which is going from strength to strength. I would also like to thank his editorial team, and especially Sam Tranum, for his advice and assistance with this project.

I would like to pay a special tribute to the many people who took the time to review or in other ways support and inform this book, in particular my close friend and colleague Dr Muiris Houston of the *Irish Times* – we are so lucky to have a medical correspondent like him in Ireland; my dear friend Cathy Kelly, the bestselling author and UNICEF ambassador, who has been so supportive for so many years; Carol Hunt of the *Sunday Independent*, a wonderful journalist and a tireless advocate for mental health, who has also been so supportive of me over the years; Paul Kelly, CEO of the excellent national suicide-prevention organisation Console, for which I am an ambassador; Maria Carmody of the Irish College of Humanities & Applied Science, for taking the time, following the recent loss of her beloved husband, to review this book; and author, media and style expert Lisa Fitzpatrick, who is always so supportive.

I would like to thank Barry McDonagh, founder of Panic Away, who does such good work helping those with anxiety; my fellow director of the board of Aware, Dr Declan Lyons of St Patrick's Hospital, for taking the time from a very busy schedule to review the book; and all the rest of the board of Aware. Also, special thanks to Dr Justin Brophy, founding member and first president of the Irish College of Psychiatry, who shares my special interest in the world of neuroplasticity. His wise advice and suggestions were particularly helpful. I cannot thank him enough.

A really special thank-you to one of Ireland's rugby greats, Alan Quinlan, for his support, and for taking time out of his busy schedule to review this book. I would also like to say a special thank-you to my THINC Task Force colleague and personal friend Professor Catherine Harmer of Oxford University, for taking the time from her hectic schedule to review this book. She is a leading expert on anxiety and depression, and I valued her comments a great deal. A special thanks to my close friend, colleague, author and brother-in-arms Enda Murphy, one of the foremost CBT proponents in the country, and to his wife Mei, for all their help and friendship through the years. Enda and I both value our national radio slot with the Sean O'Rourke show very highly, and I would like to take this opportunity to thank Sean and his wonderful team for allowing us to highlight key areas of mental health.

I would like to thank my three children: Lara, her husband Hans and my two special grandchildren, Ciaran and Sean; my son Daniel, happily working in University College London in the field of memory research; and my son Joseph, now attached to Harvard University, and his lovely wife Sue, who holds a special place in our hearts – we miss them 'round.

I reserve, as always, my biggest thank-you for my lovely wife Brenda, who is my bedrock and whose love, friendship, assistance with editing, wisdom, support, encouragement and particularly patience have made this book possible. May we continue to grow older and wiser – and in your case more beautiful – together: *Mo ghrá, mo chroí.*

Introduction

Countless people in modern Ireland live in a hidden world of fear and worry, where anxiety, in all its forms, is crippling their capacity to live normal lives. As a GP with a special interest in the use of cognitive behaviour therapy (CBT) in mental health, I have encountered so many whose lives have been paralysed by panic attacks, fear of social interaction, generalised anxiety, phobias, post-traumatic stress disorder (PTSD) and obsessive-compulsive disorder (OCD).

I decided to write this book because of the overwhelming response to a YouTube video I shot for the Panic Away website, with a friend, Barry McDonagh. At last count, it had been viewed by about 200,000 people, and there had been a hugely positive response. I have been contacted by Irish people and people from abroad whose lives have been paralysed by panic attacks. They found the video, 'Doctor Explains How to Stop a Panic Attack', very helpful.

In Ireland, I have been contacted by people who are trapped in their homes because they are afraid they will have a panic attack if they leave. I am increasingly aware of how many people's lives have been paralysed by social anxiety, general anxiety disorder and the other conditions mentioned above. Sufferers often lack the key skills to deal with them.

I dealt with some of these conditions, and the pathways in the brain underlying them, in earlier books in my 'Flagging' series, such as *Flagging the Problem* and *Flagging the Therapy*. But it is clear to me that there is a need in the wider community for a more comprehensive approach to learn the key skills necessary to challenge the hidden world of anxiety.

I am concerned by how inadequately these conditions are managed by clinicians and therapists, and how long it can take somebody in difficulty to access appropriate help. I am sometimes the last port of call for those who are deeply distressed. It is quite common to see somebody who has suffered from panic attacks for five to ten years. I find this quite sad, as, with a few sessions, or just a simple understanding of what panic attacks are, it is possible to banish them for good.

My second reason for writing this book is to explain just what happens in our brains in anxiety, what the brain structures and pathways are doing to create all of the psychological and physical symptoms of this condition.

It is important to examine how we can 'reshape' our anxious brain. The idea that we can reset our anxious brain is amazing, but modern research is proving that we can do just that.

I would like to explore just how powerful the impact of therapies such as CBT and mindfulness can be on our brains, helping us to literally remodel and improve malfunctioning circuits.

The idea that we can use our mind to reset our brain is a mind-boggling one, but that is what I hope we can do.

I hope to lay bare the hidden world of the person struggling with anxiety, and, in doing so, normalise this condition for them. Above all, I hope to share what routinely goes on in the emotional mind of the person in difficulties. We can often best deal with problems in our lives when we truly understand just 'what lies beneath'.

This book is about solutions. Many with panic attacks and other forms of anxiety can only see the problem, not the solution. And as Enda Murphy – my good friend and colleague, with whom I wrote *Flagging the Screenager* – often explains, 'The more we look at a problem, the bigger the problem gets; the more we look at the solution, the bigger the solution becomes.'

I have seen the results of these approaches. There is not only a strong academic and research basis to this book, but also years of hands-on clinical experience applying the CBT techniques outlined in it.

My colleague Enda Murphy and I use similar techniques. We believe that the deceptively simple solutions contained in this book to managing the various types of anxiety which are easily grasped and incredibly effective. They are based on classic CBT principles, with a particular emphasis on techniques used by the great psychotherapist Albert Ellis.

Combining new insights from neuroscience about what is happening in the brain during anxiety with CBT approaches, we can produce an even more effective, integrated model. This is what I am trying to present here.

This book is for everyone, from sufferers of anxiety to their families and loved ones, from counsellors, therapists, doctors and practice nurses to guidance counsellors, teachers and occupational-health nurses, from the seventeen-year-old suffering from panic attacks who is now self-harming to parents who struggle to know how to help their children and adolescents to deal with this most common of conditions. Anxiety touches almost every family in the country in some form.

It is my hope that readers will end up not only with a much richer understanding of the hidden world of anxiety, but also with practical solutions for challenging it.

If you suffer from anxiety or panic attacks, in whatever form, it is my hope that applying the techniques detailed in this book will change and reshape not only your anxious brain, but also your anxious mind.

To make it easier for you to navigate, I have laid out this book in three parts and six sections:

- Part One: Setting the Stage
- I. Setting the Stage
- Part Two: Reshaping the Anxious Mind
- II. Panic Attacks
- III. General Anxiety Disorder
- IV. Social Anxiety
- V. Phobias, PTSD and OCD
- Part Three: Reshaping the Anxious Brain
- VI. The Anxious Brain and Its Potential for Change

In part one, we set the stage. Part two is all about reshaping the anxious mind. It has been laid out with a special emphasis on clinical interactions between 'Dr Jim', who uses CBT techniques to manage anxiety, and people with the condition. (All the stories in this book are allegorical.) Part three deals with the anxious brain and how it too can be reshaped. It lays out the scientific basis underlying this exciting possibility.

You may understand your own personal story and know your particular condition: panic attacks or social anxiety or whatever it may be. Or you may be struggling to identify the type of anxiety you are suffering from. If you are unsure, it might be wise to check in with your GP or specialist.

While you might be tempted to dip in and read just the chapter that speaks to your personal situation, I encourage you to read this book from start to finish, as the lessons build on each other from chapter to chapter. The final section is a bit technical, designed to enrich your understanding of what anxiety is all about; it is important to explore the role of the brain in both the causation and the management of this condition. However you choose to use this book, I hope it will make your life journey richer.

PART ONE
Setting the Stage

I.
SETTING THE STAGE

1.
What Is Anxiety?

Let us begin by examining the following questions:

- What is anxiety? Is it an emotion or an illness?

- What is the difference between fear and worry?

- Is anxiety physical or psychological?

- What are the main types of anxiety?

- What is our stress system, how does it work and what is its role?

- What parts of our stress system are of particular importance to anxiety?

Is Anxiety an Emotion or an Illness?

We live in an anxious world. All of us can identify with feelings of anxiety. It is astonishing, therefore, when I ask an audience how many of them get anxious, and less than 10 percent will admit to it. This is because there is widespread confusion over whether anxiety is just a normal emotion, or, as many assume, an illness – and therefore, in many people's minds, a weakness.

This confusion is not limited to lay people. There is sometimes conflict between talk therapists and doctors about the nature of anxiety disorders, both in relation to causes and treatments. Therapists regard anxiety as a normal emotion, only intervening, if it is causing the person difficulties in their life. Health professionals regard anxiety disorders as mental-health conditions, or, in some case, illnesses. Who is right? In practice, both are partially correct; it's a question of interpretation/language.

Anxiety is, of course, an emotion innate to the human condition. We all experience emotions of fear and worry both acutely and chronically when faced with specific events such as exams or interviews, in the case of the former, or periods of financial difficulties or unemployment, in the case of the latter. What is important to understand here is that in these situations, anxiety is a normal negative emotion.

However, for a substantial number of people, anxiety develops a life of its own, which can, on occasion, seriously interfere with their normal activities. For this group, it moves from healthy anxiety to unhealthy anxiety.

Anxiety in such cases can become a health condition which may cause the affected person significant difficulties in their life. It is also one that simple, targeted forms of talk therapy can help to alleviate – often quite rapidly. There is little doubt that the bravery of well-known celebrities such as Niall Breslin (Bressie) in opening up to their battles with anxiety with a big 'A' has greatly assisted the public in understanding just how big a negative impact this condition can have on our lives if it is not dealt with early and effectively.

In a brilliant lecture at a conference in Dublin in 2008, Professor Paul Salkovskis, a leading psychological expert in the treatment of anxiety disorders, made the following excellent observations, which I feel are relevant:

- Anxiety is a normal reaction.

- Feelings of anxiety are normal when a person is under threat

- Physical changes are a normal part of this anxiety response.

- Avoidance and escape to safety are normal reactions to anxiety.

- Anxiety only becomes a clinical problem when it is severe and persistent.

- Anxiety disorders are exaggerations of normal emotional reactions, not 'inherited brain diseases'.

This approach to anxiety allows us to combine normal anxiety with more serious, problematic anxiety in a much more nuanced manner.

Of critical importance is the recognition that anxiety is a normal experience, and that anxiety disorders such as panic attacks, social anxiety and generalised anxiety are just exaggerations of the norm.

Prof. Salkovskis's comments are quite useful in noting that anxiety is commonly associated with physical responses, and that avoidance and safety behaviour are normal reactions to it. We will be examining both of these concepts later.

He is also quite clear that anxiety is not due to any inherited brain disease, but due to an exaggeration of normal reactions. It is worth noting that the roots of anxiety, as a condition, can often be traced back to some genetic predispositions, and, in particular, to early life and adolescent experiences.

What Is the Difference Between Fear and Worry?

It is extremely useful to divide the world of anxiety into two parts. The first relates to the world of fear, and the second to the world of worry. Most people with this condition will belong primarily to one or the other, but, as many therapists will recognise, there are often significant elements of both present.

Fear

Fear evolves, from an evolutionary point of view, from our ancestors. Fear relates to a perception that there is some immediate danger present in our environment which presents itself as an extreme threat to our safety.

If, for example, any of us heard sounds of an intruder in the middle of the night, it would usually trigger an immediate feeling of the emotion of fear or even, in some cases, panic, which is simply a more extreme form of this emotion. We could also experience such feelings if attacked by a wild dog. Fear is a sensible emotional response in such situations to a clear environmental danger which has suddenly become manifest. It is also associated with major physical bodily responses.

But what happens when the emotion of fear is acutely triggered by some unknown danger, as in panic attacks, or some seemingly innocent danger, as in phobias, and is still associated with the same physical responses? This is the situation faced by many who do battle with panic attacks, phobias and social anxiety.

Fear is usually a normal evolutionary response to danger. But when triggered irrationally, as in the above situations, it can end up paralysing the person, who does not understand why it is happening, and does not know what to do.

Worry

Worry is where we begin to reflect on and become anxious about possible dangers or unpleasant possibilities that might happen in the future. And this too can be accompanied by associated secondary physical responses.

Worry is evolution allowing human beings to work out possible consequences of different forms of action in the battle for survival, particularly in earlier times. It is this capacity that distinguishes us from animals, as we can anticipate possible outcomes, which give us an evolutionary advantage. But with this advantage comes the potential disadvantage that we may end up worrying and anxious about many situations that in practice will never occur.

For many, worry can take over their lives, and they can end up not enjoying the present as they are constantly living in a potential future scenario.

★

The common denominator between fear and worry is that both emotions are brought about by the perception of danger. In fear and panic, the danger is seen as present; in worry, the danger is seen as something that might happen in the future. In both cases, there are associated physical responses. In fear, these are usually quite pronounced and obvious; in worry, they are lower-key but often more persistent.

As we will discuss later, all of us will naturally experience both fear and worry in our lives. In general, this is healthy and normal. It is only when our experiences of fear or worry become exaggerated that anxiety begins to afflict us, often causing us extreme discomfort and difficulty.

Is Anxiety Physical or Psychological?

Most people regard anxiety as being a psychological condition, and, unfortunately, in some cases, as a psychological flaw or weakness of character. But as many who suffer from anxiety will testify, it is also associated with quite distressing physical symptoms. The classic example is panic attacks – where these physical symptoms are often overwhelming.

So is anxiety physical or psychological in nature? The answer is that the original source of our anxiety does lie in our psyche, or more accurately, in our emotional brain. But, because the latter is also in charge of our internal stress system, anxiety will often lead to a host of secondary physical symptoms. These develop because our stress system is reacting to some perceived danger.

This understanding is critical to coming to terms with anxiety and learning how to deal with it in our lives. Our brain and our body are intimately connected; there is a constant feedback loop of information between the two.

Many sufferers of anxiety do not really understand this loop. They do not realise why and how their physical symptoms happen. They tend to focus only on the psychological aspect of how they feel, and they miss out on the physical dimension. As we will see later, correcting this misunderstanding is essential if we want to learn how to banish panic attacks, for example, from our lives.

What Are the Main Types of Anxiety?

Acute Anxiety

In this form of anxiety, the main emotion is fear or panic, and, by definition, the episode is of short duration. The main types of acute anxiety are:

- Panic attacks
- Phobias

Chronic Anxiety

In this form of anxiety, episodes are more continuous. The main types are:

- General anxiety disorder (GAD)
- Social anxiety
- Post-traumatic stress disorder (PTSD)
- Obsessive-compulsive disorder (OCD)

What Is Our Stress System, How Does It Work and What Is Its Role?

One important message relates to the role that our normal, healthy stress system plays in the creation and maintenance of anxiety in our lives. The two main components of anxiety are usually associated with significant physical symptoms, so we must recognise that these originate in our stress system.

If, for example, you are suffering from panic attacks or phobias and can relate to the classic physical symptoms – heart pounding, difficulty breathing, stomach in knots, shaking, sweating, dry mouth, throat closing in, weakness and dizziness – and you want to know where they come from, read on.

Our Stress System

As human beings evolved, survival was the first priority. Threats were initially mainly physical, so the body developed lightning-fast reflexes to be able to detect and deal with dangers in the environment.

The whole body had to be able to instantly gear up to face such threats, and evolution created our internal stress system to organise such a response. Sometimes the threats would go on for longer periods, so we had to be able to keep this system on high alert during such episodes. We also had to have the ability to switch it off for periods so that we could eat and relax.

In general, a person's stress system dealt well with these situations during our ancestors' time. Firstly, they might encounter a threat to their life or the lives of their family and would have to stand and fight. Secondly, they might encounter situations where they would be fearful for their lives if they hung around, so they would flee. Thirdly, they might be under threat for a longer period, whether looking for food or coping with a sustained attack from enemies.

In all these cases, the stress system had to be able to switch on the appropriate response, the main thrust of which was to keep her and her family alive. The central controller had to be the brain. It had the job of deciding when to activate their responses to such stressors and when to calm down.

Even though we no longer live in such dangerous situations, our stress system is still vital for our day-to-day survival. Its organisation has not changed much from the time of our ancestors. What has changed, however, is the nature of the stressors that human beings are asked to face.

Whilst the dangers facing our ancestors were usually quite obvious and visceral, this is not the situation in the twenty-first century. Many of the challenges facing us now are nebulous. As a result, it is more difficult to decide on the appropriate stress response.

But whenever we encounter any form of stress, either acute or prolonged, the body initiates a cascade of automatic internal physiological responses. Understanding this process is essential for us to really grasp how to 'tame' anxiety in our lives.

The Brain's Response

All of us have a 'logical brain' situated at the front of the brain and technically called the prefrontal cortex, and an 'emotional brain' in the middle of the brain, called the limbic system (see Figure 1). Our lives are controlled by the flow of information between the two.

The coordinator of our stress system is the 'stress box', called the amygdala, which is a key player in our emotional brain (see Figure 2). When we are under attack from an internal or external stressor the amygdala swings into action to activate the body's response. How we choose to respond will sometimes depend on the final outcome of the conversation within the brain between our emotional centre and our logical centre. Once it is decided, the amygdala activates two systems within the body. One will involve an internal nervous-system response, and the other, a hormonal one. Let's look at these in more detail and then take three everyday situations and show how they work in practice.

The Nervous System's Response

The nervous system's response is carried out by a crucial internal system of nerves activated by the brain and involving almost every organ in the body. This is called the autonomic nervous system (ANS).

Every second of the day, the activity of most of the organs in the body – including the heart, lungs, gut and glands – is being monitored and altered by this involuntary internal system. Without it we would perish. Because the ANS is so important in relation to our stress system, it is worth examining it in more detail.

There are two parts to the ANS, with almost diametrically opposed functions. One is to hype up the body, to prepare it for stresses, and the other is to calm it down and give it a breather.

The first is called the sympathetic nervous system (SNS) and is the main player in activating our acute reactions to stress. It causes the heart to beat more quickly, the mouth to go dry, the pupils to dilate and the skin to sweat. It also inhibits digestion. It is all about activating the body in the face of a threat – to fight, freeze or flee.

The second is called the parasympathetic nervous system (PNS), and its job is to calm us down when we are not under stress. It causes the heart to beat more slowly, encourages digestion, constricts the pupils and makes our muscles feel more relaxed – the so called 'rest-and-digest' functions.

The activity of the SNS in response to stress is a straightforward one, with the nerves directly activating all the relevant organs, including the heart and lungs.

As we will see, it also leads to an indirect secondary hormonal response by activating the adrenal stress gland. In everyday life, it is the SNS that also keeps us alert, activated and on the ball. Whilst this function is critically important, we would struggle if our brain and body remained constantly on such high alert.

This is where the PNS comes in. Its task is to help us calm down, eat, digest our meals, take time out to rest, and, in general, just chill out. For example, all of us can relate to how relaxed we feel after sitting down to a nice meal with our family or friends. This is partly to do with our PNS firing. It is helping us to take a breather from the hustle and bustle of life.

This downtime is critically important, as our mental and physical health require a balance between our SNS and our PNS. In anxiety, this balance is often disturbed.

For example, the next time you slavishly check your mobile phone for the latest email or social-media intrusion into your life, pause and reflect. Are you not destroying this healthy balance with this relentless hyping up of your SNS?

At a large gathering recently, I was asked why anxiety was so common in our modern world, particularly amongst adolescents. My answer was simple: I just held up my mobile phone. The PNS cannot get a look in if our lives are controlled by the excessive use of this and other forms of technology.

We will see later how some therapies, such as mindfulness, help us to strengthen the role of the PNS.

The Hormonal Response

The hormonal response is activated within the brain when the stress box sends messengers to the hormone-control box, the hypothalamus/pituitary gland (see Figure 3). This, in turn, sends little hormones into the blood stream, which travel to two glands situated over our kidneys, our adrenal glands. These lie at the heart of our stress response.

The adrenal gland is divided into a central core and an outer shell, called the adrenal medulla and the adrenal cortex (see Figure 4). The former is the source of two of our key acute-stress hormones, called adrenaline and noradrenaline. It is strongly activated by the SNS. The latter, on the other hand, is strongly activated by the hormones sent from the brain, and produces the chronic-stress hormone glucocortisol. These hormones are released into the blood stream and travel around the body to activate all the various organs – the heart, lungs, gut and so on – involved in the stress response.

It is worth examining the difference between the two acute-stress hormones (adrenaline and noradrenaline) and the chronic-stress hormone (glucocortisol), as they play different roles in the stress response.

Adrenaline is released in large amounts when we encounter an acutely stressful situation where we feel mainly fear, and our natural response is to flee. For example, if we are greeted by a drug addict with a knife and decide to run for it. The physical symptoms we experience from an adrenaline rush are a pounding heart, difficulty breathing, a stomach in knots, shaking, sweating, a dry mouth, our throat closing in, weakness and dizziness. We can immediately see the similarity between our acute-stress response to a potential mugger and how we feel during a panic attack. This is no surprise, as in both cases the same adrenaline rush occurs. We will return to this later when we enter the world of panic attacks.

Noradrenaline is released in large amounts when we encounter an acutely stressful situation where our response is to get mad and stay around to fight. For example, if we were confronted by the same addict but chose (unwisely) to try to wrestle the knife from him.

Glucocortisol is released in larger amounts when we encounter a stressful situation that looks as if it is going to last for a longer period. Its main function is to provide the energy required to keep the stress response going over time. In situations of chronic stress, high levels of this hormone cause symptoms like fatigue, poor concentration, feeling wired all the time, sleep difficulties and a greater incidence of cold sores, mouth ulcers and other infections. For those who suffer from general anxiety, these symptoms will sound familiar. It is the production of consistently high levels of this hormone over long periods that lie at the heart of many of the chronic physical symptoms of general anxiety disorder.

An Overview of the Stress System and Its Responses

When we encounter acute stress, the brain, through its logical and emotional centres, will decide on the appropriate response. Both of these activate the amygdala. Then the SNS swings into action.

If the response is to flee, the SNS activates the adrenal gland to produce adrenaline and we prepare to run. The main emotion is fear.

If the main response is to fight, the SNS and the adrenal gland pump out noradrenaline, and the main emotion is anger. Should the stress become chronic, looking as if it will last, the amygdala, through the hormone control box, sends information to the adrenal gland to pour out glucocortisol, which will back up the initial acute responses. Later, we will examine the consequences of over-activation of our stress system, through these hormones and our SNS, in acute and chronic anxiety.

The role of our PNS is to allow the stress system to take a breather and encourage the body to relax and take time to digest its meals and so on. Without it, we would live in such a state of acute stress that we would quickly burn out. As a general principle, the more activated our PNS is in our lives, the calmer and less anxious we feel.

Three Examples of Our Stress System in Action

Mary is coming home late at night. She is close to home when she notices a man hanging around across the road. He has a hood up over his head and seems to be watching her intently. Her emotional brain goes into overdrive and she feels intense fear and an instinctive desire to run the last few yards to her front door. Her amygdala fires her SNS, and it, in turn, encourages the adrenal gland to pour adrenaline into her bloodstream. Her heart rate soars, her breathing becomes shallower, her pupils dilate, she begins to sweat and her stomach clenches. All this prepares her to bolt to her front door, which she does. On entering her house, she meets her brother and her body begins to gradually relax until, eventually, her adrenaline levels come back to normal.

In this situation, her natural stress reaction has probably saved her from some nasty consequences.

Dave is coming home the same night with his girlfriend when they encounter an aggressive youth who threatens them both. As he is unable to withdraw from this situation because of his girlfriend's presence, he ends up activating his acute stress system in a different way to Mary in the previous example. His emotional brain goes into overdrive, just as hers did, but the conclusion is different. His amygdala registers the emotion of anger and it strongly fires the SNS to release noradrenaline both from its own nerves and from the adrenal gland. This puts his senses on high alert. His facial features show rage and aggression, his heart rate rises, his muscles become tense and ready to strike, his vision and hearing become more acute. He is poised to face the threat presented by his assailant. He ends up beating away his attacker, who does a runner. As the night progresses Dave's noradrenaline levels drop and he ends up feeling a bit weak. Whilst many would question his wisdom in taking on such an assailant, his acute-stress response in this situation did help him to overcome a potentially difficult situation.

Peter is called in to see his boss, who explains that the financial situation in the company is very dodgy. He explains that he cannot guarantee that Peter's job will be there by the new year, which is four months away. When he hears the news, his stress system starts to pour out adrenaline due to the shock. His primary emotion is fear. As the days, weeks and months go by his stress system begins to pour out large amounts of glucocortisol. He begins to feel increasingly fatigued, his sleep becomes very fitful, his concentration wanes, his enjoyment of life begins to suffer and he feels constantly on edge – worrying, fretting and tense. He is also constantly anxious. To his wife, he describes the way he feels as 'tired but wired'. He starts to get cold sores and respiratory-tract infections. He drinks more alcohol to cope, but it makes matters worse. He even starts to get a little down in himself. He works day and night to try to make sure his boss is happy with his output. All of these symptoms are indicators of chronic stress and are due to his high glucocortisol levels. The new year arrives and the boss calls him in to say his job is safe. It takes a few days, but his glucocortisol levels wane and his physical and mental health begin to recover as his stress system returns to normal.

In real life, our stress response will vary depending on the situations we encounter. Sometimes our acute response will be more anger-based, with noradrenaline release; sometimes it will be fear-based, with adrenaline release. At other times, it may be more chronic, with glucocortisol release. We may get all three occurring regularly during each day. This is all natural, healthy and normal. It helps us to remain vigilant, protect ourselves against perceived threats and survive longer periods of strain and difficulty.

There are a few important messages about our stress system, which I want to reiterate here, as they are essential to understand when dealing with anxiety conditions:

- It is the function of our stress system to protect us, not to harm us.

- Activation of our stress system is a normal process that happens on a regular basis.

- Fear, panic and catastrophic visualisations are more associated with adrenaline; worry and ruminations are associated with glucocortisol.

- Activation of our stress system produces physical symptoms.

- These physical symptoms are often uncomfortable but not dangerous.

Key Players in Understanding Anxiety

To fully understand the stories which follow in part two, it is necessary to briefly identify the key players in the brain in anxiety, and their functions (see Figure 5).

- The right prefrontal cortex – the 'catastrophiser'. This is the part of the logical brain that creates the catastrophic visualisations so common in anxiety. A good example is when people with airplane phobias visualise what will happen when the plane doors close.

- The left prefrontal cortex – the 'worrier'. This is the part of the logical brain which creates all the worrying possibilities of what might happen in the future. A good example is when a person worries excessively about developing some major illness, with little or no evidence, in conditions such as general anxiety disorder.

- The amygdala – the 'gunslinger' in charge of the stress system. It is the main instigator of the distressing physical symptoms experienced in anxiety and panic. We call it the gunslinger as it is often trigger-happy, firing for little or no reason in these conditions.

- Adrenaline – the 'rocket fuel' that powers such symptoms. It is the main cause of the really distressing acute physical symptoms so prevalent in panic attacks and, to a lesser extent, in other forms of anxiety.

- Glucocortisol – the 'tired-but-wired' hormone. It is the main cause of the chronic, but equally distressing physical symptoms so prevalent in anxiety.

The interactions among these five players lie at the core of anxiety. Changing these dynamics is essential for the successful management of this condition. We continue this conversation in more detail in the final section, where we examine the capacity of the brain to change (neuroplasticity), and tthe effects of various therapies on the brain.

Now let's examine the world of CBT and mindfulness.

2.
Cognitive Behaviour Therapy (CBT) and Mindfulness

When we talk about cognitive behaviour therapy (CBT): 'cognitive' refers to mental processes such as thoughts, ideas, perceptions, memories, beliefs, and the ability to focus attention, reason and problem-solve; 'behaviour' refers to what we do, and, just as importantly, what we avoid; and 'therapy' refers to a particular approach used to deal with a problem or illness.

CBT is based on two simple but profound concepts: first, that our thoughts influence our emotions, which influence behaviour, so what we think affects what we feel and do; and second, that it is not what happens to us in life that matters, but how we choose to interpret it. These form the basis of all therapy disciplines within CBT. The first is self-explanatory, but it's worth exploring the second.

Mary invites six people to dinner but at the last moment cancels the event, due to a family crisis. She sends a text to all six: 'Sorry for short notice. Have to cancel out on party tonight. Talk to you tomorrow.' All six receive the same message, but not everybody interprets it the same way.

Sara takes it as an insult. *How could she do that to me?* she thinks. *Not even a proper phone call, and no attempt to explain why she had to cancel? Typical. She better not expect me at her next party!* Her inference is that Mary has deliberately shunned her. Her emotion was initially hurt and then anger. Her behaviour was to consider punishing Mary by avoiding further contact.

Jane starts to worry. *I hope Mary is all right. It's so out of character,* she thinks. *She seemed exhausted the last time I talked to her. Didn't her mother die of cancer two years ago? Maybe she is in trouble?* She rings a mutual friend to see if her fears are well-founded. Her inference is that something terrible must have happened. Her emotion is anxiety. Her behaviour is to seek reassurance that all is well.

Catherine who, six months earlier, got drunk at a dinner party, and discovered later that she had made a pass at one of her friends' partners, becomes upset. *I know Mary cancelled the party because of me. She must have decided that having me there would upset everybody,* she thinks. Her inference was that nobody wanted to be at the same party as her, because of her previous behaviour. Her emotion was shame. Her behaviour was to spend the rest of the evening replaying, over and over again in her head, the events of the previous party, desperate to change parts of the tape she wasn't happy with.

Anne, already thinking of opting out, is also upset. *I fully understand why Mary cancelled the party, she really didn't want me there, and nobody in their right mind would. I'd just be in the way, wouldn't enjoy it anyway and only spoil their night. Why would they want to talk to me? I am boring and useless. I feel so tired. I think I'll go to bed.* Her inference was to assume that Mary cancelled because she felt Anne would spoil the party, as she was uninteresting and boring. Her emotion was depression. Her behaviour was to plan avoiding future parties and retreat to the safety of her bed.

Louise also gets upset. *After all I have done for Mary and all the times I have had her and John over for meals, the one time she asks me over, she finds some reason to cancel the party. That's the last time they will eat at my table!* Her inference was that Mary did not appreciate all the effort she had put in to being hospitable. Her emotion is anger. Her behaviour is to punish Mary by ceasing to invite her to further events.

Helen is more pragmatic about the text she receives. *Poor Mary,* she thinks. *Imagine having to cancel after all those preparations. She must be embarrassed to have to do so at such short notice. I'm sure it must have been something important for her to cancel. I must ring her tomorrow and check that all is well.* Her interference was that Mary would be upset that after all her hard work she had to cancel, that there must have been a significant reason for the cancellation, and that Mary would explain when she had a chance. Her emotion is concern. Her behaviour is to contact her to offer support

From a humorous point of view, it seems like having another party in the future might be an interesting and difficult task for Mary. In reality, it's unlikely so many extremely negative interpretations would occur over a simple party cancellation. But this example illustrates how our interpretations or analyses of events in our lives powerfully affect our emotional and behavioural responses to them. As we will see later, all of us bring learned thought patterns or beliefs along with us on life's journey, and through this lens make many of the above interpretations, particularly under stress.

CBT stems from the relationship between cognition – how we interpret our environment – and behaviour. This relationship has been known for centuries. The Greek Stoic philosopher Epictetus (55-135 AD) stated that, 'Men are not disturbed by events; they are disturbed by the interpretation which they make of them.'

CBT is the most popular choice for treating depression, anxiety and addiction. The theory behind CBT is that many people with anxiety and depression develop persistent, negative thoughts, which lead to unhealthy negative emotions and destructive behaviour patterns.

In CBT, the psychologist/therapist highlights the negative and dysfunctional thoughts the person experiences when feeling depressed or anxious, and the concomitant negative behaviour patterns. Challenging these erroneous attitudes pushes the person's thoughts and behaviours towards a more logical and positive place. This technique owes much to the pioneering work of two great therapists: Aaron Beck and Albert Ellis.

Recognising Our Thoughts, Emotions and Behaviours: the ABC Model

The person credited with transforming the way in which we linked together thoughts, emotions and behaviours is Albert Ellis, arguably one of the greatest psychotherapists of the last hundred years. It was he who came up with the simple ABC model. Let's start by defining thoughts, emotions and behaviours.

Thoughts

Thoughts are best defined as the words, images, ideas, memories, beliefs and concepts that flow in and out of our conscious mind. Just because a thought comes into our mind, this does not mean that it is true. Thoughts rarely come individually. They usually come in a flow, one quickly following another in a cascade.

Sometimes we can get seemingly random automatic thoughts passing through our mind at lightning speed. Becoming attuned to these thoughts is of great importance. Thoughts can be very visual, sometimes logical, and sometimes emotional. Thoughts influence emotions, which influence behaviours. They play a crucial role in the formation of memories.

There is a major emphasis on positive versus negative thoughts in dealing with harmful stress and mental health in general. Realistic thoughts should perhaps be the goal.

Emotions

Emotions relate to how we feel. They last for relatively short durations: usually minutes or hours. If they last longer, we call them moods. Some experts join emotions and moods together, calling them feelings. I prefer to keep them separate, as it reduces confusion.

The rich tapestry of life is mediated through our emotions, as a world without them would be grey and empty. Positive emotions include joy, happiness, pleasure, love, awe, trust, contentment and peacefulness.

Emotions can be negative but not unhealthy, or negative and unhealthy. Healthy negative emotions include grief and loss, sadness, disappointment, annoyance, frustration, irritation, regret and remorse. Unhealthy negative emotions include anxiety, depression, anger, rage, emotional pain, shame, guilt, jealousy, envy and hurt. Just because emotions are negative and unhealthy does not mean that the person experiencing them is distressed or unwell.

Emotions are often associated with physical symptoms. Fear can be associated with palpitations, a dry mouth and difficulty taking deep breaths. Depression can be associated with fatigue, poor concentration and sleep and appetite problems.

Emotions play a major role in our behaviour. If we are sad, our response might be to cry or to avoid other people. If we are angry, we might become aggressive. If we are jealous, we might constantly check our partner's phone.

Decisions made in life are more influenced by emotions than logic. Modern therapists believe that suppressing our emotions is unwise. They recommend that we accept and embrace them. Because we often emphasise the role of negative emotions in illnesses like depression and anxiety, we can forget how powerful positive emotions like love, hope, joy, compassion, wonder, trust and forgiveness can be in our lives. We hear about the power of positive thinking, but we need to hear more about the power of positive emotions.

Many emotions ascribed to thoughts and events are sourced in unconscious emotional memory banks, developed during our upbringing and in our adult life. They may be triggered by internal or external events.

Emotions and thoughts are intimately interconnected, tightly woven together, creating the beautiful web of our lives. Many assume that our emotions control our thoughts, and, at first glance, this seems to be true. But many seemingly completely emotional responses to situations have their base in the thoughts or beliefs lying dormant in our mind. It's the balance between these two pathways that will often decide our mental health and also decide how we will cope with the major stressors that life will send our way

Behaviour

Behaviour is best defined as what we do. It is usually a response to events occurring in our internal or external environment. It can be influenced by both logic and emotion.

We can change our behaviour even if we struggle to change our thoughts and emotions. This can be powerful in anxiety and depression; we can't think our way into 'right being', but we can act our way into 'right thinking'. Nowhere is this more relevant than in anxiety.

Behaviour can be healthy or unhealthy. Typical examples of unhealthy behaviour are: not exercising, misusing alcohol, self-harming in depression, misusing tranquillisers in anxiety and violence in anger. Avoidant or perfectionist behaviours are also unhealthy.

To avoid experiencing distressing emotions, we commonly use safety behaviours: for example, using tranquillisers or attending the A & E when we have panic attacks. Avoidant behaviour is a similar response: avoiding public areas in phobias, or exercise in depression. Both safety behaviours and avoidant behaviours are used by people in the throes of chronic anxiety.

The Approaches of CBT Founding Fathers Albert Ellis and Aaron Beck

The Ellis Approach

Ellis's genius was to highlight what had been known for thousands of years: 'It is not what happens to us in life that upsets us and causes us so much grief, but rather how we interpret it.' He believed that the latter was based on simple inbuilt belief systems that we develop as human beings mainly due to our experiences when growing up and developing.

A simple way of looking at this is that we pick up 'viral beliefs' along the journey we call life. Like many physical viruses, we may not be fully aware of when and where we picked these up. We can, however, recognise them by how they begin to influence our lives – emotionally and behaviourally.

Ellis also demonstrated that the resulting emotions and physical symptoms have behavioural consequences. It is often the physical symptoms or negative behavioural consequences that we experience as a result of our emotions that encourage us to finally ask for help.

Ellis developed a simple ABC model.

A

'A' stands for 'activating event'. This is an event that sets up a particular chain of thoughts, emotions and behaviours. It can refer to an external event – either present or future – or an internal one, such as a memory, mental image, thought or dream. A useful way of examining the activating event is to divide it into the 'trigger', the actual event that starts the ball rolling, and the 'inference' we assign to that trigger – how we view the event. In many cases, this involves assigning a danger to the triggering event.

B

'B' stands for 'belief', an all-encompassing term which includes: our thoughts; our demands on ourselves, the world and others; our attitudes; and the meaning we attach to internal and external events in our lives. It is through our beliefs that we assess and interpret triggers.

Ellis divided them into rational beliefs and irrational beliefs. Rational beliefs – which lead to healthy negative emotions like anger, concern and sadness – are self-limiting, problem-solving and empowering. They result from a person adopting a non-demanding philosophy. They help us to adapt to life's events. Irrational beliefs – which lead to unhealthy negative emotions like rage, anxiety and depression – are self-defeating, problem-generating and disabling. They inhibit our ability to cope, making matters more difficult.

Ellis's 'rules for living', were called the 'Big MACS', which we will deal with later in the book. I regard them as the lens through which we focus on our internal and external worlds. In practice they often present as demands we make of ourselves – some reasonable, others not.

C

'C' stands for 'consequences', an all-inclusive term which can include emotional and physical experiences, and, in particular the behavioural responses that result from A and B.

Ellis's ABC Model in Action

Joe, who is due to sit his driving test in two days, becomes very stressed and anxious. If we were to do an ABC on his problem, it would look like this:

A   Activating Event: the trigger is his upcoming test; the inference/danger he sees is that he might not pass the test.

B   Belief/Demand: 'I must pass my test. If I don't then I will be a failure.'

C   Consequences: emotionally, he feels anxious; physically, his stomach is in knots, he has a tension headache and he is sighing constantly to relieve the tension; behaviourally, he stops eating, and wonders whether he should find an excuse to cancel the test.

Another simple example of this would be what happens to Sara when she finds out that a work colleague has been let go. Her ABC would look like this:

A   Activating Event: the trigger is that her work colleague has been let go; the inference/danger she sees is that she might be next.

B   Belief/Demand: 'I must be completely certain that I will not be fired. If I am, I just won't be able to cope with being unemployed.'

C   Consequences: emotionally, she is anxious; physically, her stomach is in knots, she has a tension headache and she is sighing constantly to relieve the tension; behaviourally, she stops eating, tries excessively hard to please her boss, is constantly ringing a friend in personnel, looking for reassurance that she is not next in the firing line, begins to look up future job options and is constantly checking her finances, in case she goes bust as a result of losing her job.

In general, we use Ellis's techniques to help us deal with general anxiety, social anxiety, PTSD and depression. This involves challenging irrational beliefs and behaviour. We will be using these techniques later in the book.

The Beck Approach

Beck's major contribution was to highlight how our cognitive interpretation of events in our lives could lead us to be emotionally distressed, and how this could lead to unhelpful and self-perpetuating behaviour patterns. He felt that we all had core beliefs or ways of looking at the world which lay underneath the above interpretations, and also definite rules for living, which arose out of the latter. In general, once he had identified the main emotion and behaviour, Beck would always try first to challenge our interpretations of events, getting us to logically dispute them. Only if this approach proved insufficient would he progress to examining and disputing core beliefs/rules for living.

In general, we use Beck-type approaches when dealing with panic attacks and most phobias. In the next chapter, we will examine how we use this approach to help eliminate panic attacks, in particular.

What Will CBT Mean for You?

Regardless of approach, there are a few ground rules that are important in CBT:

- We must validate and accept our emotions as having meaning for us, no matter how uncomfortable they are.

- We must examine unhealthy behaviour and be prepared to change it if appropriate.

- We have all developed – though our genes, personalities, upbring-ings and life experiences – our own personal thoughts, beliefs and ways of looking at the world. It is through these lenses that we view things that happen to us.

- In some cases, this may involve healthy thoughts or beliefs, which help us.

- In others, the view through our own personal lens can be unhelpful, causing us difficulties.

- Most of us only seek help when the consequences are causing us distress. I may, for example, be a perfectionist in my thoughts and behaviours, but, unless this is leading to emotional or behavioural difficulties, there is no reason for me to change.

- Hard work is involved in changing our thoughts or behaviours. If we are not prepared to get stuck in, success is unlikely.

- If, on the other hand, we are prepared, with help, to make such changes where appropriate, the benefits can be enormous.

For me, one of the smartest techniques to assist our brain to challenge our mind to reshape our brain is to embrace the concept of writing things down. When something is going on in our emotional mind, it is almost always going to win the battle over our logical mind. But when we write it down, then more logical parts of the brain can examine it with cold rationality. This can be a powerful tool, and it is one I favour using, together with CBT techniques, to help reshape people's thinking and behaviour, and thus their brain pathways.

Countless patients find the simple act of putting down on paper what is going on in their emotional mind a game-changer. None of us really grasp just how irrational our thinking and behaviour is until we write it down, and, in the cold light of day, rationally analyse what we have discovered through this process. The left PFC is more associated with language and cold, hard analysis. So we will be particularly recruiting this part of the brain to assist us in analysing – and also in providing potential solutions to – information which has surfaced through this simple act of writing things down. We will see Dr Jim using this potential of our brain as we progress.

CBT and Anxiety

The important players in anxiety are our amygdala, our PFC and the information pathways between them. CBT has the capacity to challenge these.

Whenever we are examining and challenging the emotional world of the amygdala, and the physical symptoms it generates, using behavioural exercises in CBT, we are reshaping negative, fearful memories buried inside this organ. This process is particularly important in panic attacks and phobias. Similarly, when we are challenging the cognitive causes of anxiety emanating from our PFC, such as our irrational beliefs and resulting negative interpretation of events, we are reshaping this part of our brain. This is very much what we do in GAD, PTSD and social anxiety. It will also end up reshaping connections between both structures.

Like all therapies, CBT has drawbacks:

- It requires genuine commitment from both patient and therapist to succeed.

- Some people will simply not click with the approach.

- Some want a quick fix and are not prepared to do the hard work involved.

- Some with significant anxiety conditions such as OCD, severe PTSD or even severe GAD may struggle without concomitant, appropriate drug therapy.

- People with major issues in their past, particularly abuse, may need more in-depth psychotherapy to move on. Depending on the type of anxiety present, drug therapy, counselling or other approaches may be more suitable.

Let's Take It Slowly

As you progress through this book, you may notice that I have set up the CBT sessions exactly as they are carried out in real life. This involves a gradually evolving revelation of just what is going on in the mind of the person with the particular anxiety condition.

I encourage readers to go through these cases slowly, and to try to elicit the key messages. If you do this, you will often notice that you are empathising with the person, sometimes because you may see yourself in them. If this happens, it will really assist you to absorb the messages you need to practise in your own life. If you rush through them, you may miss the heart of the message and end up persistently living in a world of anxiety.

If you are finding the concepts helpful and can put them into practice yourself, then this journey will have been particularly worthwhile. If you are struggling to put them into action, find a trained CBT therapist to assist you.

In this section, we have examined CBT in great detail, as it is going to form the backbone of the management of panic attacks, and, indeed, all the other forms of anxiety dealt with in this book. It is well worth reading through this section several times before progressing further. It will make it much easier to learn how best to deal with anxiety in your life.

Mindfulness

Apart from CBT, in the cases that follow I will regularly mention the importance of mindfulness in the treatment of anxiety. Let's briefly explore what this therapy entails.

This has been shown to be extremely helpful in reshaping our brain pathways in anxiety. Mindfulness is the awareness which develops when we pay attention to events experienced in the present moment within the framework of our mind/body, in a non-judgmental and accepting manner. It is increasingly recognised as a very useful tool for assisting those so distressed by negative emotions that they struggle to come to terms with the negative thoughts lying beneath. Mindfulness:

- Helps us notice what is happening in our experience, especially when engaging in compulsive patterns of thought such as rumination, which can prompt destructive or addictive behaviour.

- Offers a way for people to stay with experiences, including whatever may be unpleasant or difficult, rather than pushing them away.

- Produces a change in perspective on those thoughts or experiences, enabling people to see that their thoughts are just thoughts, not facts or reality, and that they need not be driven by them.

- Allows us choice, as a result of this new perspective. Rather than being driven by compulsive reactions to experiences, mindfulness gives us the mental space to respond differently.

- Helps us move from the world of doing to the world of being.

One wonderful mindfulness exercise of great value in anxiety is the three-minute breathing space. It can be done at any time of the day, particularly when we are under a lot of stress. It involves finding a quiet space to waste three minutes of our valuable time. Here's how it works. Finding a comfortable posture, close your eyes and engage with the following:

- Minute One: focus your mind on inner experiences, such as your thoughts, emotions and physical sensations. Do not try to change or challenge them. Just become aware of them.

- Minute Two: focus on the simple physical sensation of breathing, and particularly on your abdomen rising and falling with each breath; again, do not try to control it. This helps us to centre ourselves. This part is critical for anxiety.

- Minute Three: increase your focus or awareness on your body as a whole, including your posture, facial expression and sensations. Accept it all completely and without judgment.

This is often called a mini-meditation, and if there is one exercise that anybody with anxiety might take from this book, this is perhaps the simplest and most useful. If performed two or three times a day, the benefits are enormous.

Some people like to extend such mindfulness exercises to five minutes or even a twenty-minute body scan. In our busy lives, the simple three-minute exercise is probably much more achievable.

In the final section, I discuss in detail the impact of mindfulness on the brain. Suffice it to say here that it has the potential in anxiety to calm down both the prefrontal cortex and the amygdala. These, as we discussed earlier, are the key players in this condition.

Let's now advance to part two of this book, in which I will show you how it is possible to reshape your anxious mind. I will begin by examining the world of panic attacks.

PART TWO
Reshaping the Anxious Mind

II.
PANIC ATTACKS

3.
Panic Attacks

Panic attacks are one of the most common forms of acute anxiety, yet they are also one of the most misunderstood and often poorly managed. They cause chaos in the lives of those who regularly experience them. This can continue for long periods unless they receive expert help at an early stage. John's story, told below, is a classic example of how panic attacks can present in everyday life.

John's Story

John is twenty-five and has been working with a tech company for a year. The job is stressful, but he is enjoying the challenge. Alone in his apartment while his girlfriend is out visiting friends, John is watching the evening news when he becomes aware that his heart is pounding. Then he begins to feel short of breath. Fear courses through his body. Thoughts of dying alone from a heart attack flash into his mind. *Maybe this is it!* he thinks.

Suddenly his whole body is shaking and his mouth is dry. He struggles to breathe. His heart is now thumping at an alarming rate, and his stomach is clenched in knots. The sweat begins to pour out of every one of his pores, and he feels weak and slightly dizzy. Every muscle in his body tenses. He is terrified that he will not be able to get medical help in time. He struggles out of the apartment and starts banging on the door of the neighbouring apartment. His neighbours see him distressed and gasping for air, and immediately call an ambulance.

John is convinced that his time is up, and that he will not make it to the hospital alive. The ambulance crew administer some oxygen to him and strap ECG leads and a blood-pressure cuff onto him. They reassure him that he is not having a heart attack, but bring him to the A & E for further investigations. John continues to experience the same physical symptoms. It is only on reaching the safety of the hospital that he finally accepts that he is going to survive.

John undergoes extensive tests and is astonished when the on-duty doctor explains that his tests were normal and that he has nothing to fear medically. John's girlfriend arrives. By now, his symptoms have settled down. He begins to feel confused and embarrassed. He wonders whether he imagined the symptoms. The doctor suggests that they may have been due to a panic attack, but doesn't explain what this means or how to deal with it. He asks whether John has been under a lot of stress and whether he is an anxious person.

John has never regarded himself as an anxious person. He feels that he copes well with stress; he is always in total control, both at home and at work. He struggles to accept that what just occurred was simply down to anxiety. There has to be some more logical explanation for what he experienced. He is finally discharged, agreeing to attend his GP if he has further attacks. When he gets home, he feels quite sheepish about what happened, but also uneasy that it might recur. The following day, he goes to work as usual. Over the following six weeks, things remain settled, and he gradually forgets what happened.

Then, out of nowhere, it all begins again.

This time he is on his own in his office at work, preparing for an important presentation, when the thumping in his chest begins. *Oh no*, he thinks. *It can't be happening again.* Despite his every effort to suppress the symptoms, within minutes he has an exact recurrence of the same terrifying physical scenario as before.

Once again, his overwhelming fear is that he is going to die from a heart attack. This fear is compounded by the embarrassing thought that his work colleagues might see him in this condition. But as his symptoms worsen, he is forced to seek help from his co-workers anyway. They panic when they see how distressed his is. Once again, the ambulance comes to whisk him away to A & E.

This time he is certain the tests will be positive, revealing a serious underlying heart condition and confirming that he is going to die. He sees a different consultant this time, but once again the results come back clear. He is getting angry with both the hospital and himself. Surely there must be some explanation for these terrifying episodes.

The consultant once again mentions stress and panic attacks. But these terms mean nothing to John. He is not a person who suffers from stress, and there is nothing in his life to be anxious about. Once again, he leaves the hospital confused and apprehensive.

Over the following months, John experiences four similar episodes. Two occur at home, one in the local shopping centre and one when he is at a party with his girlfriend. All of them appear suddenly, without any warning, and for no obvious reason. After one final visit to A & E, he finally attends his GP.

The GP explains that John is suffering from panic attacks, and gives him a trial of some tranquillisers, in case it happens again. But this does not prevent John from worrying away, in anticipation of another attack. He particularly dreads them happening either at work or in a public place. No matter how often he is reassured, he is unable to shake the belief that he is going to die during one of these episodes.

Over the months that follow, John continues to have these panic episodes. Finding tranquillisers of little assistance, and concerned about the risk of addiction, he returns to his GP, who now decides to put him on a trial of an antidepressant, to help to reduce his anxiety. John starts to take these, but initially feels even more anxious and stops.

He is now becoming increasingly despairing of ever being able to live a normal life again. He becomes more and more anxious about going out socially, and this starts to lead to rows with his girlfriend. Finally, he returns to his GP, requesting a referral to a specialist. His doctor recommends Dr Jim, a colleague who specialises in CBT techniques to deal with panic episodes. Later, we will visit with John again.

What Is a Panic Attack?

A panic attack is when a person develops a sudden bout of acute anxiety with some or all of the following physical symptoms:

- Profuse sweating

- Palpitations (fast heartbeat)

- Dry mouth, stomach in knots

- Weakness, feeling faint

- Headache, muscle tension

- Chest pain

- Hyperventilation (rapid, shallow breathing)

- Trembling or shaking

- Fear of losing control or going mad

- Dizziness

- Sensations of choking

- A feeling they are going to die

Panic attacks usually occur in bursts, are unexpected and have, at first glance, no obvious cause. They are frightening in nature, and more common in women than men. They may be singular events but, in most cases, are recurrent in nature. When we get repeated episodes, we call it panic disorder. Panic attacks can also be brought on by alcohol/substances, and are often associated with other mental-health problems, such as general anxiety disorder, which we will be discussing later, and depression.

Historically, there is evidence of recognition of the nature of panic attacks by ancient Greeks as far back as the sixth century BC. Around 8 to 10 percent of the population will experience occasional panic attacks, but only 5 percent will develop panic disorder. In general, when people are anxious about panic attacks, it is panic disorder they are referring to.

What Is Panic Disorder?

Panic disorder affects an estimated 150,000 people in Ireland. It refers to a condition where a person:

- Is suffering from recurrent panic attacks.

- Is spending a lot of time worrying about their recurrence.

- Can identify a first panic attack from which subsequent panic attacks emanated.

It is quite clear that John fulfils these criteria. He has had repeated panic attacks and worries about when the next one will arrive, which are things most people with panic disorder will easily relate to.

Why do we get panic disorder at all? Research by psychologist David Barlow, an internationally recognised expert on the subject, suggests that apart from genetic predisposition, there are two psychological vulnerabilities at work.

The first is a generalised vulnerability to anxiety, created during childhood. The second is a specific psychological vulnerability, where we learn as children that some situations are dangerous – even if they are not.

Panic disorder develops when a person with these vulnerabilities experiences major stress and has a first panic attack. The latter activates the pre-existing vulnerabilities, making them more sensitive to internal and external cues associated with the episode.

Why Is Panic Disorder Such a Problem?

This condition is of major concern in the lives of many, often to the level of severe emotional distress. Why does it cause so many difficulties? The following reasons contribute to this situation:

- A person having a panic attack generally fails to understand that they are simply having a bout of acute anxiety.

- The person assumes that the physical symptoms they are experiencing are precursors to some serious potentially life-threatening illness, such as a heart attack or a stroke.

- Many with panic attacks cannot understand why there is no obvious trigger.

- The pattern of attacks may continue for a long time, until the person is finally convinced by somebody, that the symptoms are simply due to panic attacks.

- Even when they do come to believe this, they remain constantly anxious that the panic attacks will recur.

- People may feel that they are either going mad, or going to lose control and go berserk, if the symptoms keep happening.

- Many head down alternative or complimentary routes. Often they find that these are helpful – particularly yoga or mindfulness – but do not deal with the problem.

- Others end up using tranquillisers or antidepressants to try to deal with their panic disorder, but still find that they are having attacks.

- Others may use complicated breathing exercises to slow down their breathing, to assist with their panic attacks, but often find they just become more agitated.

- Many end up going around in vicious circles where, the more they try to get rid of their physical symptoms, the more panicky they become. Dr Google presents many medical reasons to explain their symptoms.

- The emotion of shame may be present – the belief that if others knew they suffered from panic attacks, they would be judged as weak. This is particularly of note in adolescents and in the workplace. Some teenagers self-harm as a result.

- There is a real lack of understanding amongst professionals as well as lay people as to just what panic attacks are, and how best to deal with them.

- There is also a lack of knowledge amongst many counsellors and therapists as to how best to deal with panic disorder. This often can be partially explained by their lack of CBT skills. Some patients end up being asked about their past, upbringing, family life, work pressures and so on. Unfortunately, although it is generally useful to know this information, it is often of little assistance in the throes of panic episodes.

Is a Holistic Approach to Panic Attacks Useful?

A holistic approach has the merit of putting together a package of useful measures to deal with the condition. What might this entail?

Lifestyle

Diet, exercise, relaxation exercises, meditation, breathing exercises, mindfulness, yoga, omega-3 oils, moderation in alcohol: these are more useful as general anxiety- or stress-reducing measures, rather than specifically anti-panic measures.

Drug Therapies

The use of tranquillisers has been a first-line approach in the past, but has fallen very much into disfavour, due to problems with addiction and sedation. They may be helpful in acute situations, but taking them can quickly develop into a form of safety behaviour. Also, tranquillisers may prevent the amygdala from reshaping its emotional memories, which is the key to long-term treatment.

The other group of drugs used to try to prevent panic disorders is the SSRI group of antidepressants. These drugs are helpful in severe cases. But it is now generally accepted that talk therapies, and particularly CBT, are the better long-term treatment. If depression is also present, drug therapy, as we will see later, has a more definite role.

Talk Therapies

If we review the role of talk therapies in the management of panic disorder, CBT emerges as the therapy of choice. Whilst others may have varying effects on underlying chronic anxiety, if present, they do not have the same short- or long-term benefits in panic disorder.

4.
The Anatomy of a Panic Attack

There is a truism that we must understand the essence of a problem before seeking a solution. This is especially relevant in teaching somebody the CBT skills to manage their panic attacks.

The reason is simple. Most sufferers are mainly anxious and fearful about panic attacks because they lack any real understanding of what is going on in their body, mind and brain during an episode. And this ignorance leads to the problem getting bigger and bigger in their emotional minds until fear and panic are all that they can see.

Developing the necessary understanding is best done by taking an actual case and breaking it down into small, easily understandable components. We are going to do this by returning to the case we examined in the previous chapter, and seeing just what happens when John goes to visit Dr Jim. He will use the ABC system that we discussed a few pages earlier to help John understand the anatomy of his particular panic attack – if you don't remember the details, you may want to review it before you proceed.

John's First Visit to Dr Jim

Dr Jim listens carefully to John's story and then asks, 'Has anyone explained to you just what happens during a panic attack?'

John admits that nobody has. Dr Jim takes out an ABC sheet and explains what the ABC system is all about. John grasps the core concepts and they move on.

'Now,' says Dr Jim, 'let's return to your first panic attack and examine it in minute detail, on paper, using this ABC model. Without really understanding just what happens in your body and mind during a panic attack, it's difficult to eliminate them.'

'Is it really possible to get rid of these?' asks John.

'That's what we hope to achieve,' says Dr Jim.

'But why is it necessary to write the details down?' asks John. 'Surely we can just talk it through.'

Dr Jim disagrees: 'When we try to analyse such situations without writing them down, the emotional brain is too strong, so the logical brain struggles to get involved in the discussion. But when we write the details down, this engages the analytical, problem-solving part of our brain. This allows us to use this part of our brain to seriously examine and even challenge the conclusions reached. So for the rest of this session it will be you that will be filling in the details on our ABC sheet. When we are finished, you will retain it, for perusal later.'

John agrees, so Dr Jim begins.

'Explain to me where you were when the first attack began, and the first thing you noticed,' Dr Jim says.

'I was on my own as my girlfriend was visiting friends,' John recalls. 'I was watching the evening news when I noticed that my heart was suddenly pounding. Is that what you are looking for? I also found it hard to breathe.'

'Now we have located the trigger which started the panic attack,' says Dr Jim.

John is confused. 'But what do you mean by a trigger? Nothing really happened at the time to cause the panic attack. That has puzzled me ever since. Are you now saying that the trigger was simply these sensations in my chest?'

Dr Jim explained that this was, indeed, the case. 'The biggest problem for most people is that they cannot identify the trigger setting off their panic attacks. It is this more than anything else that frightens them most.'

He then asked John: 'When you felt your heart pounding and had difficulty breathing, what were your emotions?'

John was able to answer this question quite easily. 'I just felt panicky.'

'And how did you feel, physically, when experiencing these feelings of panic?' asked Dr Jim.

John listed off the physical feelings that he had experienced at the time: his body shaking, dry mouth, difficulty in breathing, heart thumping at an alarming rate, stomach in knots, sweating, weakness, dizziness and tensed muscles.

'Now we have the beginnings of the skeleton of what happened to you on the night,' explained Dr Jim. 'We know what the trigger was, the emotions this caused and the physical symptoms created by the latter. Let's put these down on our ABC sheet for now. We will return to them later.'

John then wrote down this information on the ABC as follows:

A   Activating Event:
  o   Trigger: heart pounding in chest
  o   Inference/danger:

B   Belief/Demands:

C   Consequences:
  o   Emotions: panic
  o   Physical reactions: heart thumping, difficulty breathing, sweating, muscle tension, stomach in knots, weakness, dizziness, dry mouth and body shaking
  o   Behaviour

'Returning to the initial trigger where your heart was thumping,' Dr Jim continues, 'what danger did you associate with these symptoms at the time?'

'I thought my number was up,' John answers. 'I thought I was going to have a major heart attack and my girlfriend was going to find me dead when she got home.'

'And what about the subsequent attacks?' asks Dr Jim. 'Were there any other dangers that you visualised, such as other people seeing you, or losing control or feeling you were going mad? All of these can be perceived dangers in such situations.'

John decides that it was mainly dying from a heart attack, and, later, other people seeing him during an episode, that were the main dangers. John added this to the ABC.

A   Activating Event:

   o   Trigger: heart pounding in chest

   o   Inference/danger: 'I am going to have a heart attack and die.' 'Other people will see me during an episode.'

B   Belief/Demands:

C   Consequences:

   o   Emotions: panic

   o   Physical reactions: heart thumping, difficulty breathing, sweating, muscle tension, stomach in knots, weakness, dizziness, dry mouth and body shaking

   o   Behaviour

'So what demand were you making in relation to these initial physical symptoms?' asks Dr Jim.

'I just wanted the symptoms to stop,' John replies.

'And what happened when you tried to stop them?' asks Dr Jim.

'It just got worse,' John replies. 'I just became more panicky and fearful. It was just awful. I never experienced such feelings of absolute terror. The more I demanded the symptoms to stop the worse they got.'

Dr Jim asks him to add this information to the ABC sheet.

A   Activating Event:

   o   Trigger: heart pounding in chest

o Inference/danger: 'I am going to have a heart attack and die.' 'Other people will see me during an episode.'

B Belief/Demands: 'These symptoms must go away.'

C Consequences:

o Emotions: panic

o Physical reactions: heart thumping, difficulty breathing, sweating, muscle tension, stomach in knots, weakness, dizziness, dry mouth and body shaking

o Behaviour

'Now,' says Dr Jim, 'one more important question: what did you do or what was your behaviour when the full panic symptoms arrived?'

John reflects back on the night. 'Well, my first action was to seek immediate help from my neighbours before I lost consciousness and died. They contacted the emergency services, and I was transferred by ambulance to the local A & E department. On the way, they checked my blood pressure and cardiograph and told me there was no evidence of a heart attack. They also gave me oxygen in the ambulance, as I was gasping for breath at the time.'

'And what happened after this?' enquired Dr Jim.

'In the hospital, they performed loads of blood tests, further cardiographs and a chest X-ray,' says John. 'Most annoyingly for me personally, all of these tests were reported as normal. Not only that, but apart from reassuring me that I was quite healthy, they just sent me home without medications or even some sensible explanation as to what had caused the problem.'

'And what was your behaviour in subsequent episodes?' asks Dr Jim.

John explains that the same thing happened the second time, 'only this time it happened in the office. I felt so embarrassed at being carted off in an ambulance again. I was really convinced that on this second occasion they would discover evidence I had a serious heart condition, and I could finally get some help to deal with it. But once again I was told I was healthy.'

'And in subsequent episodes, did you attend your own doctor or involve yourself in any other behaviours?' enquires Dr Jim.

John goes on to explain how he attended his GP, who tried tranquillisers, which made him feel groggy. He stopped them himself, he says, as he was worried about getting hooked. He says his doctor also used antidepressants to relieve what he felt was an underlying anxiety condition, 'but this too didn't work, and I stopped these at well. I even tried breathing exercises, as somebody I knew recommended them, but I found that these made me more panicky, so stopped them as well.'

'I note from your GP's letter that you are starting to struggle to go out into public areas,' says Dr Jim. 'Is that true?'

John feels very embarrassed about admitting this, but agrees that it is becoming a problem, not just for himself but for his relationship. 'Jill is not very happy about this, but I feel it's safer to simply avoid these situations, in case they trigger a further episode,' he explains.

Dr Jim says that many of the behaviours that John has outlined are quite common. Their main function is to reduce or calm down the emotion of panic. 'For the present, let's add this final piece of the jigsaw to our ABC sheet.'

A   Activating Event:

    o   Trigger: heart pounding in chest

    o   Inference/danger: 'I am going to have a heart attack and die.' 'Other people will see me during an episode.'

B   Belief/Demands: 'These symptoms must go away.'

C   Consequences:

    o   Emotions: panic

    o   Physical reactions: heart thumping, difficulty breathing, sweating, muscle tension, stomach in knots, weakness, dizziness, dry mouth and body shaking

    o   Behaviour: left apartment to seek immediate help on first attack; sought urgent assistance from emergency services in the form of ambulance, oxygen and transport to hospital; had full hospital screen but discharged home none the wiser; on subsequent occasions sought help from work colleagues, and once again A & E department; later attended GP for further screening and reassurance; had trial of tranquillisers and even antidepressants; tried breathing exercises during the actual attack; finally, began to avoid public spaces to try to reduce chances of a further attack happening.

'We have the full picture put together now John,' says Dr Jim, 'but let's summarise what we have learnt to date. Then we will look at how to deal with the panic attack itself.' He then laid out the key parts of their skeleton:

- The initial trigger was in fact a simple physical feeling of John's heart thumping in his chest.

- John then assigned a danger to this trigger – namely, that he was going to die from a heart attack. Later, he would add the danger that other people would see him during such an attack and think less of him.

- He then began to demand, quite naturally, that the physical symptoms would go away.

- The more he demanded that the symptoms go away, the more panicky he became.

- The panicky feelings were quickly accompanied by a whole raft of physical symptoms: heart thumping, difficulty breathing, sweating, muscle tension, stomach in knots, weakness, dizziness, dry mouth and shaking.

- His behaviour was initially all about looking for safety by seeking help from neighbours or workmates, emergency services, A & E services and finally his GP, having multiple screening tests done, and then later using tranquillisers, antidepressants and even breathing exercises to try to stop the attacks.

- He later started avoiding public places, in case they triggered further attacks.

Learning Points

From John's story, we learn that:

- Contrary to what many who suffer from panic attacks think, there is actually a trigger that starts all panic attacks. Namely, the first physical feelings that they experience. This knowledge is often of great comfort to sufferers, as it answers a question that many of them struggle with: what set it off?

- It is the danger that we attribute to this initial physical symptom that is what really sets a panic attack in motion.

- This danger is usually one of four things. The first is that they will have a heart attack, stop breathing, have a stroke or die. The second is that they will lose control and run amok. The third is that they are going mad. The fourth is that people will see them.

- Most people make the mistake of then demanding that these initial physical symptoms, with their associated dangers, go away. This actually ends up worsening their emotion of panic.

- Panic is associated with a raft of physical symptoms. It is these symptoms which most frighten the person. Later we will explain just how and why they occur.

- Panic is also associated with safety and avoidance behaviours, like the ones outlined by John above. It is often these behaviours that perpetuate the duration and recurring nature of panic attacks.

5.
How to Banish Panic Attacks from Your Life

After meeting with Dr Jim, John had a better understanding of what had happened during his first and subsequent panic attacks. However, he remains unsure about how this will assist him in dealing with them. Dr Jim reassures him that they are now ready to do just that.

The Physical Symptoms

'What caused the distressing physical symptoms you experienced during this first panic attack?' asks Dr Jim.

'I assume that it was the feelings of panic that triggered them,' replies John.

Dr Jim agrees, and then asks, 'But what happened in your body to cause these symptoms?'

John struggled with this question. 'Is it my brain that is behind these physical symptoms?'

'Yes, it is your emotional brain that triggers the emotion of panic and the accompanying physical symptoms,' Dr Jim says.

Dr Jim explains that we have an emotional brain and a logical brain, and asks John which is stronger. John suggests that it is the emotional brain, and Dr Jim agrees.

'Assuming that the emotional brain is behind these physical symptoms,' says Dr Jim, 'we need to understand what it does physiologically in the body.'

Dr Jim explains that the emotional brain is in charge of our stress system, whose job it is to protect us from danger.

'When our emotional brain senses danger in any form, it ends up activating two adrenal stress glands in our abdomen, instructing them to release our fear hormone, adrenaline,' says Dr Jim. 'Let me give you an example of how our stress system works in real life. I am going to relate to you the story of a colleague of mine who met a leopard at three in the morning, in the dark, when coming back through the garden, en route from the hospital in Africa he was working in.'

'Did he survive?' asks John.

Dr Jim explains that it was this colleague's stress system firing that saved his life. Within seconds, the man had frozen. 'His heart started to pound,' says Dr Jim, 'his breathing became shallow and faster, his mouth went dry, his stomach clenched, his muscles all tightened up, he felt weak, and an overwhelming sense of dread and danger enveloped him.'

Dr Jim then asks John: 'So what caused these physical symptoms, and why were they instrumental in saving his life?'

From what he had already learned, John says he assumes it was this man's emotional brain seeing the danger that caused him to release adrenaline. 'But I still can't see how this helped him to survive,' John says.

Dr Jim explains that adrenaline is our do-a-runner hormone, whenever we encounter significant danger. 'Mother Nature, when we experience such a danger, gives us three options. The first is to freeze. The second is to stay and fight; if this happens, our adrenal gland releases our aggression hormone, noradrenaline, which prepares us to do battle. But the third and most important option is to run. In this situation, the adrenal gland releases adrenaline. Its function is to prepare us to flee. So how do you think adrenaline, by making his heart beat faster, helped my colleague escape the leopard?'

John thinks about this. 'I assume it would pump out more blood to his legs so he could run faster,' he says.

'And what about his breathing becoming faster and shallower?' asks Dr Jim.

John is beginning to see where this is all going. 'I assume, once again, it would help him to run faster,' he answers.

Dr Jim goes on to explain that the reason his colleague's mouth went dry and his stomach tied itself up into knots – and indeed, the reason that all the other physical symptoms occurred – was that his colleague's stress system, via a burst of adrenaline, was getting him ready to flee from the leopard.

'So these symptoms are simply due to the body's stress system firing if it senses the person is in danger?' asks John.

'Yes,' says Dr Jim. 'So do you think these physical symptoms are dangerous?'

John is quite definite about this. 'They must be dangerous,' he says. 'Surely they put us at risk of a heart attack from the strain they exert on the heart.'

'So are you suggesting that the function of our stress system is not to protect us but to kill us?' asks Dr Jim.

John is thrown by this possibility. 'That wouldn't make much sense,' he says.

'Well you have already decided that these symptoms can cause a heart attack,' replies Dr Jim. 'If that is the case, then every time the stress system fires, we are at risk of dropping dead.'

After further discussion, John begins to accept that these physical symptoms, caused by our body releasing adrenaline as a result of our stress system sensing danger, were not in fact dangerous themselves. They were just a normal, healthy physical response to potential danger.

Dr Jim explains that any time we attend an interview or exam we might notice similar symptoms, if we are observant. Their job, in such situations, is to make us more alert and switched on – the danger here being that we might otherwise fail the exam or interview. And yet when the interview or exam is over, we don't just drop dead.

'So what happened to my colleague when he got back to his house having escaped the clutches of the leopard?' Dr Jim asks John. 'In particular, what happened to these adrenaline-created physical symptoms?'

'I assume they gradually settled down,' says John.

'And why and how would this happen?' asks Dr Jim.

'Is it because the danger was gone so the stress system calmed down and adrenaline levels returned to normal?' John ventures.

'That is exactly what happened,' replies Dr Jim. 'So now we can see the pattern. The emotional brain sees danger and activates our stress system, which releases adrenaline. This in turn assists the person to flee from the potential danger. When the danger is perceived to be over, the same stress system recalls the excess adrenaline and all returns to normal. How long do you think it took my colleague's adrenaline rush to settle, after he escaped the leopard?'

John guesses that it took more than an hour. Dr Jim explains that, in practice, it usually only takes ten to fifteen minutes to settle down once the danger is perceived to be over.

'During the panic attack,' Dr Jim goes on, 'would you now accept that the physical symptoms you experienced were due to an adrenaline rush?'

When John agrees with this, Dr Jim goes on: 'Were the symptoms you experienced dangerous?'

By now, John is beginning to see the light. 'No,' he replies. 'I now realise they were not dangerous.'

'But were they uncomfortable?' asks Dr Jim.

This time, John replies without hesitation. 'Yes, they were extremely uncomfortable.'

Dr Jim then asks John to write down and remember the crucial maxim: 'The physical symptoms of anxiety/panic are uncomfortable but not dangerous.'

'How long do your panic attacks usually last?' Dr Jim asks.

'They could often last for an hour,' John says.

Dr Jim explains that this is common, and asks him why he thinks the symptoms took so long to settle. John struggles with this.

'It was your safety behaviour that was preventing your body's stress system from returning to normal,' Dr Jim explains.

He then demonstrates how John, through his behaviours, kept the panic attack going: for example, by seeking out assistance from neighbours or work colleagues, going to the A & E, not going into public areas or attempting to stop the panic attack by breathing exercises.

'The body is quite used to perceiving some danger and triggering an adrenaline rush,' Dr Jim says. 'But upon realising there is no obvious danger present, it shuts down this adrenaline rush – often within ten to fifteen minutes.'

When John, through his safety behaviour, continued to imply to the emotional brain that there was still a serious danger present and that the symptoms just had to go away, the emotional brain assumed a danger must be still present and continued to trigger a flow of adrenaline. So the panicky physical symptoms continued on unabated.

'So what should I do instead?' asks John. 'Are you suggesting I should do nothing?'

'That is exactly what I want you to do,' says Dr Jim. 'Suppose you were in the middle of a panic attack and I stuck your shoes to the ground so you couldn't move, what do you think would happen?'

John visualises this scenario in his head and feels slightly panicky even thinking about it. 'I would find that scary,' he replies.

'But what do you think would actually happen?' asks Dr Jim. 'I want you to think about everything we have discussed, and, in particular, about your stress system's release of adrenaline not being dangerous.'

'Well I now understand that nothing serious is going to happen to me. So I have to assume that after a while the physical symptoms would start to subside,' says John.

'How long would this take to happen?' asks Dr Jim.

John guesses that it might take up to half an hour. Dr Jim goes on to explain that, in practice, the symptoms created by the adrenaline rush would actually be gone in around ten minutes if John did absolutely nothing.

John is incredulous. 'If I do nothing, the symptoms will settle that quickly?'

'The difficulty that most people have with panic attacks is that they believe that the physical symptoms are dangerous,' Dr Jim says. 'So they keep trying to make them go away. It is this demand and the safety behaviour such as going to emergency departments, leaving shopping centres, trying to escape into fresh air, doing breathing exercises and so on, that keeps the panic attack going.'

He asks John to visualise going down to the beach and facing the sea. 'Now put up your hand and try to stop the tide coming in,' he says.

John visualises this scene and laughs. 'I would look a little foolish,' he quips.

'But that is what people who are in the middle of a panic attack are attempting to do,' explains Dr Jim, 'because trying to stop an adrenaline rush is like trying to stop the tide. But just as the tide comes in, it will also go back out. And an adrenaline rush in the body will come whether we like it or not, but it will also fade away just as quickly, as long as we don't try to interfere with the process through these safety behaviours.'

John reflected on this. 'But won't enduring these symptoms be an uncomfortable and unpleasant process?' he asks.

'Now you are coming to the nub of how best to eliminate panic attacks,' replies Dr Jim. 'The biggest difficulty with these physical symptoms is that they are really uncomfortable and therefore hard for us to bear. This is the reason that sufferers try so hard to get rid of them. All of us hate discomfort and will avoid it at all costs. What I want you to do from now on, John, is to imagine, when a panic attack strikes and these unpleasant and uncomfortable symptoms arrive, that you are stuck to the floor. Then allow these sensations to sweep over you in a whoosh, and then let them move on. A nice thought is to visualise saying to these sensations, "Come on, let's be having you. Do your worst, and then get lost!" Surrender yourself to these sensations like water flowing over you in a shower. Once you accept them as uncomfortable, but just a nuisance, you immediately start losing your fear of them. Instead of trying to get rid of them, simply embrace them. Allow them to flow over you and disappear like water in the same shower, which rapidly drains away.'

John is still concerned, like all panic attack sufferers are, that he would be overwhelmed by the discomfort. Dr Jim then asks him the key question: 'Is it in your interest, John, to learn how to deal with panic attacks once and for all?

Or would you prefer to experience the lifelong discomfort of living in a permanent state of fear that these attacks will keep recurring, often at the most inopportune times?'

John quickly acknowledges that no matter how difficult it was going to be, it was preferable to banish panic attacks for life.

'In that case,' Dr Jim goes on, 'you have to put these ideas into practice. You see, the more you embrace and challenge the physical sensations, the less the emotional brain is bothered about them, and the more quickly the adrenaline rush and physical symptoms will completely subside.'

'But what if this happens in a public place, like a shopping centre?' asks John.

'You would have two choices,' answers Dr Jim. 'You could simply pop into the restrooms, sit down in a cubicle, and wait for the symptoms to wash over you and disappear. Or simply sit down somewhere like a café or seating area, and do the same.'

Explaining the Role of the Amygdala and the PFC to John

Dr Jim then introduced John to the importance of the amygdala in panic attacks. He explained how it is in charge of his stress system and is a primitive organ whose function is to seek out danger in the environment, and, if it encounters any, to fire instantly. It was the amygdala that had triggered the fight-freeze-or-flight response in the leopard example. This organ is vital for our survival and extremely efficient in this function, but its motto is, 'Act first and leave the thinking to more advanced parts of the brain.' This was why the amygdala is not amenable to talk therapy. It would leave that to the PFC, our more advanced, logical brain.

Dr Jim explains that the amygdala also has a long memory of emotions, such as fear and panic. But it does respond to the flooding-exposure technique outlined above. Once it relearns that there is no real danger associated with the physical symptoms, or, as we will see later, the trigger in panic attacks, its emotional memory banks are reshaped for the future. He also mentions the importance of exercise and mindfulness in assisting this process.

Dr Jim then discusses with John the PFC, its role, and how, during a panic attack, it gets sidelined because the amygdala has temporarily taken over control of the brain and the stress system. This was why we can't talk or think our way out of a panic attack, Dr Jim emphasises. Instead, we have to practise the amygdala-based approaches above.

John finds all this information extremely helpful in grasping what was going on when he had a panic attack – not only in his mind, but also in his brain. He now realises why the flooding-exposure technique was more likely to be effective than many other approaches he had tried. He really likes the idea of resetting his amygdala for the future.

Challenging the Danger

Dr Jim then asks John to return to the 'A' section of the ABC, because he wants to dispute with John the danger that he might die of a heart attack or that people might see him.

  A   Activating Event:
    o   Trigger: heart pounding in chest
    o   Inference/danger: 'I am going to have a heart attack and die.'
       'Other people will see me during an episode.'

Dr Jim starts by asking John what caused the original symptom – his heart pounding – and what the proof was that it was dangerous.

John struggles to explain why his heart should suddenly start pounding.

'Could it be a symptom of just being anxious?' Dr Jim asks.

'Are you saying that if we are anxious or stressed, our emotional mind can simply trigger our stress system to cause this physical symptom?' John asks, putting it all together.

'You are absolutely correct,' Dr Jim says. 'Now let's examine the first danger you expressed. Does a simple physical symptom of anxiety like this actually lead to heart attacks?'

'Probably not, otherwise we would all be at risk every time we became anxious,' John says, based on what he has learned about his stress system.

'What happens in panic attacks,' Dr Jim explains, 'is that we simply become anxious, possibly due to being subconsciously stressed from work or other pressures in life. This triggers our stress system, which leads to our heart going slightly faster or our breathing becoming shallower. We then fall into the trap of assuming this symptom is actually dangerous, and demand that it go away. This leads to the emotions of panic, and the subsequent cascade of physical symptoms so well-known to the sufferer.'

But in practice, the physical symptoms of anxiety – such as the ones John presented with – are never dangerous, Dr Jim explains. 'They do not cause us to suffer heart attacks or strokes, to collapse or to die. They are simply the normal physical symptoms of anxiety – uncomfortable, but not dangerous.'

'Now,' he asks John, 'what is the real chance of people seeing you in the middle of a panic attack?' He explains that, in practice, people do not see the symptoms of anxiety or panic in others, as they are far too engrossed in the most important thing in their lives: themselves.

They both have a good laugh at that, and John finally agrees that this perceived danger was also not real. In fact, he now agrees with Dr Jim that the original presenting trigger, his heart pounding, was not dangerous in any way.

Putting It All Together

Dr Jim summarises John's story so far:

- The initial trigger, heart pounding, was simply a physical symptom of routine anxiety that we all get from time to time.

- The danger John attached to this physical trigger was imagined. We don't get heart attacks or strokes from the physical symptoms of anxiety. Nor do people see the physical symptoms of anxiety.

- The more we demand that such physical symptoms go away, the more our emotional brain will disobey this demand and trigger further panic, with associated physical symptoms.

- These physical symptoms are caused by our stress system assuming we are in danger and then firing and releasing an adrenaline rush.

- Such symptoms are in no way dangerous, although they are very uncomfortable.

- The more we dread and try to push away such physical symptoms, the worse they will get and the longer they may last during an attack.

- The various safety behaviours that we use to try to push away such symptoms – going to the A & E, taking tranquillisers, taking anti-depressants, doing breathing exercises – just extend the duration of the panic attack.

- The key is to accept that the physical symptoms of anxiety are uncomfortable but not dangerous.

- Imagine that you were stuck to the ground, allowing the waves of physical sensations to just wash over you and move on.

- If you do this, the panic symptoms will be gone in ten minutes or less. If you try to stop them, they may last for hours.

- It is very much in your interest to take this approach, even if it is very uncomfortable, because if you do, your fear of panic attacks will disappear for good.

- This flooding-exposure technique is the best way to reshape your amygdala's emotional memory of panic for the future.

The Panic Exercise

Dr Jim finishes by giving John a most unusual exercise, which he calls the panic exercise.

'I want you to go into as many busy areas as you can, such as shopping centres and public areas in the next two weeks. Each time you get there, try to bring on a panic attack,' the doctor says. 'I would also like you to do this when you are on your own in the apartment – again, just bring them on. So I am actually asking you to have as many panic attacks as you can in the next two weeks, and then return to me and we will see how you have got on.'

'Why are you asking me to perform this panic exercise?' John asks, aghast. 'Is this not going to make the next few weeks intolerable?'

'Do you think I would ask you to perform this exercise if I had the slightest concern it would harm you mentally or physically?' Dr Jim asks. 'Why am I asking you to do this exercise?'

John reflects, and then replies: 'Is it that you want me to put what I have learned here into practice, so that the more panic attacks I have during this period and actually deal with, the better I will be able to cope with them in the future?'

'That is certainly one possible positive outcome that could come out of this exercise. But there is something else that I want you to consider. But firstly, will you close your eyes and don't think of a pink duck on top of your head,' Dr Jim says.

Feeling slightly foolish, John does as he is told.

When he opens his eyes again, Dr Jim asks him, 'Now what did you think about?'

John starts to laugh. 'All I could see was a pink duck on top of my head,' he says.

'Welcome to the world of your emotional mind,' explains Dr Jim. 'We all have a logical mind and an emotional mind. The latter is much more powerful, but also very disobedient. So when I asked your emotional mind not to think of a pink duck, it did just the opposite. And that is what happens to people suffering from repeated panic attacks. They keep demanding of their emotional minds that they must not have any further panic attacks. They then become so anxious about this possibility that the emotional brain overrules this demand, and keeps on triggering further episodes. Because you now realise that panic attacks are not dangerous, and know what to do when you get them, the emotional brain and mind are no longer interested. So the more you demand that you must have them, the fewer panic attacks, if any, you will actually get.'

Dr Jim explains to John that he has given this panic exercise to patients on numerous occasions. Amazingly, the vast majority returned complaining that they had been unable to trigger any panic attacks. They were bewildered, but relieved. The small number who had experienced panicky symptoms found that they were now not as severe, and easily dealt with them, as they were much better equipped after all they had learnt.

John is really excited about this whole approach. He feels more in control of his world of panic, with a much better understanding of what panic attacks are and how to deal with them. After all, they just involve 'being anxious about being anxious', as John and Dr Jim had finally agreed.

★

Two weeks later, John is back to see Dr Jim, incredulous that he had no further panic attacks, and, in particular, that no matter how hard he tried, he was unable to trigger one. He still got anxious, but now he understood just what this was, and was no longer concerned about it. He was no longer fearful of a future episode, as he now had the skills to deal with it.

Six months later, he remains panic-attack free. His fear of fears is gone. He has conquered and reshaped his amygdala.

6.
How Others Banished Panic Attacks from Their Lives

Let's meet three other sufferers: Mary, Susan and Simon.

We will then examine the place of panic attacks in other conditions, such as depression and addiction.

Mary's Story

Mary is a thirty-five-year-old busy mother of two small children who also works part-time. In the middle of her weekly shopping with her two boys, she suddenly noticed that her heart was beating faster than normal, and that she felt like she had a tight band around her head.

Her breathing began to get shallower and faster, her stomach went into knots, her muscles became tense, she got a slight headache, her mouth went dry and she began to feel dizzy. She was terrified of collapsing and leaving her small child alone in a busy, crowded supermarket.

As her breathing worsened, she left her shopping and grabbed her child to run out into the open air, hoping that this would make it easier for her to breathe. She rang the emergency services and requested that an ambulance to take her to the hospital.

Eventually, she found herself in A & E with her child, and managed to contact her husband to join her. By then, her symptoms were subsiding. She was informed that her symptoms were due to a simple panic attack, and allowed to go home.

Mary remained anxious for several months that this so-called panic attack would return. She also became anxious about being out and about, or visiting busy areas, like the church or the local supermarket, for fear that one would strike again.

Then, out of nowhere, it struck. This time she was on her own, in the house, with the younger of her two children, when, once again she began to feel short of breath and got a dull headache. She visualised the episode finishing with her having a heart attack or lying paralysed on the ground following a major stroke. She became distressed about who would look after her child. She made a panic-stricken phone call to her husband. By the time he arrived, she was extremely distressed and demanded he bring her back to the hospital.

Following a further battery of tests, she was told she was physically quite healthy. She was administered a tranquilliser and sent home with instructions to visit her doctor to learn how to cope with stress and anxiety. She did so, and was reassured by her GP that what she was having were indeed panic attacks. She was given tranquillisers to take if she had another.

Thus began a five-year ordeal for Mary, as she suffered from irregular, recurrent bouts. She spent as much time worrying about when and where they might occur as about the episodes themselves. She became convinced that she was slowly losing her mind. A therapist explored possible causes in her early life and taught her some breathing exercises.

None of these approaches helped. Indeed, the more she tried to regulate her breathing during the attacks, the more distressed she became. She was increasingly frustrated and ashamed when such episodes occurred in front of her children. On one occasion, following a very severe, prolonged episode, thoughts of doing something to end it all started to come into her mind. But the thought of leaving her two children behind without a mother was sufficient to prevent her from progressing down that dark road.

Finally, she was referred to Dr Jim, who empathised with her long story of distress, and her sense of hopelessness about ever feeling normal again.

'Has anyone explained just what a panic attack is?' Dr Jim asks.

Mary reveals that nobody has ever really done so. Dr Jim takes out an ABC sheet and explains what the ABC system is all about. He asks her to fill in the sheet as they progress.

'So,' says Dr Jim, 'let's return to the first panic attack you experienced and examine it in great detail, on paper, using this ABC model.'

He asks her what the first symptom she noticed was, and learns that it was her heart beating faster, followed by a dull headache, that triggered the episode. He also notes that her emotional response to this trigger was severe panic, followed by a cascade of physical symptoms: her breathing getting increasingly shallow and fast, her stomach going into knots, her muscles becoming tense, a slight headache beginning, her mouth going dry and the feeling coming on that she was going to faint.

Dr Jim then asks her to write down this information on their ABC sheet, which she does.

A   Activating Event:
  o   Trigger: faster heart rate, followed by dull headache
  o   Inference/danger:

B   Belief/Demands:

C   Consequences:
  o   Emotional reactions: panic
  o   Physical reactions: heart rate faster, fast shallow breathing, muscle tension, stomach in knots, headache, dry mouth, weakness and feeling of going to faint

'Let's examine the initial trigger of your heart beating faster. What danger did you associate with these symptoms at the time?' he asks.

Mary replies that her major danger the first time was that she would have a heart attack, or a stroke, and die. And her child would end up abandoned in the supermarket.

'And what about subsequent attacks?' asks Dr Jim. 'Were there any other dangers you visualised, such as other people seeing you, or losing control or feeling you were going mad? All of these can be perceived dangers in such situations.'

Mary replies that with subsequent episodes, apart from her worries about having a stroke and dying, she became convinced she was losing her mind. She adds that she became increasingly fearful that such episodes might occur in front of other people, particularly her small children, which would make her feel ashamed.

Dr Jim asks Mary to add this new information to the ABC:

A   Activating Event:
  o   Trigger: faster heart rate, followed by dull headache
  o   Inference/danger: 'I am going to have a heart attack or stroke and die.' 'Other people, particularly my children, will see me during an episode.' 'I am going to lose my mind and go mad.'

B   Belief/Demands:

C   Consequences:
  o   Emotional reactions: panic
  o   Physical reactions: heart rate faster, fast shallow breathing, muscle tension, stomach in knots, headache, dry mouth, weakness and feeling of going to faint

'So what did you want the physical symptoms to do during that first panic attack?' asks Dr Jim.

'I just wanted them to stop,' Mary says.

They added this to the ABC.

A   Activating Event:

    o   Trigger: faster heart rate, followed by dull headache

    o   Inference/danger: 'I am going to have a heart attack or stroke and die.' 'Other people, particularly my children, will see me during an episode.' 'I am going to lose my mind and go mad.'

B   Belief/Demands: these symptoms must stop

C   Consequences:

    o   Emotional reactions: panic

    o   Physical reactions: heart rate faster, fast shallow breathing, muscle tension, stomach in knots, headache, dry mouth, weakness and feeling of going to faint

'One more important question: what did you do or what was your behaviour when the full panic symptoms arrived?' Dr Jim asks.

Mary notes that she just left her shopping where it was, grabbed her child and ran out into the open air, hoping it might make it easier for her to breathe. She then rang the emergency services for an ambulance.

'And after that?' asks Dr Jim.

'Well, they checked me out and then discharged me without any treatment other than telling me that I had suffered a panic attack,' says Mary.

'And what did you do when these attacks struck again?' asks Dr Jim.

Mary went on to enumerate the various things she had tried, including a further visit to the A & E, taking tranquillisers, counselling and breathing exercises – none of which had made any difference. 'Then I considered suicide as an option,' she admitted, with tears in her eyes. 'I am so ashamed of that' she says, clearly upset that she could have even considered this option. 'I would never have gone through with it though. I couldn't do that to my children.'

Dr Jim empathises, saying that sometimes we can get so distressed emotionally with repeated panic attacks that this option can enter into our minds, but this rarely happens. He also comments that many of the behaviours Mary has outlined are common. Their main function was to calm down her emotion of panic.

'For the present,' Dr Jim says, 'let's add this final piece of the jigsaw to our ABC sheet.'

A   Activating Event:

- o   Trigger: faster heart rate, followed by dull headache

- o   Inference/danger: 'I am going to have a heart attack or stroke and die.' 'Other people, particularly my children, will see me during an episode.' 'I am going to lose my mind and go mad.'

B   Belief/Demands: these symptoms must stop

C   Consequences:

- o   Emotional reactions: panic

- o   Physical reactions: heart rate faster, fast shallow breathing, muscle tension, stomach in knots, headache, dry mouth, weakness and feeling of going to faint

- o   Behaviour: left shopping centre during first attack to seek immediate help; sought urgent assistance from emergency services in the form of an ambulance and transport to hospital A & E; had full hospital screen but was discharged home none the wiser, other than being told she had panic attacks; on subsequent occasion, sought help again from A & E and was given tranquillisers; later attended GP for further reassurance; tried breathing exercises during the actual attack; finally began to consider the possibility of suicide, but rejected this as an option.

They have now put together the anatomy of her first and subsequent panic attacks, so Dr Jim moves on to assist Mary in how best to banish them for good.

'What caused the distressing physical symptoms you experienced during this first panic attack?' he asks.

Mary says it was her feelings of panic that caused them, and Dr Jim asks her what happened in her body that caused them.

'It must be my brain that caused it,' she replies.

Dr Jim agrees that it was her emotional brain that triggered the emotion of panic and the accompanying physical symptoms. He explains the difference between her logical brain and her emotional brain, and that it is her emotional brain that is in charge of her stress system, whose job it was to protect her from danger. He helps her to see that it is the stress system releasing a rush of adrenaline into her bloodstream that ends up creating this burst of intense physical symptoms. He explains what adrenaline is, and, using the leopard example from the previous chapter, helps her to see that it is simply our do-a-runner hormone, and that the symptoms it causes are uncomfortable but not dangerous.

'How long do your panic attacks usually last?' Dr Jim asks.

Mary explains that they could often be there for over an hour.

'Why do you think it took so long for them to settle down?' Dr Jim asks.

When she struggles to answer this, he suggests that it was her safety behaviour preventing her body's stress system from returning everything to normal. They then discuss how Mary, by leaving the shopping centre, going to the A & E, taking tranquillisers and trying to stop the panic attack using breathing exercises, had prolonged the duration of her attacks.

'Suppose that in the middle of a panic attack,' Dr Jim says, 'I stuck your shoes to the ground so you could not move. What do you think would happen?'

Mary visualises this as a terrifying scenario and feels panicky even thinking about it. 'I can't even conceive of how awful that would be,' she replies.

'But what do you think would actually happen?' asks Dr Jim. 'Think about everything we have discussed – and, in particular, about the physical symptoms created by adrenaline as not being dangerous.'

'I suppose that nothing serious would really happen to me, and that after a while the physical symptoms would start to abate,' Mary says.

'And how long do you think it would take for this to happen?' asks Dr Jim.

Mary guesses that it could take from half an hour to an hour.

'In practice,' Dr Jim says, 'the symptoms created by the adrenaline rush would actually be gone in around ten minutes if you did absolutely nothing. The difficulty that most people have with panic attacks is that they believe the physical symptoms are dangerous and keep trying to make them go away. It is this demand, and safety behaviours such as going to emergency departments, leaving shopping centres, trying to get out into fresh air, taking tranquillisers, trying to do breathing exercises and so on, that keeps the panic attack going.'

He asks Mary to visualise going down to the local beach and facing the tide. 'Then put up your hand and try to stop the tide. That is what people in the middle of a panic attack are trying to do. Because trying to stop an adrenaline burst is like trying to stop the tide. Just as the tide comes in and the tide goes out, so too an adrenaline rush will come, whether we like it or not, but it will also fade away just as quickly. The major proviso, of course, is that we don't try to interfere with the process through these safety behaviours.'

He continues: 'What I want you to do from now on, Mary, is to imagine, when a panic attack strikes and these unpleasant and uncomfortable symptoms arrive, that you are stuck to the floor, and these sensations are simply washing over you like the tide and then moving on. Try to visualise that you are saying to the sensations, "Do your worst and then get lost!' Then surrender yourself to the sensations, as if they were cascades of water flowing over you in a shower, which disappear quickly down the drain. Once you can learn do this, you will quickly lose your fear of the physical symptoms. So instead of trying to get rid of them, simply embrace them, allowing them to flow over you – to quickly disappear.'

Dr Jim then introduces Mary to the importance of the amygdala in panic attacks, and how it is a primitive organ whose function is to seek out danger in the environment, and, if it encounters any, to fire instantly. He explains how it is the amygdala that triggers the fight-freeze-or-flight response, and how this organ is vital for our survival. Its motto, 'Act first and leave the thinking to more advanced parts of the brain,' means that the amygdala is not very amenable to talk therapy, Dr Jim explains. However, it does respond to the flooding-exposure technique outlined above, he says.

Once the amygdala relearns that there is no real danger associated with either the trigger or the physical symptoms in panic attacks, its emotional memory banks will be reshaped for the future, Dr Jim says. He also mentions the importance of exercise and mindfulness in assisting this process. He goes on to discuss the PFC, its role, and how, during a panic attack, it gets sidelined by the amygdala, which temporarily takes control of the brain and stress system. This is why, Dr Jim explains to Mary, we can't talk or think our way out of a panic attack. This really helps Mary to understand why she has to face down the physical symptoms.

Dr Jim then asks Mary to return to the 'A' section of the ABC, because he wants to dispute her visualised dangers, starting with the worry that she was going to have a stroke and die. 'What was the cause of the triggering symptom – your heart going faster – and where is your proof that it was dangerous and going to kill you?' he asks.

Mary struggles to answer.

'Could it be just a symptom of being anxious?' Dr Jim asks.

Mary agrees that this might be the case.

'How could a simple symptom of anxiety actually lead to a heart attack or stroke or kill you?' Dr Jim asks.

Mary agrees that this is actually not likely.

'What happens in panic attacks,' Dr Jim explains, 'is simply that we become anxious because, subconsciously, we are stressed from work or other pressures in life. This triggers our stress system, which leads to our heart going slightly faster or our breathing a little shallower. We then fall into the trap of assuming this is actually dangerous, and we demand that these symptoms go away, leading to the emotions of panic and the uncomfortable physical symptoms which ensue.'

He then queried her second major danger: that she was going to go mad. 'How likely do you think this is?' he asks her. 'Do you have many friends or colleagues who have gone mad from panic attacks?'

When Mary thinks about this, she starts to laugh. 'I might be the first!' she jokes. She agrees that this was simply a perceived danger, rather than a genuine possibility.

Dr Jim agrees. Such physical symptoms of anxiety have nothing to do with our mental health, and therefore there was no danger, he says, reassuring her further.

'And,' Dr Jim asks, 'what are the chances of people seeing you in the middle of a panic attack? In practice, people generally do not see symptoms of anxiety or panic in another person, because they are far too engrossed in the most important thing in their lives: themselves.'

As to the potential of Mary's children seeing her during a panic attack, once again this was more of a danger in her mind than a reality, Dr Jim says.

He finishes by giving Mary the panic exercise he gave to John. 'I want you to go into as many busy areas as you can, such as shopping centres, and bring on as many panic attacks as you can in the next two weeks,' he tells her.

When Mary becomes alarmed, he performs the pink-duck exercise to explain to her the power of the emotional mind.

'This is what happens to people suffering from repeated panic attacks,' he explains. 'They keep demanding of their emotional minds that they must not have any further panic attacks, and they become so anxious about this possibility that the emotional brain overrules this demand and keeps on triggering further panic attacks. But when you realise that panic attacks are not dangerous, and know what to do when you get them, the emotional brain and mind become less interested. So the more you demand that you must have them, the fewer panic attacks you will get.'

Mary is quite excited at the possibility of eliminating her fear of recurrent panic attacks. She also reasons that if they do occur, now she will at least know what to do. She agrees to give the panic exercise a try.

★

Two weeks later, Mary returns to see Dr Jim again. She is like a new woman. She did actually have a minor panic attack, but she was much better prepared to deal with it. She found, to her surprise and delight, that she was able to embrace the symptoms and let them wash over her and fade away. She was no longer afraid of them recurring.

Six months later, her panic attacks were a thing of the past. She had reset her own amygdala, and would never allow this unruly organ take over her life again.

Susan's Story

Susan, at the age of seventeen, finally arrives in the office of her school guidance counsellor after suffering three years of emotional distress. She had been repeatedly cutting herself, which was her way of dealing with the mounting emotional distress created by relentless panic attacks. Following a talk with a close friend, she finally plucked up the courage to talk to the school counsellor, Ms Ryan.

Her panic attacks began when she was fourteen. She was in her bedroom when the first symptoms arrived. She was alone, checking her social media, when suddenly she found it difficult to breathe. Aware that she was on her own, she found herself starting to panic. Her heart was pounding, her mouth was dry and it became increasingly difficult to breathe. She felt weak and sweaty and her stomach tied itself into knots. She tried to stand up, but felt weaker, and this panicked her more.

Susan rang her mum, who raced back to find her shaking and crying, certain she was going to die. She brought her daughter straight to the local hospital emergency department, where, after a while, the symptoms slowly receded. The doctor on duty fully checked Susan out and reassured her that everything was OK. She advised Susan to go home and relax, as she seemed a little stressed or anxious.

Susan was mortified; there was nothing wrong with her! And she had made such a fuss, upsetting her mother and wasting the time of the busy doctor. She felt really confused. Had she just imagined all the sensations? She tried to talk to her mother, but her mother was already dismissing the event. From that moment on, Susan began to dread that these horrible feelings would recur.

Sure enough, they began to reappear regularly. But because of her previous experiences with both her mum and the hospital, Susan hid her distress. She was particularly anxious that the attacks would not happen in front of her classmates or friends. *It would be just awful if they saw me like this*, she thought. *What would they think?*

In the beginning, she was anxious that she was going to die, but experience taught her that she was not seriously at risk, physically. Still, she dreaded the thought of completely losing control and 'making a complete fool' of herself in a public place, particularly at school.

She confided in her older brother, but he just reassured her that everything would be fine; it was her hormones, he said. Eventually, her distress came to a head, and, at sixteen, she started to self-harm. It was such a relief when she cut herself, as her body felt so much more 'relaxed' afterwards. Initially, she made small lacerations on her wrists, but when some of her friends noticed the marks, she switched to cutting herself in areas that were harder to notice.

By this stage, she was getting panic episodes once or twice a month. How was she going to get through the Leaving Cert cycle if this continued? she wondered. And what would happen if it occurred during one of her mock exams, or, worse, during the real thing? Her distress levels increased, and so did her self-harming.

What bothered her most was that she could see no obvious reason for the attacks. It was not as if she were anxious or bothered by any particular difficulties at school. She had always been a good student and got on really well with her classmates. So why were they happening?

Ms Ryan empathised with Susan's story and suggested that the most likely cause of her symptoms was panic attacks. She had seen this pattern regularly over the years with other students. The good news for Susan was that they were completely treatable with some professional assistance.

Ms Ryan suggested that Susan open up to her mum, and ask her to arrange an appointment with Dr Jim, who had helped some other students. Susan agreed with Ms Ryan that the cutting was not helping her deal with the problem, and that she would end up with scarring. They decided that Susan would cease this behaviour, and would instead attend Dr Jim for assistance with her panic attacks.

Susan initially attends Dr Jim with her mother, who is mainly concerned about the level of self-harm that has surfaced.

'But why do you think Susan is self-harming?' asks Dr Jim.

Her mother becomes very upset. 'I just don't know,' she says, 'but I find it so distressing that Susan would want to harm herself in this way. I spend every waking moment worrying she will do something more serious. I could never live with myself if that happened.'

Dr Jim turns to Susan and asks her the same question: 'Why were you self-harming?'

Susan explains that cutting herself became the only way she could deal with the constant fear of another panic attack. 'I found them so distressing,' she adds, 'and felt I couldn't talk to my mum because I felt ashamed. I was only wasting her time over something I felt I should be able to deal with myself – but I didn't know how.'

Dr Jim explains to Susan's mother that self-harm, including cutting, was simply a behavioural response to Susan's emotional distress. This distress, he says, was caused by her difficulties in trying to deal with constant panic attacks. 'Remember,' he says, 'that all behaviour, including self-harm, has a purpose, and that is usually to calm some emotion. In this case, it is to get relief from the emotions of fear and anxiety that Susan's panic attacks were engendering in her.'

He then asks Susan, 'Was your intention ever to do something more serious, or was it just to relieve the distress temporarily?'

'It was just to relieve the distress,' she replies. 'In some ways it almost became a habit.'

Dr Jim eventually calms Susan's mother, reassuring her that Susan has no intention of more serious self-harm. Her mother is happy to learn that Susan realises such behaviour is not solving the problem.

Dr Jim is now able to begin the process of helping Susan to deal with her panic attacks. He starts by asking Susan whether anyone has explained to her what a panic attack is. She shakes her head. 'Apart from Ms Ryan, who tried to give me some information,' she says.

Dr Jim takes out an ABC sheet and explains what the ABC system is all about.

'Now,' he says, 'I am going to return to the very first panic attack you had, and we are going to examine it in great detail, on paper, using this ABC model. And we are going to get you to write in the details as we go along. This is so you will have a copy to take with you when you go home.'

He returns to the first panic attack and asks her what the first symptom she noticed was. He learns that it was her difficulty breathing that triggered the episode. He also notes that her emotional response to this trigger was severe panic, followed by a list of physical symptoms, including her heart pounding in her chest, a dry mouth, increasingly difficulty breathing, sweatiness, a stomach in knots, difficulty standing up and sudden weakness.

Dr Jim gets Susan to write this information on the ABC sheet:

A   Activating Event:

- o   Trigger: difficulty breathing

- o   Inference/danger:

B   Belief/Demands:

C   Consequences:

- o   Emotional reactions: panic

- o   Physical reactions: heart pounding in her chest, dry mouth, increasing difficulty breathing, sweating, stomach in knots, difficulty standing up, sudden weakness

'Let's return to when you first felt this difficulty breathing,' Dr Jim says. 'What danger did you associate with this sensation at the time?'

'That I was going to stop breathing and die on my own,' Susan says.

'And what about subsequent attacks?' asks Dr Jim. 'Were there any other dangers that you visualised might happen, such as other people seeing you, or losing control or feeling you were going mad? All of these can be perceived as dangers in such situations.'

Mary replies that with each subsequent episode, she became increasingly afraid that other people in her class or school would see her experiencing a panic attack. She was particularly afraid of losing control and making a complete fool of herself. She is not really sure what would happen in such a situation, but in her mind she sees it as absolutely awful. 'If this happened,' she adds, 'I just don't know how I would handle it.'

They added this new information to Susan's ABC.

A   Activating Event:

- o   Trigger: difficulty breathing

- o   Inference/danger: 'I am going to stop breathing and die.' 'I am going to lose control and something awful will happen.' 'Others, particularly my classmates will see me.'

B   Belief/Demands:

C   Consequences:

- o   Emotional reactions: panic

- o   Physical reactions: heart pounding in her chest, dry mouth, increasing difficulty breathing, sweating, stomach in knots, difficulty standing up, sudden weakness

Once Susan finishes adding to her ABC, they continue talking.

'So,' Dr Jim asks, 'what did you want to happen to this symptom of difficulty breathing, during that first panic attack, if you were so fearful of these dangers?'

'I just wanted these awful symptoms to stop,' she replies.

They add this to the ABC.

A   Activating Event:

- o   Trigger: difficulty breathing

- o   Inference/danger: 'I am going to stop breathing and die.' 'I am going to lose control and something awful will happen.' 'Others, particularly my classmates will see me.'

B   Belief/Demands: these symptoms must stop

C   Consequences:

- o   Emotional reactions: panic

o   Physical reactions: heart pounding in her chest, dry mouth, increasing difficulty breathing, sweating, stomach in knots, difficulty standing up, sudden weakness

'Now,' says Dr Jim, 'just one more question, Susan. What did you do, or what was your behaviour – in the first and subsequent attacks – when the full panic symptoms arrived?'

Susan says that she rang her mum, and then went with her straight to the hospital. She adds that she had a full check-up and was told that there was nothing wrong with her – that she was simply stressed or anxious. She explains that she felt so stupid, that she never again looked for help, and even hid her panic attacks from her family, friends and teachers.

'I did, on one occasion try to ask my brother what to do, but he dismissed me as just being a fusspot, so I didn't ask anyone else,' Susan says. 'I kept trying to make the symptoms go away myself. On a few occasions, I tried to do breathing exercises, as I read somewhere that they were helpful if you were stressed. But this didn't work very well, and I stopped them quite quickly. I would also try to get out into the fresh air as fast as I could, as I felt it would at least help me breathe better. But this didn't work out either. It was only when I started to cut myself that I got any relief from the distress.'

Dr Jim asked Susan to add these behaviours to her ABC.

A   Activating Event:

o   Trigger: difficulty breathing

o   Inference/danger: 'I am going to stop breathing and die.' 'I am going to lose control and something awful will happen.' 'Others, particularly my classmates will see me.'

B   Belief/Demands: these symptoms must stop

C   Consequences:

o   Emotional reactions: panic

o Physical reactions: heart pounding in her chest, dry mouth, increasing difficulty breathing, sweating, stomach in knots, difficulty standing up, sudden weakness

o Behaviour: sought urgent assistance from her mum; went straight away with her to hospital A & E; had full hospital screen, but was discharged none the wiser, other than being told she was just a little anxious and to try to relax; tried to do breathing exercises, but they were unsuccessful; tried to get out into open spaces and fresh air during attack, but this was also unsuccessful; tried to make the symptoms go away herself; did on one occasion seek help from her brother, to no avail; other than this, hid her difficulties from her family, friends and teachers; eventually discovered that self-harm in the form of cutting herself was the only way she could relieve her distress.

Dr Jim starts the process of helping Susan to deal with her panic attacks by explaining the ABC they have put together, and detailing what had happened to her during her first attack. He then explores with her the physical symptoms she experienced during this attack.

'What caused the distressing physical sensations you experienced during this first panic attack?' he asks.

Susan says she assumes, from what she has learnt, that her fear and panic caused it. Dr Jim asks what happened in her body that created these physical sensations, and Susan ventures, 'It must be my brain that causes them.'

Dr Jim explains the difference between her logical brain and her emotional brain, and that it is her emotional brain that is in charge of her stress system. He helps her to see that it was her stress system, whose job it is to protect her, which released an adrenaline rush that created this burst of intense physical symptoms. He discusses with her what adrenaline is, and, using the leopard example from the previous chapter, helps her to see that it is simply our do-a-runner hormone, and that the symptoms it causes are uncomfortable but not dangerous.

'How long do your panic attacks last?' he asks, and Susan replies that they often last up to an hour or more. Dr Jim asks why she thinks they take so long to settle down. When she struggles to answer, he explains that it was her safety behaviour that was preventing her body's stress system from returning everything back to normal. He goes on to explain how Susan – by urgently seeking help from her mum in the first attack, going to the A & E, trying to stop the panic attacks herself, using breathing exercises, and, in particular, hiding everything from her loved ones and friends and self-harming – had helped to make her panic attacks last longer and recur more frequently.

'Suppose,' he says, 'that when you were in the middle of a panic attack, I stuck your shoes to the ground so that you could not move. What do you think would happen?'

Starting to visualise this scenario, Susan feels panicky and starts to tremble a little. 'I can't even begin to explain how awful that would be,' she says.

'But what do you think would actually happen?' asks Dr Jim. 'I want you to think about what we have discussed about the physical symptoms created by your fear hormone, adrenaline, not being dangerous.'

'I suppose that if what you have told me about my stress system being there to protect me is true, then maybe nothing serious would happen to me,' Susan says. 'So I guess that after a while the physical symptoms would start to subside.'

'How long do you think it would take for this to happen?' asks Dr Jim.

Susan figures that it might take half an hour to an hour.

'In practice, the symptoms created by the adrenaline rush would actually be gone in around ten minutes if you did absolutely nothing,' Dr Jim says. 'The difficulty that most people have with panic attacks is that they believe the physical symptoms are dangerous and keep trying to make them go away. It is this demand, and the various safety behaviours we have talked about, that keep the panic attack going.'

Dr Jim asks Susan to visualise going down to the beach and facing the tide. 'Then visualise putting up your hand and trying to stop the tide from coming in,' he says. 'That is what people who are in the middle of a panic attack try to do. Trying to stop this adrenaline burst is like trying to stop the tide. But just as the tide comes in and the tide goes out, so too will an adrenaline rush in the body come and go. It will fade away quickly as long as we don't try to interfere with the process through all of these safety behaviours.'

Dr Jim continues: 'What I want you to do from now on, Susan, is to imagine – when a panic attack strikes and these unpleasant and uncomfortable symptoms arrive – that you are stuck to the floor. Try to visualise that you are saying to the sensations, "Do your worst and then get lost!' And then surrender yourself to the sensations as if they were water flowing over you in a shower. Once you learn do this, you will lose your fear of the physical symptoms. Then, instead of trying to get rid of them, you will be able to simply embrace them, allowing them to flow over you and quickly disappear.'

Susan worried that she might not be able to put up with the extreme distress that these physical sensations might cause.

'How distressing has it been for you, trying to prepare, in fear and trepidation for when the next panic attack will arrive in your life?' Dr Jim asks her.

Susan agrees that it has been a nightmare trying to cope with this fear, which is why she has self-harmed so much.

'Would it be easier to put up with the discomfort of letting these physical sensations wash over you, if it helped you deal with these episodes and banish them from your life?' asks Dr Jim.

Susan agrees that it sounds like the lesser of the two evils, and says that she would, at this stage, be prepared to do anything to get rid of these attacks. She says she will try to put Dr Jim's advice into practice.

Dr Jim then introduces Susan to the importance of the amygdala in panic attacks, explaining to her that it is a primitive organ whose function is to seek out danger in the environment, and, if it finds any, to fire instantly. He explains how it is the amygdala that triggers the fight-freeze-or-flight response, and that this organ is vital for our survival. He tells her that the amygdala's motto, 'Act first and leave the thinking to more advanced parts of the brain,' means that it is not very amenable to talk therapy. But, he says, the amygdala does respond to the flooding-exposure technique he has outlined to her.

Once the amygdala has relearnt that there is no real danger associated with the physical symptoms or the trigger in panic attacks, its emotional memory banks will be reshaped for the future, Dr Jim tells Susan. He also mentions the importance of exercise and mindfulness in assisting this process, and gives her the three-minute breathing exercise to practise.

Dr Jim discusses the role of the PFC, and how, during a panic attack, it gets sidelined while the amygdala temporarily takes control of the brain and stress system. This is why we can't talk or think our way out of a panic attack, he says. This information really helps Susan to understand why she has had so much difficulty over the years She now feels that she has a concrete picture of the 'enemy' in her mind. It makes her even more determined to face down the physical symptoms.

Dr Jim then asks Susan to return to the 'A' section of the ABC, because he wants to challenge the dangers she visualised: that she was going to stop breathing and die, or lose complete control and do something awful, or that others would see her – particularly her classmates. He begins by asking her what was the cause of the triggering symptom, her difficulty breathing. Where was her proof that it was dangerous and was going to kill her?

When Susan struggles with this, Dr Jim asks, 'Could it be a symptom of just being anxious?' Susan thinks about this and says she feels it might be the case. 'How could a simple symptom of anxiety actually lead you to stop breathing or kill you?' Dr Jim asks her. Susan agrees that this was not a real danger.

'What happens in panic attacks,' Dr Jim explains, 'is that we simply become anxious. We may be subconsciously stressed from school or other family or social pressures in life. This triggers our stress system, which leads to our heart going slightly faster or our breathing becoming a little more laboured. We then fall into the trap of assuming that this is actually dangerous and demanding that the symptoms go away, which leads to the emotions of panic and the physical symptoms which follow.'

Dr Jim then queries her second major danger: that she was going to lose control and do something awful like running wild through the school. 'How likely do you think this is?' he asks. 'Do you have many friends who have completely lost control and gone screaming through the school as a result of just being anxious or having a panic attack?'

Susan starts to laugh. 'I would definitely be the first,' she admits, and agrees that this is simply a perceived danger in her head, rather than a real possibility.

Dr Jim reassures her further, explaining that the physical symptoms of anxiety have nothing to do with our mental health, and so there was no real danger.

'Now,' he asks, 'what is the real chance of people seeing you in the middle of a panic attack? People do not see symptoms of anxiety or panic in another person. They are far too engrossed in the most important thing in their lives: themselves.'

Dr Jim finishes by giving her the panic exercise. 'Susan, I want you to try to bring on as many panic attacks as you can in the next two weeks. It doesn't matter where you have them. It can be at home on your own or with others around, or at school – preferably in some central area, where, in your mind, other classmates might see you,' he says. 'Why do you think I am asking you to do this?'

Susan is both at a loss to answer this question and somewhat alarmed at the exercise. 'Is it because you want me to try to learn how to deal with panic attacks?' she asks.

'You are on the right track, but I probably need to explain further why this is such a great exercise for you to do,' Dr Jim says.

He then goes on to do the pink-duck exercise to explain the power of the emotional mind. 'What happens to people suffering from repeated panic attacks,' he says, 'is that they keep demanding of their emotional minds that they must not have any further panic attacks. They become so anxious about this possibility that their emotional brain overrules this demand and keeps on triggering further panic attacks.'

Dr Jim continued: 'But because you now realise that panic attacks are not dangerous and you know what to do when you get them, your emotional brain and mind are no longer interested. So the more you demand that you must have them, the fewer panic attacks you will get.'

Susan agrees to give this a try. She is becoming increasingly excited that she might be able to eliminate her fear of panic attacks occurring, for once and for all. She also reasons that if they do occur, she now at least knows what to do.

★

Two weeks later, Susan returns to see Dr Jim again. She says she tried as hard as she could to bring on panic attacks, but was unable to do so. She still found herself getting anxious, but now realised that this was quite normal. She felt much more comfortable accepting this.

Three months later, she was still free of panic attacks. Six months later, she still had no further panic attacks and her self-harm was in the distant past. She was proud that she had taken on her enemy, the amygdala, and finally conquered it.

What Susan did not realise was that she had actually reshaped her amygdala's emotional memory. She had used the power of her mind to understand what was going on in a panic attack and then used that information to challenge her amygdala – and she had won.

She became a mental-health champion in her own school and succeeded in helping other girls to open up about their difficulties in this area.

Simon's Story

Simon was a man who liked to be in complete charge of all aspects of his life and was considered a 'control freak' by those who knew him. He was a forty-five-year-old manager who ran his section of the factory like a sergeant major, and his family on similar lines.

He was in his office working on his computer when the first symptoms began. He felt his throat closing in and his breathing getting shallower. His first thought was that he might die. *Are these the first signs of a major heart attack?* he wondered. Only a few months previously, he had lost a close friend to a sudden heart attack, and the memory of the funeral was still quite fresh in his mind.

His heart began to pound, and he became even more panicky. He felt himself getting weaker, the sweat rolled off him and his stomach tightened. He noticed his throat closing in more, and his mouth was by now completely dry. He felt all his muscles tense up and the beginning of a slight headache. This made him feel even more panicky. *Maybe this is the beginning of a stroke rather than a heart attack*, he thought.

He felt foolish looking for help. He was not a man who sought assistance unless no other option was available, but this was a medical emergency and his life was at risk. He contacted a colleague, and very soon he was in the back of an ambulance on oxygen, completely convinced that his time had come.

A few hours later, Simon and his wife, who had responded quickly when she got word that her husband was in A & E, were stunned when the hospital specialist reassured them he was not in any danger, and that he was in fact physically quite healthy for his age.

Simon was initially relieved, but then he became annoyed at the implication that he had imagined it all. He challenged the doctor to explain what had happened to him. The specialist explained that Simon had most likely suffered a typical panic attack, and suggested that he was a man under too much stress. Horrified, Simon told the specialist that he was not a man who got stressed or anxious. He struggled to come to terms with the idea that he could get anxious or panicky about anything.

But four weeks later, Simon had a similar episode at work. This time he refused to return to the hospital for assistance, though the attack went on for more than an hour. He kept trying to get rid of the symptoms himself, but this proved ineffective. As a result of this episode, he attended his doctor to seek reassurance that he was not suffering from any serious medical condition. He had a raft of tests done, and his doctor reassured him that he was quite healthy. The doctor agreed with the A & E specialist that Simon was probably suffering from panic attacks, and suggested some breathing exercises to use during the attacks, and also some tranquillisers – neither of which turned out to be particularly helpful. The doctor also suggested that Simon attend Dr Jim. Reluctantly, Simon agreed.

Dr Jim meets Simon and listens intently to his story. He asks Simon about his workplace and his family, building up a picture of his life. Simon surprises himself by feeling quite comfortable with Dr Jim. *Maybe this is the person to help me*, he thinks.

'I agree with your doctor and the specialist from the hospital,' Dr Jim tells him. 'These are classic panic attacks. But I am also sensing that you may suffer from an underlying general anxiety disorder as well. So what I am going to suggest is that we deal with your panic attacks first, and maybe later explore your general anxiety.'

Simon, like most men, immediately rejects any notion that he might be somebody who suffers from anxiety. 'I am not sure if I agree with this view,' he counters. 'I can accept that I get very stressed on occasion in the job, but would that not be considered quite normal?'

'We men are all the same,' Dr Jim says. 'We can handle being told we are stressed, but we can't cope with the idea of anxiety. Let's just park that debate for the present and focus on your panic attacks. Has anyone explained to you what a panic attack is?' Simon says nobody has.

Dr Jim takes out an ABC sheet and explains what the ABC system is all about, and how they are going to use it as a template to understand Simon's panic attacks. 'Now,' says Dr Jim, 'we are going to revisit the first panic attack you experienced and examine it in great detail, on paper, using this ABC model. And you are going to write in the details as we progress. What was the first sensation you noticed?'

Dr Jim learns that it was Simon's throat closing in followed by shortness of breath that triggered the episode. Simon also notes that his emotional response to this trigger was severe panic, followed by a raft of physical symptoms: his heart pounding, sudden weakness, sweating, his stomach clenching, his throat closing in even more, his mouth going completely dry, his muscles tensing up and the beginning of a slight headache.

Dr Jim asks Simon to write down this information on their ABC sheet, which he does.

A   Activating Event:

    o   Trigger: throat closing in and difficulty breathing

    o   Inference/danger:

B   Belief/Demands:

C   Consequences:

- o   Emotional reactions: panic
- o   Physical reactions: heart pounding, sudden weakness, sweating, stomach clenching, throat closing in more, mouth going completely dry, muscles tensing up, the beginning of a slight headache
- o   Behaviour:

'Let's return to the first symptoms – your throat closing in and your difficulty in breathing. What danger did you associate with these sensations, at the time?' Dr Jim asks.

Simon replies that his major danger at the time was that he was going to have a heart attack and die. And then, later, when the headache arrived, he thought he was going to have a stroke and end up paralysed or die.

'And what about subsequent attacks?' asks Dr Jim. 'Were there any other dangers that you visualised, such as other people seeing you, or losing control or going mad? All of these can be perceived dangers in such situations.'

'Well I did become quite bothered that my work colleagues would see me like that when it happened the second time,' replies Simon.

They added this new information to their ABC.

A   Activating Event:

- o   Trigger: throat closing in and difficulty breathing
- o   Inference/danger: 'I might have a heart attack and die.' 'I might have a stroke and end up paralysed or dead.' 'Others might see me.'

B   Belief/Demands:

C   Consequences:

- o   Emotional reactions: panic
- o   Physical reactions: heart pounding, sudden weakness, sweat-

ing, stomach clenching, throat closing in more, mouth going completely dry, muscles tensing up, the beginning of a slight headache

o   Behaviour:

'So what were you hopeful would happen, Simon, during that first panic attack if you were so fearful of these dangers?' asks Dr Jim.

'I just wanted these awful symptoms to stop,' Simon says.

'Just one more question,' Dr Jim says. 'What did you do, or what was your behaviour, when the panic symptoms arrived?'

Simon replies that he sought help from colleagues, who rang for an emergency ambulance, and then he received oxygen, and was checked out with multiple tests in the A & E. And that, later, he attended his doctor, did breathing exercises, and even took some tranquillisers, none of which were of any real assistance

They added this information to their ABC list.

A   Activating Event:

   o   Trigger: throat closing in and difficulty breathing

   o   Inference/danger: 'I might have a heart attack and die.' 'I might have a stroke and end up paralysed or dead.' 'Others might see me.'

B   Belief/Demands: these symptoms must stop

C   Consequences:

   o   Emotional reactions: panic

   o   Physical reactions: heart pounding, sudden weakness, sweating, stomach clenching, throat closing in more, mouth going completely dry, muscles tensing up, the beginning of a slight headache

   o   Behaviour: sought urgent assistance from his work colleagues; went by emergency ambulance to hospital A & E; had oxygen en route; had a full hospital screen; and tried doing breathing exercises and taking tranquillisers.

Now that they have pieced together what happened during Simon's first panic attack, Dr Jim begins the process of exploring with Simon how best to deal with future attacks. He starts by explaining the ABC they have put together, showing Simon what had happened to him during the attack. He then explores the physical symptoms Simon experienced during the attack.

'What do you think caused you to feel the physical symptoms during the first attack?' Dr Jim asks Simon. Simon suggests that it was his fear and panic that caused them. Dr Jim asks him what happened in his body that created those physical sensations, and Simon ventures, 'It must be my brain that causes them.' Dr Jim explains the difference between his logical brain and his emotional brain, and how it was his emotional brain that was in charge of his stress system. He helps Simon to see that it was his stress system releasing an adrenaline rush that created this burst of intense physical symptoms. He then discusses with Simon what adrenaline is, and, using the leopard example, helps him to see that it is simply our do-a-runner hormone and that the symptoms it causes are uncomfortable but not dangerous.

'Let's examine how long your panic attacks usually last,' Dr Jim says. Simon notes that they could last for up to an hour, sometimes longer.

Dr Jim asks why he thinks it takes so long for them to settle down. When Simon struggles to answer, Dr Jim explains that it was his safety behaviour that prevented his body's stress system from returning everything to normal. He goes on to explain to Simon how he was not actually helping his panic attacks by urgently seeking help from work colleagues, getting oxygen in the emergency ambulance, going to the A & E, using breathing exercises and taking tranquillisers.

'Suppose you were in the middle of a panic attack, and I stuck your shoes to the ground so you could not move. What do you think would happen?'

Simon visualised this scenario. 'I don't really know,' he admitted.

'I want you to think about everything we have discussed about the physical symptoms created by your fear hormone, adrenaline, not being dangerous,'

Dr Jim says.

'I suppose, on thinking about it, nothing serious is going to happen to me,' Simon says.

'If this is the case, how long do you think it would take for these physical symptoms to subside?' asks Dr Jim.

Simon guesses that it might take up to an hour. Dr Jim explains that the symptoms created by an adrenaline rush would actually be gone in around ten minutes if Simon did nothing.

'The difficulty that most people have with panic attacks,' Dr Jim says, 'is that they believe the physical symptoms are dangerous, and they keep trying to make them go away. It is this demand and the safety behaviour that maintains the panic attack.'

He asks Simon to visualise going down to the beach and facing the sea. 'Then put up your hand and try to stop the tide. That is what people in the middle of a panic attack try to do,' explains Dr Jim, 'because trying to stop this adrenaline burst is like trying to stop the tide. But just as the tide comes in and the tide goes out, so too an adrenaline rush in the body will come, whether we like it or not, but it will also fade away quickly, as long as we don't try to interfere with the process through all of these safety behaviours.'

Dr Jim continued: 'What I want you to do from now on, Simon, is to imagine, when a panic attack strikes and these unpleasant and uncomfortable symptoms arrive, that you are stuck to the floor and these sensations are simply washing over you like the tide. Try to visualise that you are saying to the sensations, "Do your worst and then get lost!' And then surrender yourself to them, as if they were water flowing over you in a shower. Once you can learn do that, you will lose your fear of the physical symptoms. Instead of trying to stop them, simply embrace them.'

Simon was a little bit sceptical that this would work in real life. Were the physical symptoms not so overwhelmingly unpleasant that he might struggle to do this? he asks Dr Jim.

'How distressing would it be for you to live for the rest of your life with the fear that one of these episodes might occur, particularly at work?' asks Dr Jim. 'Would it not be easier to put up with the discomfort of letting these physical sensations wash over you as I have described? Suppose that by doing this you learnt how to deal with these episodes permanently?'

Simon agrees that it is at least worth a try, because the alternative is unthinkable.

Dr Jim then introduces Simon to the importance of the amygdala in panic attacks, and explains that it is a primitive organ whose function is to seek out danger in the environment, and, if it finds any, to fire instantly. He explains that it is the amygdala that triggers the fight-freeze-or-flight response, that this organ is vital for our survival, and that it is not very amenable to talk therapy. But, Dr Jim says, it does respond to the flooding-exposure technique. And once it has relearnt that there is no real danger associated with the physical symptoms or the trigger in panic attacks, its emotional memory banks are reshaped for the future. Dr Jim goes on to discuss the PFC, and how, during a panic attack, it gets sidelined by the amygdala, which is why we can't talk or think our way out of a panic attack.

To a logical man like Simon, this made much more sense than the 'psychobabble' that he perceived talk therapy to be. If he could grasp that there was a sensible reason he was experiencing the panic attacks, then he was more amenable to the flooding-exposure technique Dr Jim had suggested. He is not going to let a 'bully' like the amygdala take over his life. He is now completely on board, and agrees to put Dr Jim's suggestions to the test.

Dr Jim asks Simon to return to the 'A' section of the ABC, because he wants to challenge the dangers Simon visualised: that he was going to have a heart attack or major stroke and die, or that workmates would see him in distress. Dr Jim starts by asking Simon what caused the triggering symptoms – his throat closing and his difficulty breathing. Where was his proof that it was dangerous and was going to kill him? Dr Jim asks. Simon struggles to answer.

'Could it be a symptom of just being anxious?' Dr Jim asks. 'Or, in your case, a result of stress?' Simon says this might be the case.

'How could a simple symptom of anxiety actually lead to your having a heart attack or kill you?' Dr Jim asks. Simon agrees that this is actually not likely.

'What happens in panic attacks,' Dr Jim explains, 'is that we simply become anxious. We may be subconsciously stressed from family or work pressures, and this might trigger our stress system. This leads to our heart going slightly faster or our breathing becoming a little more laboured or our throat closing in. We then fall into the trap of assuming that these symptoms are dangerous, and this leads to panic and the subsequent physical symptoms.'

Dr Jim then queries Simon's second major danger – that he was going to have a stroke and either become paralysed or die. 'How likely do you think this is?' he asks. 'Or is it just like the fear of having a heart attack?'

Simon nods. He is beginning to get the message. Dr Jim assures him that such physical symptoms of anxiety have nothing to do with our physical health, and pose no danger.

'Finally,' Dr Jim says, 'what is the real chance of people at work seeing you in the middle of a panic attack? In practice, people do not see symptoms of anxiety or panic in others, as they are far too engrossed in the most important thing in their lives: themselves.' Simon agrees that this is probably the case.

Dr Jim finishes by giving Simon the panic exercise. 'I want you to try to bring on as many panic attacks as you can in the next two weeks,' he says. 'I don't mind where you have them. It can be at home, on your own or with others present. Or at work, where, in your mind, your workmates might see you. Can you see why am I asking you to perform this exercise?'

Simon was at a loss to answer this, and alarmed at the idea of performing the exercise. 'Is it because you want me to learn how to deal with panic attacks?' he enquires.

'You are on the right track. But I need to explain further why this is such a great exercise,' Dr Jim says. He does the pink-duck exercise with Simon to explain the power of the emotional mind. 'And that is what happens to people suffering from repeated panic attacks,' he says. 'They keep demanding of their emotional minds that they must not have any further panic attacks. They become so anxious they might, that their emotional brain overrules this demand and keeps on triggering further panic attacks. But because you now realise that panic attacks are not dangerous and know what to do when you get them, your emotional brain and mind are no longer interested. So the more you demand that you must have them, the fewer panic attacks you will have.'

Simon agrees to give this a try. Maybe it is possible to eliminate his panic attacks once and for all, he hopes. He reasons that if he does have one, at least he will know what to do.

★

Two weeks later, Simon returns to see Dr Jim. He is much more positive. He had another panic attack, and he approached it as Dr Jim had recommended. To his great surprise, the attack was gone in less than five minutes. It was also less severe than his previous attacks. No matter how hard he tried, he could not bring on a panic attack intentionally. As a result of these two positives, he is no longer worried about having another episode.

Three months later, after two more visits to Dr Jim, Simon's panic attacks are completely gone. Following some further discussions, he accepts that he does, in fact, have some deeper issues with anxiety. But that was for another day.

What About the Link with Addiction and Depression?

Let's now briefly explore the links between panic attacks and two other key mental-health issues – addiction and depression.

Addiction

Whilst the vast majority of panic attacks are caused by an underlying anxiety about anxiety, there is also a link between panic attacks and addiction.

When we are addicted to alcohol or other legal or illegal substances, the part of our emotional brain linked to our pleasure system becomes tolerant of the substance in question, and, in fact, craves it.

When we abuse the substance and then withdraw from it, information is sent from our pleasure system to our amygdala, and we start to become more anxious. This can trigger panic attacks. Let's take three people who end up with Dr Jim and see what happens.

Thomas's Story

Thomas, who is thirty-three years old, is a construction worker who has become a binge alcoholic. He presented to his doctor with panic attacks. The doctor explained that solving Thomas's problems would involve facing his addiction. Otherwise, it would be extremely difficult to eliminate the panic. He also asked Thomas to attend Dr Jim.

Dr Jim, after going through his history in detail, is quite honest with Thomas 'There is little point in me trying to help you to deal with your panic attacks if you keep drinking.' He makes an agreement with Thomas to assist him further if he will:

- Attend an alcohol counsellor

- Attending AA (Alcoholics Anonymous)

- Keep off alcohol

Thomas, who has also been under severe pressure from his wife to change or lose her, agrees to these conditions. He promises to come back when he has made the changes. Three months later, he is in a new space. He is off alcohol, attending AA and working with an alcohol counsellor. He has noticed a significant reduction in the number of panic attacks he has been having. But he still wants to try to banish them from his life altogether. Dr Jim begins the process of helping Thomas in much the same way as he helped the four previous patients. One year later, Thomas is still off alcohol and is having no further panic attacks, which ceased after two sessions with Dr Jim.

Paul's Story

Paul is a twenty-nine-years-old successful businessman. He has gradually slipped into a weekend cocaine habit. He presented to his doctor with a history of panic attacks, admitting his substance-abuse problems. He was referred to Dr Jim, who makes it clear that the cocaine habit Paul has fallen into is playing havoc with both his brain and mental health. Dr Jim explains what is happening in Paul's brain and how it is a complete waste of time for him to give Paul advice on panic attacks unless he makes a clear decision to:

- Attend a drugs counsellor

- Attending NA (Narcotics Anonymous)

- Keep off cocaine and other substances

Paul is quite angry with Dr Jim and challenges him. 'I only use these drugs for recreational purposes. Surely it should be easy to give me something – like a tranquilliser, or at least some techniques to deal with the panic attacks,' he says.

Dr Jim holds quite firmly to his decision, and shakes hands with Paul. 'Come back to me when you are clean and we will have a further conversation about your panic attacks,' he tells Paul.

Two years later, Paul reaches a crisis point. His habit has deteriorated further; his panic attacks have become continuous and very distressing. His fiancée has given him a clear ultimatum: stop using cocaine or she will leave for good.

Paul returns to Dr Jim, and this time just asks for help. Dr Jim refers him to a drugs counsellor, and Paul ends up doing a three-month stint in a treatment centre. By the time he returns to Dr Jim, he is feeling like a new person, and his panic attacks have almost completely subsided. Dr Jim gives him some advice on how to deal with them.

Two years later, Paul is happily married, completely clear of his drug habit, his panic attacks a distant memory.

Joan's Story

Joan is sixty years old. She became increasingly anxious following the sudden death of her husband and the social isolation which followed. She struggled to come to terms with his loss, using alcohol to deal with periods of low mood. She began to get panic attacks and became increasingly isolated as a result. She finally went to see her doctor with her daughter, who had become increasingly concerned. Her doctor referred her to Dr Jim.

Dr Jim is very sympathetic, but quite firm with Joan. It will be impossible for him to assist her with her panic attacks unless she is prepared to face her alcohol abuse, he tells her. He suggests:

- Attending an alcohol counsellor

- Attending AA

- Keeping off alcohol

He promises that if she is willing to do what he asks, he can teach her techniques to deal with her panic attacks. Dr Jim, and Joan's daughter, suggest that Joan might also benefit from bereavement counselling, getting a dog for company and as a guard, and trying to reintegrate into her local community by joining some local groups involved in gardening, historical trips or other hobbies that interest her.

With her daughter's assistance, Joan takes on board Dr Jim's advice and eliminates her alcohol use, realising that it is better to deal with her grief and loneliness in healthier ways. Within three months she is back with Dr Jim, and her panic attacks have completely gone away. He is delighted, but says that if they return, he will show her how to deal with them. She remains well.

Depression

Many people are surprised to learn that panic attacks can be a presenting symptom for depression. Are they not a symptom of anxiety, and nothing to do with mood? they ask.

The amygdala, which triggers many of the feelings of low mood in depression, is also involved when we are anxious, so there is crossover. Most people, when they are feeling very down, observe that they often also feel quite anxious and agitated. Because of this link, it is not a major step to developing panic attacks.

Peter's Story

Peter is a twenty-five-year-old postgraduate. He presented to his GP with a history of three months of severe, recurrent panic attacks. But he also admitted that he had been experiencing significant depression for the previous six months, and having suicidal thoughts. He had been misusing alcohol to lift his mood, and the more he drank the more his panic attacks deteriorated. His doctor started him on a modern SSRI antidepressant and referred him to Dr Jim to assist him in dealing with his panic attacks.

Dr Jim explains to Peter that it is most likely his depression, together with his use of alcohol, that is triggering his panic attacks. He lays out a holistic package for Peter and explains how it would work: firstly, he advises Peter on the importance of exercise and nutrition; secondly, that it is better for Peter to abstain from alcohol completely for at least three months; thirdly, to take a month off from work to try to remove some of the pressure from his life; fourthly, to wait for a number of weeks before starting any significant CBT exercises in relation to his depression; fifthly, to wait for a month to see if the antidepressant is effective in lifting his mood; finally, to see if his panic attacks continue when his mood lifted.

A month later, on his return to see Dr Jim, Peter is feeling much better. Many of his depression symptoms have receded. He is able to return to work and is now off alcohol and exercising. His panic attacks are now completely gone.

III.
GENERAL ANXIETY DISORDER

7.
The World of
General Anxiety Disorder

Anxiety is a word we all commonly use. None of us are strangers to being anxious; it is an inherent part of the human condition. For some, this normal anxiety becomes heightened to such a level that significant physical and behavioural consequences intrude on their everyday lives, and, in some cases, takes over. Just as depression with a little 'd' is an emotion we all experience, while depression with a big 'D' is a significant mental-health condition, there is anxiety with a little 'a', the normal emotion, and anxiety with a big 'A' – the condition.

At the heart of anxiety is worry, worry and more worry. And it is this constant worrying that ends up producing the physical and behavioural difficulties that make this condition so distressing for the sufferer. For many decades, this form of persistent, general anxiety was not really recognised as a condition in itself. It was regularly – and still is – misconstrued as being part of a depression cycle.

Eventually, it was accepted as being a definitive mental-health condition called general anxiety disorder (GAD), with specific physical, emotional, cognitive and behavioural characteristics. A diagnosis of general anxiety disorder was made when a significant number of these characteristics were present.

Before meeting some people who suffer from this condition let's examine these criteria.

General Anxiety Disorder

General anxiety disorder (GAD) is a state of chronic anxiety in which the person presents with persistent feelings of:

- Intense anxiety and foreboding
- Excessive worry about their health, family or job
- A constant sense of impending disaster

This is often combined with the following physical and psychological symptoms, many of which are more distressing than the above:

- Mental and physical fatigue – in some cases very severe
- Poor concentration
- Mind going blank in common social and domestic situations
- Difficulties with memory
- Muscle tension
- Restlessness, tremors
- Sleep difficulties (in up to 70 percent of sufferers), often associated with nightmares and grinding teeth
- Indecisiveness
- Hypervigilance at all times
- Regular avoidance of situations in everyday life due to fatigue and worrying about ability to cope
- Never wanting to begin a new task because of worries about not having the energy to finish it, becoming apathetic about such ventures and thus limiting the richness of their lives

- Irritable-bowel-type symptoms like abdominal pain and loose bowel motions

The sufferer is also vulnerable to bouts of acute anxiety, panicky-type episodes, with the following typical types of physical symptoms:

- Tension headaches
- Constant sighing
- Palpitations
- Stomach cramps and disturbance
- Loss of appetite, with associated weight loss

Severe stress, particularly in relation to loss, major health issues or financial concerns will lead to bouts of extreme inner anxiety. All the usual symptoms of GAD are magnified in such cases, and the person quickly becomes exhausted. It is the mental and physical fatigue that are most underestimated, and that cause the greatest upset in the life of the person with GAD – and that often prompt them to seek help.

Sufferers – mainly women, who are at least twice as likely to have this condition – begin to accept the symptoms as normal and live in a twilight world of worry and exhaustion. It often worsens with age, as the mounting stresses of life build up, and it takes less and less stress to trigger acute bouts. Many misuse alcohol to cope. The wine epidemic amongst women, so regularly encountered by alcohol counsellors as a major issue in modern Ireland, has some roots in this often unrecognised disorder. Most people who sufferer from GAD will experience at least one episode of depression during their life.

The pathways leading to this disorder are probably set up from early in our childhood, due to a combination of genetic predisposition, family and environment. These combine epigenetically to produce an oversensitive amygdala, which reads all situations through a lens of fear and apprehension. (Increasingly, environmental influences are felt to be a major deciding factor as to whether GAD appears later in our lives.) Normally it is the role of our

PFC to quieten the emotional brain's amygdala, but in this disorder it fails to do so, particularly when exposed to stressors.

If we take an overview of the psychological and neurobiological data available to date, we build up the following picture of this illness:

- Some of us are born with a genetic predisposition to being anxious. If you want to know more about the role of specific genes in this process, I recommend reading *Flagging the Therapy*. Whether these genes are switched on or off will often depend on environmental factors encountered during childhood and adolescence.

- Of those with such a genetic predisposition towards anxiety, some will be reared in secure, calm households, where fear pathways are modulated, and risks of developing this disorder diminish.

- Others will be reared in more anxious households, difficult social circumstances or perfectionist/non-validating environments. By the time they are adults, they develop a hyped-up amygdala and a higher risk of developing GAD.

- In such cases, life stresses and strains put pressure on their coping skills, creating multiple possibilities for the emotional brain to be fearful and negative.

- Higher brain centres – in the form of our PFC – struggle to keep a check on these fear pathways, and are quickly overruled. So anxiety rules the roost.

- Because the amygdala is in charge of our stress system, its state of constant hypervigilance leads to the stream of the secondary physical symptoms that are so prevalent in this condition.

- Of great relevance is the fact that when our amygdala is hypersensitive like this, we may experience some of the typical amygdala physical symptoms, even in the absence of a significant trigger.

- This explains why sufferers may complain of both acute and chronic physical symptoms of anxiety in GAD, with no obvious cause: it is almost like background noise.

- Our stress hormone glucocortisol plays an important role in relation to many of the physical symptoms, such as fatigue. High levels, during episodes, can lead to increased risks of depression, osteoporosis, heart attacks, stroke and infections.

- Acute stressors, which might not affect others, can further trigger this whole system, activating, through the amygdala, our stress system and releasing adrenaline, leading to typical symptoms of acute anxiety.

- Once this general anxiety pathway is set in motion, from our late teens or early twenties onwards, our emotional brain will perpetuate the process, unless we identify it and make relevant changes.

- This explains why matters deteriorate as we get older, as stresses build up and the GAD pathway strengthens.

- The positive news is that major changes in relation to thinking and behaviour can be made, reshaping this negative pathway, and transforming lives in the process.

Many people suffering from GAD end up attending their family doctor on countless occasions, seeking reassurance that their physical symptoms are not due to some serious underlying illness. Many will also end up having multiple hospital investigations performed, for similar reasons. It can often take years for the actual diagnosis to come to the surface.

Part of the difficulty is that the more the sufferer is told that there is nothing wrong with them, and that they are perfectly healthy, the more anxious they become. Since they are still complaining of the physical symptoms, they remain convinced there is something wrong.

Many never consider anxiety as a possibility, and often react negatively if it is suggested. This is because the physical symptoms themselves are so real to the person that they cannot link them to just being anxious.

How to Treat General Anxiety Disorder

Lifestyle Changes and Complimentary Therapies

The following have been shown to be of benefit:

- Regular exercise – thirty minutes a day if possible. Any form of exercise is beneficial. Walking, cycling or jogging can easily be built into our lives.

- Proper nutrition – one of the most common concerns in anxiety is the sufferer's poor diet. Avoid all wonder diets, as they are usually of limited value.

- B vitamins/omega-3 fish-oil supplements – particularly for the fatigue.

- Avoiding caffeine – to ease fatigue, in particular. This may be in the form of coffee or Coke or energy drinks such as Red Bull.

- Avoiding chocolate or other sugar hits – they just dial up the anxiety.

- Being extremely wary of using any form of alcohol, particularly wine, as a crutch to ease feelings of anxiety or their physical consequences. It will drop your mood and increase your risk of developing tolerance or addiction.

- Being extremely wary of using over-the-counter drugs, such as those containing codeine, for similar reasons.

- Yoga, meditation/mindfulness courses and general relaxation and breathing exercises.

- If teeth grinding is a big problem, visiting your dentist for a night guard.

- Examining stressors in your life and trying to deal with them. This can be done with your close family, or friends or with the assistance of a counsellor or therapist.

Drug Therapies

These have a place in the treatment of GAD, but are less effective than talk therapies:

Minor Tranquillisers

These drugs combat GAD by acting on key receptors in the amygdala, with a view to calming it down. Their effect is immediate, with a rapid reduction in all symptoms, which makes them popular with anxiety sufferers. Tranquillisers can be useful for short periods, but longer-term use leads to tolerance, increasing misuse and finally, in some cases, actual addiction, perpetuating the problem. But the bigger, hidden problem is that they prevent the amygdala being reset with therapies such as CBT.

Antidepressants

The main drugs used nowadays are the SSRIs. These have been shown to decrease the symptoms of anxiety. By increasing activity in the serotonin mood system, they calm the amygdala. Where there are profound physical symptoms – such as intractably irritable bowels, total exhaustion or associated low mood, in particular – such drugs may be useful. They may help the person with severe GAD to arrive at a point where they can become involved in talk therapies. When the talk therapy has taken over, the SSRIs should be discontinued. In reality, some people remain on these drugs for life. In long-term treatment, there is an issue of side effects, particularly sexual ones.

Lyrica

This is a drug used for chronic pain, but it is now also used as a therapy to relieve symptoms of GAD. It is fast-acting and non-addictive. It does have some significant side effects in higher doses, however, such as oedema and drowsiness. Lyrica should ideally be used for relatively short intervals whilst talk therapies such as CBT are employed.

Herbal Remedies

In the case of GAD, St John's wort is used in many countries. It mimics the actions of the SSRIs, and it comes with its own dangers and interactions. Another herb commonly used is valerian.

Talk Therapies

Are particularly helpful in dealing with GAD, and should ideally be the treatment of choice. The options include:

- Counselling
- Psychoanalysis
- Behaviour therapy
- Acceptance and commitment (ACT) therapy
- Mindfulness
- CBT therapy

We have already dealt with CBT in detail. This method – perhaps accompanied by mindfulness in some situations – is most effective in dealing with GAD, and, indeed, anxiety of any type. This is the talk therapy we will be using to assist you in dealing with GAD.

Let us now look at how three different people with GAD presented and received assistance from our resident expert, Dr Jim, to deal with their anxiety using the above therapy approaches, and particularly CBT.

Paula's Story

Paula, a thirty-two-year-old primary-school teacher and mother of two, attended her GP with the classic opening line: 'I am constantly tired.' She felt tired and forgetful, lacked concentration, struggled to both start and finish new tasks, and was grinding her teeth at night. She was also drinking excessive amounts of wine, especially at night, when her exhaustion became overwhelming.

Her doctor examined her and performed some blood tests. On her next visit, he ruled out underlying anaemia, thyroid disease, diabetes and depression. Paula was unhappy with this and asked to be referred to a specialist, just to be sure. Her GP suggested that it might be anxiety that was triggering all of the symptoms, but agreed to refer her to a specialist.

Six weeks later, she returned, having had a complete check up with a physician. He had reassured her that she was physically healthy and suggested that she might be stressed. Her GP explained that she might be suffering from a chronic-anxiety state called GAD. He discovered that her mother, in Paula's own words, had been 'a constant worrier' while Paula was growing up. And that she could see similar traits in her older sister.

Paula wondered if some tranquillisers would help to calm her down. Her GP was unhappy with prescribing these, explaining that they could be quite addictive and would not sort out the problem. He suggested that she try some simple lifestyle changes, such as exercising more and eating properly, which she clearly was not doing, as well as severely curtailing her alcohol consumption and taking up mindfulness or yoga as stress-reducing measures.

Paula agreed to try some of these and found them of assistance, but six weeks later a further stressor – a visit from a school inspector – retriggered all her symptoms with a vengeance. She returned to her GP for further advice. 'I just can't cope with the way I am feeling, either physically or mentally,' she explained. 'I am just a wreck.'

Her GP suggested a course of an antidepressant SSRI. 'I know you are not depressed,' he explained, 'but these sometimes help with GAD.' Paula was not very happy taking them, and when she developed some side effects, she stopped. She returned to her family doctor, asking for referral – this time, to a therapist. Her GP referred her to Dr Jim, who, he explained, uses CBT techniques to assist people with anxiety.

Paula meets Dr Jim, who concurs with her GP that the symptoms are coming from general anxiety disorder.

'This is simply medical jargon to explain that you are suffering from significant anxiety with physical and behavioural consequences,' he explains.

He agrees with the lifestyle changes her doctor recommended. He notes that she has not responded well to any form of drug therapy.

'This is not unusual,' he says, 'as there is significant evidence that talk therapies such as CBT can be more effective in the long run.'

Paula asks him to explain just what GAD is, as she is still a little confused about the diagnosis. He gives her the analogy of the central-heating system in her house, and how it can be turned up or down depending on outside temperatures. In GAD, it is seems as if our whole stress system is dialled up all the time, and that most of the physical symptoms we are experiencing are simply a response to this overactive stress system.

He explains that through our genes, and, in particular, our environment as we grow up, we develop ways of looking at the world that make us feel constantly anxious. It is our physical responses to that anxiety – and also our behaviours – that end up causing most of our difficulties. He adds that some people might develop secondary panic attacks as a result of these physical symptoms, but that this was not the case for her.

Paula can relate to this information. 'That makes so much sense to me,' she says. 'I would always have seen myself as an anxious worrier, from my childhood right through my teens and into my twenties. And I can definitely relate to both of my parents having such anxiety traits. So I may have picked up some of these traits from them.'

Dr Jim suggests that it doesn't really matter where her anxiety came from. What matters, he says, are the irrational beliefs that lie behind this emotion, beliefs that are constantly being triggered in her everyday life. He explains what rational and irrational beliefs are.

'It is these beliefs – particularly our irrational beliefs – that are the lens through which we view everything that happens to us in life, and, in the case of anxiety, this is particularly the case,' he says.

'So,' asks Paula, 'are you saying that my emotions of anxiety and all of these physical symptoms are caused by these irrational beliefs?'

'Yes,' says Dr Jim. 'They are most likely the main cause of your problems, including the unhelpful behaviours you described, such as drinking alcohol to relieve the anxiety and physical symptoms.'

'And if I were to learn some way of changing such beliefs, could that help to reduce my anxiety and dampen down all of these horrible physical symptoms?' asks Paula.

'In my experience,' Dr Jim says, 'this is one of the most powerful ways of treating this condition. We will have to look at some ways of dealing with the physical symptoms as well, but learning to reshape your irrational beliefs, which involves a lot of hard work and effort, can be really effective.'

'But how can simply changing how I think calm down the stress system you mentioned?' Paula asks. 'Is it not preset now for life as a result of my past?'

'The great news is that we now know from research that we can literally reshape pathways in our brain by challenging our thinking and behaviour with CBT,' Dr Jim says, 'and that this, in turn, helps to dial down our overactive stress system in GAD.'

Paula is now definitely on board. She asks for a more information about CBT, and how it will work. Dr Jim gives her an example. Imagine that four people are mugged in Dublin, he says. One comes home anxious and shaking and avoids going out for the next few weeks. A second arrives home angry, and, if he could have found the mugger, would have assaulted him with a golf club. A third arrives home feeling depressed, isolates himself and goes to bed. A fourth is annoyed, but feels it is a risk of living in the city, and gets on with his life.

'Why,' Dr Jim asks, 'did these four people feel and behave differently in response to the same event?'

'Because of how they thought about it,' Paula says.

'Right, and how they thought about the event was really decided by whether it triggered a rational or irrational belief,' Dr Jim says. 'We all have rational and irrational beliefs. It is just that my set is different from yours.'

Dr Jim explains that CBT is based on two major principles:

- Our thoughts influence our emotions, which influence our behaviour. So what we think affects what we feel and do.

- It is not what happens to us in life that matters, but how we choose to interpret it.

Dr Jim then goes on to explain the ABC concept to Paula, and how they will use it to try to locate and deal with her irrational beliefs. He asks her for an example of something that will regularly trigger a bout of anxiety for her. This will give them a concrete example to work on. Paula describes how she becomes incredibly anxious if one of her children becomes ill. Dr Jim asks her to be more specific.

'Two weeks ago, Darragh developed a really high fever at seven in the evening,' she replies.

'What was your emotion?' he asks.

'I became incredibly anxious – almost panicky,' she answers.

Dr Jim then asks her to write down this information on the ABC sheet:

A   Activating Event:

    o   Trigger: son develops high temperature

    o   Inference/danger:

B   Belief/Demands:

C   Consequences:

    o   Emotional reactions: anxiety, slight panic

    o   Physical reactions:

    o   Behaviour:

'Now what were your physical responses when you became extremely anxious about Darragh's fever – both at the time and also later?' Dr Jim asks.

Paula thinks about it.

'It was the usual for me,' she replies. 'My stomach going into knots, my breathing getting very shallow, my heart beating a little faster, a headache coming on, all my muscles becoming very tense and the tiredness and fatigue just getting so much worse.'

'It is important to realise,' Dr Jim says, 'these physical symptoms are simply down to your emotion of anxiety. We will go after them later. For now, let's just add them to our ABC.'

A   Activating Event:

    o   Trigger: son develops high temperature

    o   Inference/danger:

B   Belief/Demands:

C   Consequences:

    o   Emotional reactions: anxiety, slight panic

    o   Physical reactions: stomach going into knots, breathing getting very shallow, heart beating a little faster, headache, muscles getting very tense, tiredness and fatigue increasing

    o   Behaviour:

'So what was it about Darragh developing this fever that caused you to become so anxious?' Dr Jim asks. 'In general, almost every case of anxiety means the person is assigning some danger to a trigger. In this case, what danger were you assigning to his temperature? What did you visualise was going to happen?'

'My real fear,' explains Paula, 'was that this was something serious, like bad pneumonia.'

'This would be an understandable concern for any mother,' he agrees, 'but was that the real worry? Was it something even more serious?'

Paula suddenly has tears in her eyes. 'I could see it all in front of my own eyes. I just saw him unconscious in a hospital bed and then had these awful images of him lying in a coffin.'

'So if we were to summarise your danger here, it was that Darragh might go on to develop a very severe infection such as pneumonia – or, even worse, meningitis – and then possibly end up acutely ill in hospital. And that he might actually die.'

Paula agrees.

'Were you anxious that he was definitely going to die, or was it just that he might die?' Dr Jim asks.

Paula has to think about this.

'I suppose it was more that he might die,' she says.

'So what you are really saying is that it was more your visualisation of what might happen, rather than what had actually happened that was really behind your anxiety at that moment,' Dr Jim says.

He asks her to add this information to their ABC, which she does.

A   Activating Event:

  o   Trigger: son develops high temperature

  o   Inference/danger: 'His fever might be due to serious infection like pneumonia or meningitis.' 'His condition might quickly deteriorate.' 'He might end up acutely ill in a hospital bed.' 'He might eventually die.'

B   Belief/Demands:

C   Consequences:

  o   Emotional reactions: anxiety, slight panic

  o   Physical reactions: stomach going into knots, breathing getting very shallow, heart beating a little faster, headache, muscles getting very tense, tiredness and fatigue increasing

  o   Behaviour:

'Let's move on to see what irrational belief was triggered by this situation and the danger you assigned to it,' says Dr Jim. 'This usually takes the form of some absolute demand you are making about the trigger. So what demand were you making, at the time, about Darragh's fever?'

Paula reflects on this.

'Well I suppose my demand was that Darragh must not get very sick and die. That was what was making me so anxious,' she says.

'Suppose he did become very ill, Paula, what would you then feel about yourself?' Dr Jim enquires.

'I would feel really awful – a complete failure for not being able to stop this happening,' she says.

'So what you were really demanding was that Darragh must not get very ill and die. If this were to happen, you would feel you were awful and a real failure,' Dr Jim says.

With tears in her eyes, Paula nods.

Dr Jim adds the new information to their ABC.

A   Activating Event:

   o   Trigger: son develops high temperature

   o   Inference/danger: 'His fever might be due to serious infection like pneumonia or meningitis.' 'His condition might quickly deteriorate.' 'He might end up acutely ill in a hospital bed.' 'He might eventually die.'

B   Belief/Demands: 'My son must not get very sick and die. If this happens, I am awful and a failure for letting it happen.'

C   Consequences:

   o   Emotional reactions: anxiety, slight panic

   o   Physical reactions: stomach going into knots, breathing getting very shallow, heart beating a little faster, headache, muscles getting very tense, tiredness and fatigue increasing

   o   Behaviour:

'So what did you do when you became very anxious as a result of this demand?' Dr Jim asks. 'It is often our behaviour in such situations that causes us difficulties.'

'The first thing I did was to contact the out-of-hours service, but even after being reassured by the doctor, I still remained very anxious,' she says. 'So I rang my mother, and then my sister, looking for reassurance that what I was doing was right.'

'And did this work?' asks Dr Jim.

'It worked for an hour or two, but the anxiety came back even worse than before: *Maybe they were all wrong, and he really was ill*, I thought. So I contacted the out-of-hours service again and insisted that the doctor come and see Darragh, which he did,' says Paula.

'And what was the result of that?' asks Dr Jim.

'He did a thorough examination and reassured me that it was simply a throat infection, and started Darragh on antibiotics and the usual measures to keep his temperature down,' replies Paula.

'So did this settle down your anxiety?' enquires Dr Jim.

'For a while,' she replies, 'but I still couldn't eat and found myself back on the phone to my sister seeking reassurance that the doctor had really got it right. Were there not many situations where even experienced doctors missed pneumonia or meningitis in small children? I asked her. And the doctor who had seen him seemed so young.'

Paula continued: 'She tried to reassure me, but still all I could see was Darragh arriving to the hospital too late to be saved. I even went on the Internet seeking reassurance, but that made things worse, as all I could see were possible serious reasons for his high temperature.'

'So what happened after that?' asks Dr Jim.

'Eventually, my husband realised that I was just going to keep on worrying unless he intervened,' replied Paula. 'Because by that stage I had got myself into a terrible state. I was crying, not eating, constantly checking and rechecking Darragh's temperature, and also checking and rechecking his skin for even the smallest spot that might suggest the possibility of meningitis. So my husband just put both of us in the car and brought us down to the emergency department in the local children's hospital. The minute I got to the hospital, I felt myself starting to relax, because I knew for sure that Darragh would be safe.'

Paula explains that once again a full examination of Darragh was carried out in the hospital and blood tests were performed. 'They reassured me that he was going to be fine and that the diagnosis by the previous doctor was correct,' she says. 'They kept him for a few hours more to make sure his temperature was settled, and then they allowed us home.'

'And did your anxiety settle when you went home?' asks Dr Jim.

Paula laughs. 'It did for another while, but then it recurred in a minor way when his temperature went back up for a few hours. It settled on treatment, but I still couldn't sleep for a few nights and didn't eat properly for days and even lost a few pounds. I was constantly hovering over him, looking for the slightest change in his appearance. I didn't really settle down until he was back up and running around.'

Dr Jim added all this information to their ABC.

A   Activating Event:

o   Trigger: son develops high temperature

o   Inference/danger: 'His fever might be due to serious infection like pneumonia or meningitis.' 'His condition might quickly deteriorate.' 'He might end up acutely ill in a hospital bed.' 'He might eventually die.'

B   Belief/Demands: 'My son must not get very sick and die. If this happens, I am awful and a failure for letting it happen.'

C   Consequences:

o   Emotional reactions: anxiety, slight panic

o   Physical reactions: stomach going into knots, breathing getting very shallow, heart beating a little faster, headache, muscles getting very tense, tiredness and fatigue increasing

o   Behaviour: contacted out-of-hours services and sought reassurance from doctor on duty; telephoned mother and sister on few occasions, seeking reassurance; stopped eating and sleeping properly; arranged for GP to visit house to check on child; got husband to bring child to hospital for further check-up and bloods to be completely reassured that he was not going to die from meningitis; even when child was recovering, hovered excessively to make sure he was not showing any new symptoms.

When they finish adding to the ABC, Dr Jim says, 'So if we were to summarise all the information that we have put together on our ABC, Paula, it would look like this.'

- Darragh developed a fever, which is quite common in small children, and you became very anxious, with multiple physical symptoms.

- Your main danger was that he might have some very serious condition like pneumonia or meningitis, and so he might die.

- In fact, you could almost visualise him in the coffin.

- Your interpretation of his fever and your accompanying danger were seen through the irrational belief or lens that, 'Darragh must not get very ill or die, and if he does I am a failure for letting it happen.' This is what was really making you so anxious.

- All your subsequent behaviour was to allay and reassure your anxiety. This was what we call safety behaviour.

8.
How Paula Learned to Challenge Her Anxiety

'Now that we have some understanding of what made you so anxious about this event and what your resulting behaviour was,' says Dr Jim, 'let's see if we can help you to reshape your thinking and your behaviour. Because if we can do that for this event, we can apply the same ideas to similar situations in the future.'

Together they review her ABC, which they wrote at the end of the previous chapter. You may also want to review it before proceeding, if you don't remember the details.

Challenging Paula's 'A'

'We could challenge your "A", your interpretation of Darragh's fever,' Dr Jim explains. 'The difficulty is that we would probably dispute your proof that the dangers you laid out were really going to happen. But this would only deal with this one situation where you became very anxious. What happens next week when one of the other children develops a fever, or your husband develops a headache? Isn't the whole pattern just going to repeat itself?'

Paula agrees that this is what kept happening to her. 'I just go from one anxious situation to the next. I just can't break the cycle,' she says.

'What is much more effective, Paula,' Dr Jim says, 'is to challenge the "B" and the "C". What I mean by this is to challenge the irrational belief which is the real driver of your anxiety, and also challenge the emotional and behavioural consequences of this belief.'

Challenging Paula's 'C'

'I would like to start by challenging the "C", the consequences,' Dr Jim says. 'Would it make any sense if I asked you to just stop being anxious?'

Paula looks puzzled. 'I don't think that would work,' she replies. 'If it were that easy, I would have done it already.'

Dr Jim agrees. 'The first important message is that we must learn to simply accept our emotions as they are, whether we are anxious or depressed or hurt. Emotions are part of who we are, and learning to absorb and accept them is essential to becoming well again. So many people rail against such emotions and demand that they go away. But the more we tell our emotional brain to stop being anxious, the more anxious we will become.'

'So what you are saying is that I must learn to accept that it is OK to be anxious and stop trying to make it go away?' asks Paula.

'Yes,' says Dr Jim. 'It is one of the most common errors that people with anxiety make. They feel that to be anxious is in some way abnormal, and then they try to stop the emotion, and that ends up making them even more anxious. Now, moving on, what caused all of the physical symptoms you experienced when you became so anxious about Darragh's fever?'

'I assume it was my anxiety that caused them,' Paula says.

'But what happened in your body that caused them?' Dr Jim asks.

'It must be my brain that caused it,' says Paula.

Dr Jim agrees, and explains the differences between her logical brain and her emotional brain. It is her emotional brain that is in charge of her stress system, he says, and it is her stress system firing that gives rise to these physical symptoms.

'So whenever our emotional brain senses a danger, whether real or perceived, it immediately activates our acute stress system, which prepares us to fight or flee,' says Dr Jim. 'It does so by activating internal nerves and also by releasing our fear hormone, adrenaline.'

Dr Jim then introduces Paula to the importance of the amygdala. He explains how it is in charge of her stress system, and how it is a primitive organ whose function is to seek out danger in the environment, and, if it detects any, to fire. It was the amygdala that triggered the fight-freeze-or-flight response in the leopard example discussed in previous chapters. This organ is vital for our survival and extremely efficient in its function, Dr Jim explains. He then discusses with Paula what adrenaline is, and helps her to see that it is simply our do-a-runner hormone, and that the symptoms it causes are uncomfortable but not dangerous.

'But in your case,' Dr Jim says, 'because the danger – as you perceived it – was there for days, your stress system ended up being on constant high-alert. This resulted in you experiencing these very uncomfortable feelings for days. In fact, your stress system only went back to sleep when Darragh was back running around again, and you were no longer worried. The danger was gone.'

'But are these symptoms not dangerous for the body?' asks Paula. 'Surely, we must be more at risk of heart attacks, for example, from the stress they are putting on our bodies.'

Dr Jim explains that, in fact, these physical symptoms pose no danger to us, even though they are extremely uncomfortable. He explores with Paula the idea of simply learning to accept that the more she demands that the symptoms go away, the more the symptoms will increase; and the more she accepts and just goes with them, the more they will start to become background noise. He also explains how, when we are constantly anxious, we release our chronic-stress hormone, glucocortisol, and this causes fatigue, difficulties with concentration and a tired-but-wired feeling at night.

Paula asks why she experienced some of these physical symptoms at times when there was no obvious trigger for them. Dr Jim explains that this was probably because our amygdala is hypersensitive in GAD and can trigger these symptoms of its own accord. The best way to manage them is a combination of exercise, treating the symptoms like background noise and just learning to go with them, and mindfulness. These have been found to retrain our amygdala to be calmer, he says.

Paula finds it extremely helpful to understand why she felt the way she did at such times. She thinks she would be better able to cope in the future. She also understands how her behaviour added to her difficulties, and how to avoid such behaviour in the future.

'But it is what is going on in my head that I can't cope with,' she adds. 'That is what is making me so distressed.'

Challenging Paula's 'B'

'Now we need to examine and challenge your "B", your irrational belief,' Dr Jim says. 'This took the form of an absolute demand: "Darragh must not get very sick and die. If this happens, I am awful and a failure for letting it happen." So what is it about this demand that makes it irrational?'

Paula, on reflection, suggests that it was probably the 'must' part.

'Is there anything else?' he enquires.

She ventures that it might be the suggestion that she would be 'a failure'. Dr Jim agrees.

'What lies at the heart of anxiety,' explains Dr Jim, 'is that we make some impossible demand of ourselves, and, when we can't achieve this goal, rate ourselves as a failure.'

He goes on to show Paula the big MACS (see Figure 6), and explains that they are going to use it to challenge her demand. He challenges her 'B' as follows.

★

'M' stands for 'must', Dr Jim says. He explains that people who suffer from anxiety live in the 'land of must', where they use absolute terms like 'ought to', 'have to', 'should' and 'must' in relation to much of what happens to them in their lives.

'Returning to your absolute demand that "Darragh must not get very sick or die," Dr Jim says, 'what would be a healthier demand?'

After some discussion, they agree that a more rational, healthier demand from Paula in this situation might be that she would prefer if Darragh did not get very sick or die, but that whether this happened was out of her control. That led to a discussion on the importance of control in Paula's life.

'My husband has so often called me a control freak,' she laughs, 'down to the smallest detail. I really struggle when I am not in control.'

Dr Jim asks her what she can really control in her life. After a few attempts to answer, Paula begins to realise that, in reality, she is able to control very little. Dr Jim explains that when we are seeking control, we are looking for one or more of the following: 100-percent certainty, order, security or perfection.

'So which of these, Paula, were you looking for in relation to Darragh's illness?' he asks.

Paula decides that she wanted 100-percent certainty that Darragh's condition would not deteriorate, and, above all, that he would not die.

'Can we be 100-percent certain of anything in life?' Dr Jim asks her. 'Can you be certain that you will be home in time this evening?'

They agree that anything could happen. She could have a flat tire, an accident and so on.

'Most of the time,' Dr Jim says, 'we can be reasonably certain we can achieve our objectives, but we can never be absolutely certain. In real life, there is always going to be a chance that something may or may not happen, and we have to learn to accept this as a reality. So with that in mind, when we examine the demand you were making in relation to Darragh's fever, is it really possible to ever be absolutely certain that any child or indeed any adult, will not get really ill, or, in a tiny percentage of cases, actually die?'

They agreed that no one could ever be 100-percent certain.

'And what about looking for 100-percent order, Paula?' he asks. 'Is that something you seek in your everyday life?'

Paula laughs. 'I wish my husband was here! He is forever bemoaning my constant quest for total order at home.'

'But in real life, Paula, is there any such thing as 100-percent order?' Dr Jim asks.

Once again, after further discussion, they agree that there isn't. They go on to discuss demands for 100-percent security and perfection, and Paula accepts that these simply are not achievable either.

Dr Jim then gives Paula two exercises to try to teach her to understand, emotionally, just what not being in control is really all about. 'The reason that we struggle with the big things in life is that we imagine we are in control of our everyday routines,' Dr Jim says. 'So we have to dismantle your sense of control in relation to these.'

Firstly, he gives her a coin-toss exercise: she must designate particular activities that she is looking forward to enjoying, either on her own or with her husband. An hour before the activity is to take place, she has to toss a coin. If it comes up heads, she can go; if it comes up tails, she cannot. The exercise is designed to help her experience what uncertainty feels like in practice, rather than in theory.

Secondly, he gives her a disorder exercise: her husband – who will really enjoy this role – is designated to pick a room each week and create complete chaos in it. Her role is to work around the mess for a designated period, without cleaning it up. The proviso is, of course, that he will clean it up after the exercise.

Paula is distraught about this latter exercise.

'I just don't know how I will cope with that kind of disorder in the house!' she exclaims. 'My anxiety levels will go through the roof.'

Dr Jim agrees that it is going to be difficult. 'But you know, Paula,' he explains, 'when you have experienced what it is like to have your everyday routines so disordered and out of control, you will find it much easier to cope with the uncertainty and disorder that comes with more serious issues, such as Darragh's fever.'

Paula is beginning to understand what Dr Jim is trying to get her to see. 'You want me to experience the feeling of a situation being out of my control, and learn how to cope with it,' she says. She is finally beginning to understand what anxiety is really all about: the desire for absolute control.

*

In the big MACS, 'A' stands for 'awful', Dr Jim explains. He points out that many who suffer from anxiety imagine the worst case scenario. Everything becomes a 'catastrophe'.

'If you feel there is a tiny chance that something will go wrong and a much bigger chance that it won't, you will spend all your time and effort reflecting on the former,' he says.

Paula immediately recognises herself. 'I spend so much of every day worrying about all kinds of things that never happen,' she says. 'In that way, I am so like my mother, who always worried about everything – but especially about health matters.'

Dr Jim asks her how this played out in relation to Darragh's illness.

'Whenever he became unwell from even the most minor of ailments,' Paula says, 'I visualised him ending up dead – even in a coffin. It was all I could see that night,' she adds, with tears in her eyes, 'that white coffin.'

'The reason you struggled to get this image out of your mind,' explains Dr Jim, 'is that your emotional brain was swamped by this thought, and your logical mind couldn't get a look in.'

This tendency comes from her PFC, he explains, and specifically her right PFC. It is particularly active when we are visualising such negative possibilities.

'I will show you how to challenge such visualisations,' he says.

Paula finds it helpful to understand why she had such catastrophic visualisations, and that she could learn to reduce them.

'Did you have any proof,' Dr Jim asks her, 'that your visualisation of Darragh becoming extremely ill and dying was actually going to happen?'

Paula agrees that she did not – it was just her natural reaction to always assume the worst was going to happen. 'Until now, I did not know how to prevent this from happening,' she adds.

Dr Jim agrees that it is very difficult to switch off these catastrophic visual images and irrational assumptions. 'But I am going to give you a simple aid to help you deal with them,' he says. 'What do you visualise when I ask you to think of spilt milk?'

'A complete mess,' Paula immediately answers. 'When you rear a few children, you get used to cleaning up such messes. And as for the smell . . .'

'But what if I told you that spilt milk could also be the smallest drop on the table,' counters Dr Jim. 'Would that not also be spilt milk?'

Paula has to agree that this is true.

'In practice,' he explains, 'most people make the same automatic assumption – that spilt milk must always mean a real mess. When we are catastrophising, as you were when Darragh was ill, we are doing the same thing.'

'So what you are trying to get me to see is that I have to start challenging whether what I am worrying about is just a drop rather than a mess or a puddle,' Paula says.

'Yes. Unless you can prove that what you are catastrophising about is actually true and definitely going to happen, then it is only a drop of spilt milk,' Dr Jim says.

Paula agrees to try to keep this visual idea in her mind whenever she is imagining the worst.

'So if we apply this concept to Darragh and his fever, did you have any proof that he was going to die?' Dr Jim asks.

Paula agrees that she did not, and that, in fact, on looking at his fever logically, the chances of him dying were slight indeed.

*

In the big MACS, 'C' stands for 'can't stand it', Dr Jim explains. That feeling is quite common in those who suffer from anxiety, he says.

Paula says she regularly feels that she would not be able to cope if her son became very ill. 'I would just disintegrate,' she says. 'I wouldn't be able to handle how I would feel.'

'Suppose Darragh did actually become very ill?' he asks. 'Would you cope if you had to?'

Paula replies that she would most likely have to, as a mother.

'So you would cope if it were in your own and Darragh's interest?' he asks. 'You might not cope the way you think you should, but you would cope?'

Paula replies that she would. Dr Jim continues.

'We all think that we just won't cope if something terrible happened in our lives, but, in reality, we have no option other than to cope. We do not have the luxury of just lying down, because others are often relying on us. We have to keep going – both for them and for ourselves. If we take the worst case scenario, if Darragh were to die, would you cope?'

Paula now grasps what he is trying to get her to see. 'I would have to cope,' she answers. 'I would still have my husband and my other two children, all of whom I love so much.'

Dr Jim gives her a maxim to remember: 'We can put up with anything in life if it is in our own interest to do so, or in the interest of those we love.'

★

In the big MACS, 'S' stands for 'self-/other-rating', Dr Jim explains. This lies at the heart of the emotions of anxiety and depression, he says. This is where we not only judge ourselves, but also accept others' opinions of us.

'So when you wrote down that you would be "a failure" if you could not fulfil your irrational demand that Darragh must not get very ill and die, you were in fact rating yourself,' Dr Jim says. 'Let's challenge this irrational belief. Where do you rate yourself as a person, between one and one hundred?'

Paula replies that she would rate herself quite highly, probably around eighty. He draws a scale and marks in her estimate (see Figure 7).

'And where do you feel others rate you?' he asks.

'Around the same,' he replies.

So he adds this.

'And if Darragh had become very ill, where would you rate yourself?' he asks.

Paula replies that she would drop her rating down to ten. He marks this in.

'And others? How do you feel they would rate you if that happened?' he asks.

'Also about ten,' Paula says.

'And now for the most important message of the day,' says Dr Jim. 'Can we rate a human being? Where's the measuring tool?'

On reflection, Paula agrees that we can't rate humans, as we are too complex.

'Would you like to join a very special club – the Raggy Doll Club?' Dr Jim asks (see Figure 8).

Intrigued, Paula asks him for more information.

'This is a highly exclusive club,' he explains. 'There are three important criteria for membership: 1) we cannot rate ourselves; 2) we cannot accept other people's ratings of us; and 3) we can rate our behaviour, but not ourselves.'

Dr Jim explains that the Raggy Doll Club is a concept created by leading CBT therapist Enda Murphy, based loosely on a former TV series. The Raggy Dolls were the rejects in the basket, and the cartoon was about their adventures. 'To join in the Raggy Doll Club, you just have to decide to meet the three criteria,' he says.

Dr Jim goes on to explain that he is a member of the Raggy Doll Club: a normal human being who tries to do his best. He accepts that he will make mistakes on some occasions and get it right on others, and accepts that he can't judge or rate himself, no matter what happens. He also doesn't accept others' ratings of him. In life, he explains, we can rate our behaviour but not ourselves. And it's the same for others.

'Who else is a member of this club?' Paula asks. 'It sounds like a great space to be in.'

'The other members of the club are the rest of the human race,' Dr Jim says. 'All of us are fallible, imperfect and at the mercy of the arrows that that life throws. We have to learn to accept to ourselves unconditionally. To join is easy. Membership is free and makes us invulnerable to the arrows life throws at us.'

Paula begins to smile, realising the power of the allegory. 'I need to join,' she says.

★

Dr Jim summarises all the work they have done in challenging her demand that Darragh must not get ill or die and if he did, she would be a failure.

- She was looking for 100-percent certainty that if Darragh developed a fever he would not become really ill or die. In practice, this was an impossible demand. It would be better to say she would prefer he did not become very ill or die.

- She had been imagining the worst, without any proof.

- She had assumed she would not be able to cope if Darragh became very ill. In reality, she *would* cope, because it would be in her son's interest to do so.

- She was being critical of herself and assuming others would do likewise.

- Paula needed to become a Raggy Doll.

Dr Jim explains that if Paula can apply these lessons, she can reshape her thoughts and feelings. But it will require a lot of work over a period of time if she wants to get better. 'The skill of life is not learning how to succeed, but how to fail,' he says.

Paula is enthusiastic and agrees to continue.

Dr Jim asks her to keep a notebook. When she gets very anxious, he says, she should document it in this notebook – in the ABC manner they have worked on. He also challenges her to regularly carry out the coin-toss and dis-order exercises, until she finally learns to accept that life is largely out of her control.

★

Six months later, after a series of such sessions, Paula is experiencing a lot less anxiety and fatigue, and she is recognising triggers and demands much more easily. She has become more realistic in the demands she places on herself, and has found herself a real-life Raggy Doll, which she regularly communicates with when she finds she is rating herself. She is learning about mindfulness, and has begun to practice the three-minute breathing space every day.

She still suffers from GAD, and acute stressors will still occasionally throw her off line, but, overall, she is doing much better. She has techniques to deal with any issues that arise, and she can return to Dr Jim if she gets into difficulties. She has also built into her life some key lifestyle changes: she exercises regularly, continues her mindfulness exercises, eats better, takes fish oils and has significantly moderated her wine consumption. She avoids caffeine and practices yoga. She has taken up painting to fulfil the creative side of her personality.

Most importantly, and almost unknown to Paula, the subtle CBT messages she has absorbed have helped her to reshape crucial neural pathways between her emotional brain and her logical brain – she has reshaped her own brain. And the even better news is that these changes will persist into the future.

If you suffer from GAD, if you can learn to apply some of these concepts in your life, then you too can reshape your brain.

9.
How Carol and John
Overcame Their Anxiety

Let's now visit Carol and John and listen to their stories, and see how they too learned to reshape their minds and brains to deal with GAD.

Carol's Story

Carol is thirty-three. She is married with three children, combining a busy home life with a part-time job as a receptionist. Her widowed mother struggled both with anxiety and with making ends meet. This has led to Carol being quite insecure, always struggling to be in control of every part of her life, and particularly her finances. This has led her into the world of GAD.

Carol presented to her GP complaining of extreme exhaustion; irritable bowels; teeth-grinding at night, with secondary facial pain; and increasing forgetfulness and difficulty concentrating. She had also lost some weight. If she encountered stress, her symptoms worsened. She sometimes felt slightly panicky, with her heart pounding and her stomach in knots, shaking, sweating, sighing and breathing shallowly. She had become increasingly reliant on drinking wine each evening to try to reduce her anxiety levels, and she was concerned that this was getting out of hand.

A good friend had become concerned that she might be developing depression, and had suggested that she go see her GP. Before doing so, Carol spent a fortune on alternative remedies, including homeopathy, hypnotherapy, aromatherapy and reflexology, to name but a few. Some of these helped her feel better, but they did not prevent her from slipping further into trouble. On the advice of an alternative therapist, she tried St John's wort, but she had a negative reaction and stopped using it.

She opened up to her GP, expressing her fear that she had become depressed, and detailing the therapies she had tried. She requested some blood tests and asked whether medication might be the way forward. The doctor listened to her story, examined her, and did some blood tests. She explained that she did not feel Carol was depressed, as her mood seemed normal. But she might be suffering from a more general form of anxiety called GAD, she said.

'In relation to using drug therapy, it is something we can consider if other therapies are not helping or if depression itself were to appear,' she said. 'But because you reacted badly to St John's wort, I would be inclined to avoid it.'

She gave Carol some general advice on diet, exercise, supplements, moderation in alcohol and yoga/meditation therapies. She also suggested visiting a colleague of hers called Dr Jim, who he said used CBT techniques to help people with GAD. Carol agreed.

When Carol attends Dr Jim, he agrees with her GP that her symptoms are suggestive of general anxiety disorder. He also agrees with the lifestyle changes her doctor recommended, especially on exercise, yoga, mindfulness, diet, supplements and avoiding the use of wine daily to calm her anxiety. He suggests she consider doing a number of CBT sessions. Carol agrees to this approach.

Dr Jim begins by describing what GAD is, as she is still unsure of what the diagnosis means. He gives her the analogy he gave Paula, of the central heating system in her house, and how it can be turned up or down, depending on the outside temperature. 'In GAD, Carol,' he explains, 'it is as if our whole stress system is dialled up all the time. Most of the physical symptoms we feel are simply a response to this overactive stress system.'

Carol asks whether her problems with anxiety stem from her childhood, and Dr Jim explains that this is possible, but that it doesn't really matter. 'We are much more concerned with how these problems are impacting your life now, and what to do about them,' he says.

He explains to Carol about rational and irrational beliefs, and how they are the lens through which we view everything that happens to us. He adds that we can pick them up – almost like viruses – in childhood, adolescence or adult life.

Dr Jim goes on to explain the ABC concept to Carol, and how they will use it to try to locate her irrational beliefs and learn how to deal with them. He adds that she will be the one writing the information on the ABC sheet. He asks her for an example of something that often triggers a bout of anxiety, as this will give them a concrete example to work on.

Carol gives him the example of receiving a telephone call from a friend and learning that a close associate at her workplace had just been fired. Following this conversation, she began to feel very anxious, she says.

'So now we have the trigger, which was the telephone call, and your emotion, which was anxiety,' says Dr Jim.

He asks Carol to write this information down on their ABC sheet, which she does.

A   Activating Event:

    o   Trigger: hearing that a close associate has been fired

    o   Inference/danger:

B   Belief/Demands:

C   Consequences:

    o   Emotional reactions: anxiety

    o   Physical reactions:

    o   Behaviour:

'Now,' asks Dr Jim, 'what were your physical responses when you became extremely anxious following this telephone conversation?'

'I just felt awful,' she replies. 'My stomach was in knots, I had difficulty taking a deep breath, and my heart was beating a little faster. I felt weak and shaky, all my muscles were very tense and the fatigue was overwhelming. I also had terrible nightmares and my husband told me I was grinding my teeth for nights after the conversation.'

'And what did you do?' he asks.

Carol says she began ringing work colleagues for reassurance that her job was not at risk, and started checking her mortgage-insurance details. She stopped eating and exercising and began drinking more wine to reduce her anxiety.

'But it was the thoughts going round and round in my head that really exhausted me,' she says. 'I kept replaying all of the potential scenarios that might happen if I were let go, particularly in bed at night and first thing in the morning. When I did sleep, I was grinding my teeth, so I must have been having nightmares.'

'These are typical of the kinds of behaviours that distress us so much in anxiety,' says Dr Jim. 'We will be examining them in detail later. For now, let's just add them to our ABC.'

A   Activating Event:

- o   Trigger: hearing that a close associate has been fired

- o   Inference/danger:

B   Belief/Demands:

C   Consequences:

- o   Emotional reactions: anxiety

- o   Physical reactions: stomach going into knots, difficulty taking a deep breath, heart beating a little faster, shaking, muscles very tense, teeth grinding at night and significantly increased fatigue

- o   Behaviour: rang a work colleague looking for reassurance that her job was not at risk; checked her mortgage-insurance details; drank more wine than usual; struggled to eat; had difficulty sleeping; spent hours replaying in her mind what would happen if she were let go; and stopped exercising.

'So what was it about this phone call that caused you to become so anxious?' Dr Jim asks. 'Anxiety usually means you are assigning some danger to a trigger. So, in this case, what danger were you assigning to the news of a close associate being let go? What did you visualise was going to happen?'

'My first thought was that I was going to be next in line,' Carol says.

'And what was it about that possibility that led you to feel so anxious?' Dr Jim asks.

Carol decides that her immediate concern was that it would become a real struggle for her and her husband to pay their mortgage. Dr Jim asks her to elaborate.

'All I could see was the repossession court, the eviction and a real battle to find somewhere for our family to live,' she says. 'At night, the scene replayed itself over and over in my mind. I could even visualise Paul, my husband, and I separating due to the stress of it all. I know of a few friends who have gone down that road. It was all a complete nightmare.'

'Were you anxious that all of this was actually going to happen, or was it just that it might happen?' Dr Jim enquires.

Carol thinks about the question. 'I suppose it was more that it might happen,' she decides.

'So what you are really saying is that it was your visualisation of what might happen – rather than what had actually happened – that was really behind your anxiety?' Dr Jim asks.

When Carol agrees, Dr Jim asks her to add this information to their ABC.

A   Activating Event:

- o   Trigger: hearing that a close associate has been fired

- o   Inference/danger: that she was next in line to be fired; if that happened her family's finances would be badly affected; they would struggle to pay the mortgage; they would end up in the repossession courts and lose their house; they would struggle to find somewhere to live; and they would end up homeless and possibly separated.

B   Belief/Demands:

C   Consequences:

   o   Emotional reactions: anxiety

   o   Physical reactions: stomach going into knots, difficulty taking a deep breath, heart beating a little faster, shaking, muscles very tense, teeth grinding at night and significantly increased fatigue

   o   Behaviour: rang a work colleague looking for reassurance that her job was not at risk; checked her mortgage-insurance details; drank more wine than usual; struggled to eat; had difficulty sleeping; spent hours replaying in her mind what would happen if she were let go; and stopped exercising.

'So now let's examine what irrational belief was triggered by this situation and the danger you assigned to it,' says Dr Jim. 'This usually takes the form of some absolute demand you are making about the trigger. So what demand were you making of yourself after this telephone conversation?'

'I was demanding that I must not lose my job,' says Carol. 'It really was that simple, because if I could achieve that demand then none of the rest would happen.'

'Suppose you were not able to achieve this demand and you did lose your job, then how would you feel about yourself?' Dr Jim enquires.

'I would feel a complete failure for not being able to prevent this happening,' she says.

'So what you were really demanding was that you absolutely must not lose your job, and if this were to happen you would feel you were a real failure,' Dr Jim says.

Carol agrees and they add this to their ABC.

A   Activating Event:

    o   Trigger: hearing that a close associate has been fired

    o   Inference/danger: that she was next in line to be fired; if that happened her family's finances would be badly affected; they would struggle to pay the mortgage; they would end up in the repossession courts and lose their house; they would struggle to find somewhere to live; and they would end up homeless and possibly separated.

B   Belief/Demands: 'I absolutely must not lose my job. If this happens, I am a complete failure for letting it happen.'

C   Consequences:

    o   Emotional reactions: anxiety

    o   Physical reactions: stomach going into knots, difficulty taking a deep breath, heart beating a little faster, shaking, muscles very tense, teeth grinding at night and significantly increased fatigue

    o   Behaviour: rang a work colleague looking for reassurance that her job was not at risk; checked her mortgage-insurance details; drank more wine than usual; struggled to eat; had difficulty sleeping; spent hours replaying in her mind what would happen if she were let go; and stopped exercising.

'So if we were to summarise all the information that we have put together on our ABC, Carol, it would look like this,' says Dr Jim.

- You had a conversation with a friend and heard he had lost his job. As a result, you became very anxious, with multiple physical symptoms.

- Your main danger was that you would lose your job, struggle to pay your mortgage, lose your house and end up homeless.

- You interpreted this conversation through the irrational belief or lens that you absolutely must not lose your job, because if you did you would be a failure for letting that happen.
- That was what was really making you so anxious.
- All of your subsequent behaviour – some of which was what we call safety behaviour – was to allay and reassure your anxiety.

'Now that we have some understanding of what made you so anxious about this event,' says Dr Jim, 'and your resulting behaviour, let's see if we can assist you to reshape both your thinking and behaviour in relation to this. If we are successful for this event, we can apply the same ideas to similar situations in the future.'

Challenging Carol's 'A'

'We could dispute or challenge your "A", your interpretation of the telephone conversation with your friend,' Dr Jim explains. 'To do this, we could probably dispute where your proof was that the dangers you laid out were really going to happen. But what is much more effective, Carol, is to challenge the "B" and the "C". What we mean by this is to challenge your irrational belief, which is the real driver of your anxiety – and the emotional and behavioural consequences of this belief.'

Challenging Carol's 'C'

'Let's start by challenging the "C", the consequences. It's not useful or realistic to just try to stop being anxious. We have to learn to simply accept our emotions as they are,' Dr Jim says. 'Now, what causes all of the physical symptoms you experienced when you got anxious after this telephone conversation?'

Carol says she thinks it was her anxiety that was the cause. Dr Jim agrees, but says that in practice her stress system lay behind the physical symptoms.

'Whenever our emotional brain senses a danger, whether real or perceived, it immediately activates our acute stress system, which prepares us to fight or flee,' Dr Jim explains. 'It does so by activating our internal nervous system, and also by releasing our fear hormone, adrenaline.'

Dr Jim introduces Carol to the amygdala. He explains that it is in charge of her stress system. It is a primitive organ whose function is to seek out danger in the environment, and, if it perceives any, to fire. It is the amygdala that triggers the fight-freeze-or-flight response, he says. This organ is vital for our survival, and extremely efficient in its function. He then discusses with her what adrenaline is, helping her to see that it is simply our do-a-runner hormone, and that the symptoms it causes are uncomfortable but not dangerous.

When we are constantly anxious, he explains, we also release our chronic-stress hormone glucocortisol. It was this that caused her to feel fatigue, have difficulties with concentration and have tired-but-wired feelings at night when she was trying to sleep.

Dr Jim explains that there is no actual danger from these physical symptoms, but stresses that they are extremely uncomfortable. It is this discomfort that so many with anxiety struggle the most to deal with. He then explores the idea of learning to accept that the more she demands the symptoms go away, the more they will increase; the more she accepts and just goes with them, the more they will start to become background noise.

Carol queries why she would experience these physical symptoms at times when there was no obvious trigger for them. He explains that this is probably because our amygdala is hypersensitive in GAD, and can trigger these symptoms of its own accord. The best way to manage them is a combination of physical exercise, mindfulness exercises, and treating them like background noise and just going with them, Dr Jim says.

'Now let's examine your behaviour when you became anxious about your demands in relation to this assignment,' Dr Jim says.

This leads to a discussion of many of the unhealthy behaviours that Carol fell into.

'They are what I always do in such situations,' she admits.

Following a frank conversation, Carol agrees that stopping exercise, heading for the wine bottle, eating poorly and binning her dinners were definitely not of assistance. Dr Jim and Carol agree that persistently seeking advice from work colleagues was not helping to solve the issues. It was also not really of help to be constantly ruminating and visualising all of the scenarios that might result from her losing her job.

Next, Dr Jim and Carol revisit more positive behaviours, like exercising more, eating better, not using alcohol as a crutch, doing some mindfulness exercises, taking up yoga, and writing down things that are upsetting her (using the ABC sheets) and learning to challenge them. The latter would help her to learn how best to encourage her more logical mind to examine situations, rather than leaving her emotional mind to run the show, Dr Jim says. Carol accepts these suggestions.

She finds it very helpful to understand why she felt the way she did – both emotionally and physically – when she was anxious. She believes she will be able to cope better with such situations in the future. She has also learned the importance of behaviour, and how it can be changed.

Challenging Carol's 'B'

'Let's examine and challenge your "B", your irrational belief. This took the form of an absolute demand that you must not lose your job, because if you did you would be a failure for letting it happen,' says Dr Jim. 'So do you think this demand is rational or irrational?'

Carol says it was probably irrational.

'What lies at the heart of anxiety,' explains Dr Jim, 'is that we make some impossible demand of ourselves, and, when we can't achieve this goal, we rate ourselves as a failure.'

He then challenged her 'B'.

'So, returning to your absolute demand that you must not lose your job,' Dr Jim says, 'what would be a healthier demand?'

After some discussion, they both agree that a more rational or healthier demand might be that she prefers not to lose her job, but whether this happens is out of her control. That leads to a discussion on the importance of control in Carol's life. Dr Jim asks her what she can really control. After a few attempts to answer this, she realises that she is able to control very little.

When we seek control, Dr Jim explains, we are looking for one or more of the following: 100-percent certainty, order, security or perfection. He and Carol have a good conversation about Carol's need for 100-percent certainty that she will not lose her job, and her demand for 100-percent security for herself and her family. She begins to realise that these are impossible demands to fulfil. To teach her this at an emotional level, he gives her the coin-toss and disorder exercises that he gave to Paula.

Dr Jim goes on to challenge Carol's catastrophising in relation to the situation. Did she have any proof that her visualisations of what might happen would, in fact, occur? he asks her. He shares with her the spilt-milk analogy he used with Paula. He also explains the role of her right PFC in creating these catastrophic visualisations, and how applying the spilt-milk analogy on paper would assist this part of her brain to reduce this tendency.

When Dr Jim introduces Carol to the Raggy Doll Club, she is more than willing to become a lifelong member.

Dr Jim then summarises all the work they have done in challenging her demand that she must not lose her job, and if she does, that will make her a failure.

- Carol had been looking for 100-percent certainty that she would not lose her job. This was an impossible demand, as nothing in life is guaranteed. So it was better to change this to a demand that she would prefer not to lose her job.

- Her need for 100-percent security in relation to her family's financial situation was also not realistic. Was 100-percent certainty possible in any other area of our lives?

- She had been imagining the worst without any proof that it would occur. If she re-examined her assumption that she was certain to lose her job, was there any clear evidence to back that up?

- She then criticised herself, put herself down and assumed others would do likewise.

- Carol needed to become a Raggy Doll.

Dr Jim explains that this ABC example is a microcosm of what happens to us when we become anxious. If Carol can apply the lessons learnt through it, she can reshape her thoughts and feelings, he says.

Carol is enthusiastic about continuing, so Dr Jim asks her to document in a notebook periods when she becomes very anxious. She should write down the trigger and all the rest, in the ABC manner they have worked on, he says. He also challenges her to regularly perform the coin-toss and disorder exercises.

★

After a series of such sessions, Carol is experiencing a lot less anxiety and fatigue, and she is recognising triggers and demands much more easily. She has become more realistic in the demands she places on herself, and has found herself a real-life Raggy Doll, which she regularly communicates with when she finds she is rating herself. She is learning about mindfulness, and has begun to practice the three-minute breathing space every day.

She still suffers from GAD, and acute stressors will still occasionally throw her off line, but, overall, she is doing much better. She has techniques to deal with any issues that arise, and she can return to Dr Jim if she gets into difficulties. She has also built into her life some key lifestyle changes they have agreed on.

Most importantly, and almost unknown to Carol, the subtle CBT messages she has absorbed have helped her to reshape crucial neural pathways between her emotional brain and her logical brain – she has reshaped her own brain. And the even better news is that these changes will persist into the future.

Sean's Story

'It's there first thing in the morning when I wake up, before I have time to worry about anything. I am just a freak,' Sean tells Dr Jim on his first visit.

Sean is twenty-five and has had trouble with anxiety from a very early age.

He was the typical anxious child, brought up by an equally anxious mother, seeing their family doctor so many times it was embarrassing. The list of physical ailments seemed endless: from limb pains to abdominal pains to headaches. His doctor was constantly referring him for specialist opinions. Eventually, he was diagnosed as an 'anxious child', and the label stuck.

Sean's anxiety reached its zenith in his adolescence. He spent most of his schooldays complaining of physical symptoms such as unexplained headaches, abdominal pains, intermittent diarrhoea, weak spells and panic attacks. With the support of a special guidance counsellor, he somehow made it through. His exam years were a nightmare. Picking up on his mother's desire for him to achieve, he strove to be the perfect student. His panic attacks were so bad that eventually he had to be placed in a separate room to do his Leaving Cert exams, along with a few other classmates.

When he got to college, his anxiety reached new levels. As a result, he began to miss lectures and tutorials. His anxiety began the minute he woke up and continued for most of the day, a mixture of dread, worry, constant ruminations and catastrophic visualisations, against a background of unpredictable panic attacks. He stopped eating properly and began to lose weight. His concentration waned and he began to self-harm, unable to cope with the distress and discomfort created by the classic mix of fear and worry.

Other students in Sean's class were achieving their objectives more easily than he was, which made him even more anxious. And the more anxious he got, the more disturbed his sleep became, the more weight he lost and the more panic attacks he began to experience. He began to see himself more and more as a weak person, incapable of dealing with life.

Sean attended the college doctor, concerned that maybe he was suffering from depression. The doctor confirmed that the issue was more anxiety, as his mood was occasionally low but not consistently so. The doctor suggested that drug therapy was not the most effective way to deal with this issue. Instead, he referred Sean for counselling. When this was unsuccessful, he suggested that Sean visit Dr Jim, who used CBT to help people deal with their anxiety.

Dr Jim agrees with Sean's college doctor that the main problem is anxiety, not depression. He explains what GAD is, and how it is often accompanied by panic attacks. There are two types of anxiety circuits in our brains, he says, and in Sean's case both are quite active.

'The lower circuit is the one that is probably causing your panic attacks and the way you are feeling when you wake up,' Dr Jim says. 'The upper one is causing most of your difficulties with constant worrying. I am going to show you some techniques to calm both of these circuits down. Which is causing you the greatest distress? That is where we should start.'

'I would love to be able to live my life without the fear of further panic attacks,' Sean says. 'After that, I would like to be able to cope better with the panicky feelings I have first thing in the morning, and then the nonstop stream of negative worrying thoughts that are constantly filling my head for the rest of the day.'

For the rest of the visit, Dr Jim shows Sean how to use the ABC system to understand and deal with panic attacks. He encourages Sean to exercise more and to enlist in a mindfulness course. After two visits, Sean is no longer having panic attacks, and he is comfortable that they no longer pose a threat to his psychological well-being.

'Now,' says Dr Jim, 'let's move on to the second issue that was bothering you: what happens when you wake up each morning. Can you give me an example?'

'Two days ago, on Monday morning, I woke up feeling incredibly anxious,' says Sean. 'I was not thinking about anything at all, but I still felt tense. Not knowing what was making me anxious made it even worse. Within five minutes, my mind was full of thoughts about an assignment that I had to have ready by the end of this week, one that I had kept putting off making a start on. As the deadline was looming, I was becoming increasingly anxious to have it ready in time, and, more importantly, to deliver the perfect assignment to my tutor.'

'So there are really two separate issues going on here,' Dr Jim says. 'The first is the presence of these feelings when you wake up in the morning, and the second is your upcoming assignment. So let's do a separate ABC on each of these triggers and see what we can learn.'

They start with the trigger of Sean waking up feeling very tense and anxious.

'Just what were these feelings like?' Dr Jim asks.

Sean has never really examined this before. He takes a minute to reflect, before answering. 'My muscles were all tense, my jaw was sore from clenching it, my stomach was in knots, I was shaky and trembling, I had difficulty breathing and my heart was pounding,' he says.

'And after the work we did on your panic attacks, can you guess what caused these symptoms?' Dr Jim enquires.

'I assume these were simply the physical symptoms of me being anxious,' Sean says.

'So what was your emotional reaction to waking up feeling so tense?' Dr Jim asks.

Sean says he became extremely anxious and slightly panicky, and then the physical symptoms he had woken up with became much worse.

Dr Jim starts an ABC sheet, and Sean writes down this information.

A   Activating Event:

- o   Trigger: waking up in the morning feeling very tense

- o   Inference/danger:

B   Belief/Demands:

C   Consequences:

- o   Emotional reactions: anxiety

- o   Physical reactions: tense muscles, shortness of breath, jaw sore from clenching, stomach in knots, body shaking and trembling, heart was pounding

- o   Behaviour:

'So what was it about waking up feeling so tense that caused you to become so anxious and panicky?' asks Dr Jim. 'In general, as we saw in dealing with your panic attacks, this usually means that you are assigning some danger to the trigger. So what danger were you assigning to waking up feeling like this?'

'For me, the really scary bit was that I could see no reason why I was feeling like that,' Sean explains. 'I wasn't worrying about anything at time. To be honest, I just thought that I was going slowly mad.'

'So your real danger was that if there was no obvious cause for feeling like that, it must have meant that you were going insane,' says Dr Jim.

Sean agreed, and so Dr Jim asked him to add this to their ABC.

A Activating Event:

> o Trigger: waking up in the morning feeling very tense
>
> o Inference/danger: 'As there is no obvious reason I am waking up feeling so tense, it must mean I am going slowly mad.'

B Belief/Demands:

C Consequences:

> o Emotional reactions: anxiety
>
> o Physical reactions: tense muscles, shortness of breath, jaw sore from clenching, stomach in knots, body shaking and trembling, heart was pounding
>
> o Behaviour:

'So what was your demand then, Sean, and what did you do when you became increasingly anxious?' asks Dr Jim.

'My demand was simply that this awful feeling of tension and the other physical symptoms must go away,' says Sean. 'As for what I did, I simply tried everything I could to banish them, and I also tried to distract myself by focusing on tasks for the day. But then I started to get anxious about my upcoming assignment.'

They then added this information to their ABC.

A Activating Event:

> o Trigger: waking up in the morning feeling very tense
>
> o Inference/danger: 'As there is no obvious reason I am waking

up feeling so tense, it must mean I am going slowly mad.'

B   Belief/Demands: 'These physical symptoms must go away.'

C   Consequences:

o   Emotional reactions: anxiety

o   Physical reactions: tense muscles, shortness of breath, jaw sore from clenching, stomach in knots, body shaking and trembling, heart was pounding

o   Behaviour: tried to make the symptoms go away with the power of his thoughts, and then tried to distract himself from the feelings by focusing on his work for the day, in particular his upcoming assignment.

Dr Jim then lays out what he felt were the key parts of the ABC.

- The initial trigger for Sean waking up tense was that he was experiencing the simple physical feelings of being anxious.

- He assigned a danger to this trigger: that because he could not identify the reason for it, he was going slowly mad.

- He began to demand that the physical symptoms go away.

- The more he demanded they go away, the more anxious he became.

- The more anxious he became, the more his physical symptoms increased.

- His attempts to make the physical symptoms go away were not been helpful, nor were his attempts at distracting himself.

Dr Jim then asks Sean if he notices any similarity between this ABC sheet and the sheets they did on his panic attacks. Sean immediately sees the link.

'In both cases,' Sean ventures, 'the initial triggers were just the physical symptoms of being anxious.'

'That's true, but what else is similar?' Dr Jim asks.

When Sean really examines the sheet, he notices that in both cases he was anxious about being anxious, and that he was demanding the symptoms go away.

'I also can see that my danger is the same in both cases, namely that I thought I was going mad,' says Sean. 'Also, by trying to demand that the symptoms go away, I was making things worse in both situations.'

Dr Jim and Sean also agreed that his behaviours – trying to make the symptoms go away, and trying to distract himself – were not helpful. Dr Jim then explains that he wants Sean to take the same approach to the physical symptoms as he had with his panic attacks, and accept them as uncomfortable but not dangerous. Sean agrees to try to do this from now on.

'But now,' asks Dr Jim, 'let's return to your initial danger: that there was no obvious cause for waking up first thing in the morning with these symptoms, and therefore they were a sign that you were going mad. Does experiencing the simple physical symptoms of anxiety caused by your stress system firing really mean that you are going mad?

Sean agrees that this is unlikely. 'But I still don't really understand why I wake up with all of these symptoms,' he says. 'I can now accept that they are uncomfortable but not dangerous, and feel I can now learn to live with them, but I would still like to know why they are present so many mornings when I awake.'

What Was Going on in Sean's Brain When He Was Asleep?

'Suppose I asked you something completely different,' says Dr Jim. 'What happens to your brain when you are asleep?'

'I assume it is also resting,' says Sean, unsure. 'Although I know we also dream at night, so I assume that in some way it must at times still be active.'

Dr Jim explains that we are normally asleep for around eight hours a night. He says this can be broken up into some periods when the brain seems to be resting, but is actually carrying out essential repairs, and other periods – REM sleep phases – when we are strengthening and reorganising our memories. He explains that REM sleep is characterised by rapid eye movements, and that it is during REM sleep phases that we dream.

'Dreams are simply the result of the brain taking all of the information from the previous day's activities and filing and refiling it in various places,' Dr Jim says. 'This activity can create confused visual and emotional constructs, so the brain tries to put them together to form a story. When we wake up in the middle of such a story, we call it a dream – or a nightmare, if it is really unpleasant. We now know that more than two-thirds of all dreams are anxious dreams. When we have one of these, the amygdala triggers the same physical sensations it would if we were awake. But because we are asleep, we are unaware of them.'

Sean is starting to put it all together now. 'So what you are saying is that if I had such a dream – or, more likely, nightmare – shortly before I woke up in the morning, but I don't consciously remember it, I can still end up with the emotional and physical feelings I experienced during it?'

'That is exactly what happens,' says Dr Jim. 'We dream more, or have more REM phases, during the last two hours before we wake than we do earlier in the night. So this makes it possible to wake up either during such an anxiety-laden dream, or shortly after it. If you are inclined to be more anxious during the day, it makes sense that the dreams you have will involve a lot of emotions of fear and associated physical symptoms.'

'Let me get this clear,' says Sean. 'What you are saying is that many of these physical symptoms that I wake up with are then really coming from my unconscious mind when I am asleep, where my memories or dreams, as you described them, are being activated, with the result that I am either panicky or anxious when I am asleep?'

'It was not being able to remember the dream in the morning when you awoke that was really making you so anxious,' says Dr Jim. 'This is because you were unaware of all of this happening in your brain when you were asleep. So when your stress system was firing due to fear or anxiety in your dream, the result was all of the physical symptoms you were experiencing when you woke up.'

Suddenly, Sean has a thought. 'Is it possible that the assignment that I was worrying about for the few days before was making my brain more anxious when I was asleep?' he asks.

'Yes,' Dr Jim says. 'If you were anxious about something like your assignment, it was inevitable that your brain, as it was reorganising memories while you slept, would be more likely to trigger an anxiety-laden dream.'

For Sean, this is a light-bulb moment, as he realises there is an explanation for the morning symptoms he has been experiencing for years. He vows never to allow these early morning physical sensations to bother him again. While they are uncomfortable, he is determined to accept them and not assign a danger to them. Above all, he knows he is not going mad.

On his next visit with Dr Jim, Sean is coping much better with his panic attacks gone and also with the early morning physical symptoms. But he is still anxious during the day, his mind filled with worrying, negative thoughts, and some associated physical symptoms. He asks Jim for some assistance with this.

Dr Jim returns to the second trigger Sean told him about on the previous visit: his anxiety about the assignment that was due to be handed in that week. He takes out an ABC sheet for this issue, and begins explaining to Sean the role of rational and irrational beliefs in our lives.

'We know that when we get extremely anxious about something,' Dr Jim says, 'it usually means that one of our irrational beliefs has been triggered. So we are going to use the example you have given us to see if we can track down which irrational belief is causing you to feel so anxious, with all the physical and behavioural difficulties that this unhealthy negative emotion can lead to. Let's start with the trigger again, and your emotion.'

'My trigger here was the assignment that was due to be handed in, and my emotion was anxiety,' says Sean, who is now quite comfortable with this process.

'And what physical symptoms did you experience when you became very anxious about this trigger?' enquires Dr Jim.

'During the day in question, I began to get the usual symptoms: tiredness, difficulties with concentration, tension headaches and stomach pains,' says Sean. 'To be honest, I knew they were due to anxiety, but it didn't help – I just felt like crap.'

Dr Jim asks Sean to add these to their ABC.

A Activating Event:

- o Trigger: upcoming assignment to be handed in
- o Inference/danger:

B Belief/Demands:

C Consequences:

- o Emotional reactions:
- o Physical reactions: initially, tense muscles, shortness of breath, jaw sore from clenching, stomach in knots, body shaking and trembling and heart pounding; later developed persistent fatigue, difficulty concentrating, stomach pains and a tension headache
- o Behaviour:

'So what was it about this assignment that caused you to become so anxious?' asks Dr Jim. 'This usually means that you are assigning some danger to the trigger. So what danger were you visualising as a result of this particular assignment?'

'There were a number of things really bothering me,' explains Sean. 'The first was that I am a bit of a perfectionist. In this, I take after my mother. I really struggle to hand an assignment unless I feel I have done as perfect a job as I can on it. But as a result of procrastinating about writing it, I found myself running out of time. I felt so stupid that I had let that happen. I am in college long enough now to know that you cannot leave things until the last moment.'

'That's the first danger Sean,' Dr Jim says, 'but what else was bothering you about the assignment?'

'Well, I was also bothered that if I did not get it lodged with my tutor in time, it might not be accepted, and I would fail this part of my exam. If that happened, I could visualise myself getting further behind, and finally having to repeat the exams in the autumn, as I would not pass them in summer,' says Sean. 'I also found myself increasingly bothered that using up all the energy necessary to write up the assignment would leave me feeling more fatigued and more anxious. In the past, before I met you, I would also have worried that if that happened, it might trigger a panic attack.'

'So let's summarise your dangers,' Dr Jim says.

- 'The assignment might not be done as perfectly as I would like, and I would feel I have let myself and my tutor down if this were to happen.'

- 'I might run out of time to do it due to my procrastination.'

- 'I might not get the assignment in to my tutor in time, and so I might end up failing this module.'

- 'This might lead me to end up failing the whole course in the summer and having to repeat in the autumn.'

- 'The energy I might have to use to write up the assignment will lead me to feeling more fatigued and eventually more anxious.'

- 'If this happened, in the past, I would have been bothered that I might end up having a panic attack.'

Dr Jim asks Sean to add these to the ABC.

- A Activating Event:
  - o Trigger: upcoming assignment to be handed in
  - o Inference/danger: 'The assignment might not be done as perfectly as I would like, and I would feel I have let myself and my tutor down if this were to happen; I might run out of time to do it due to my procrastination; I might not get the assignment in to my tutor in time, and so I might end up failing this module; this might lead me to end up failing the whole course in the summer and having to repeat in the autumn; the

energy I might have to use to write up the assignment will lead me to feeling more fatigued and eventually more anxious; if this happened, in the past, I would have been bothered that I might end up having a panic attack.'

B Belief/Demands:

C Consequences:

o Emotional reactions:

o Physical reactions: initially, tense muscles, shortness of breath, jaw sore from clenching, stomach in knots, body shaking and trembling and heart pounding; later developed persistent fatigue, difficulty concentrating, stomach pains and a tension headache

o Behaviour:

Dr Jim continues: 'Let's now examine which irrational belief was triggered by this situation and the danger you assigned it. This usually takes the form of some absolute demand you are making about the trigger. So what demand were you making, Sean, in relation to this assignment?'

'I suppose I was demanding a few things,' ventures Sean. 'The main one being that the assignment must be done perfectly and be in on time.' He reflects for a moment and then continues. 'I also suppose that I was demanding that I don't fail this module or, in particular, the whole year. And, of course, I was demanding that I would not get more anxious, and, in particular, would not have a panic attack. Although, after the work we have done, I no longer have to worry about this.'

'Well done,' Dr Jim says. 'These are, indeed, the demands being triggered by your irrational beliefs. But suppose you were unable to satisfy these demands, such as your demand that you must hand in the perfect assignment on time. How would you feel about yourself?'

Sean sees what he means. 'I would feel I was a complete failure,' he replies.

Dr Jim then explains that this was the typical irrational belief and absolute demand we make of ourselves when significant anxiety is triggered. 'We make some impossible demands of ourselves, and when we can't fulfil these demands, rate ourselves as failures,' he adds.

They added this new information to their ABC.

A Activating Event:

    o Trigger: upcoming assignment to be handed in

    o Inference/danger: 'The assignment might not be done as perfectly as I would like, and I would feel I have let myself and my tutor down if this were to happen; I might run out of time to do it due to my procrastination; I might not get the assignment in to my tutor in time, and so I might end up failing this module; this might lead me to end up failing the whole course in the summer and having to repeat in the autumn; the energy I might have to use to write up the assignment will lead me to feeling more fatigued and eventually more anxious; if this happened, in the past, I would have been bothered that I might end up having a panic attack.'

B Belief/Demands: 'My assignment must be done perfectly and be in on time with my tutor, and if this does not happen then I am a failure; I must not fail this module or the whole year, and if I do I am a failure; I must be certain that I do not get more anxious or have more panic attacks, and if I do it will be awful and I am a failure for letting it happen.'

C Consequences:

    o Emotional reactions:

    o Physical reactions: initially, tense muscles, shortness of breath, jaw sore from clenching, stomach in knots, body shaking and trembling and heart pounding; later developed persistent fatigue, difficulty concentrating, stomach pains and a tension headache

o   Behaviour:

'So what did you do Sean, when you became very anxious as a result of this demand?' asks Dr Jim. 'It is often our behaviour in such situations that causes us difficulties.'

'I did my usual trick of putting off doing the assignment until the last second,' says Sean. 'It was as if the more I put it off, the more I was convincing myself that I was really planning it out and that when I got around to it I would do an even better job. But, of course, I was only fooling myself.'

'And what else did you do?' prompts Dr Jim.

'I spent more time thinking about it, day and night, rather than doing anything to get it started,' says Sean. 'When I did start, I just found myself checking and rechecking what I was doing, to see if it was done as perfectly as possible. I also struggled to sleep because of these thoughts in my head, and distracted myself by going on to my social media or by going on drinking binges. I checked with fellow students about how they were laying out their projects, but if I were to be brutally honest, I mostly just stopped eating, lost weight, drank too much and self-harmed to deal with the constant worrying thoughts and horrible physical sensations brought on by my anxiety.'

They then added this new information to their ABC.

A   Activating Event:

o   Trigger: upcoming assignment to be handed in

o   Inference/danger: 'The assignment might not be done as perfectly as I would like, and I would feel I have let myself and my tutor down if this were to happen; I might run out of time to do it due to my procrastination; I might not get the assignment in to my tutor in time, and so I might end up failing this module; this might lead me to end up failing the whole course in the summer and having to repeat in the autumn; the energy I might have to use to write up the assignment will lead me to feeling more fatigued and eventually more anxious; if this happened, in the past, I would have been bothered that I might end up having a panic attack.'

B Belief/Demands: 'My assignment must be done perfectly and be in on time with my tutor, and if this does not happen then I am a failure; I must not fail this module or the whole year, and if I do I am a failure; I must be certain that I do not get more anxious or have more panic attacks, and if I do it will be awful and I am a failure for letting it happen.'

C Consequences:

o Emotional reactions:

o Physical reactions: initially, tense muscles, shortness of breath, jaw sore from clenching, stomach in knots, body shaking and trembling and heart pounding; later developed persistent fatigue, difficulty concentrating, stomach pains and a tension headache

o Behaviour: kept avoiding starting the assignment; when he did start, was constantly checking and rechecking to see if it was done as perfectly as possible; stopped eating and lost weight; constantly ruminated on the issue; constantly checked in with classmates about how they were doing their projects; struggled to sleep; used alcohol as a crutch; self-harmed.

'So now that we understand, Sean, what made you so anxious about this assignment, and your resulting behaviour, let's see if we can help you to reshape both your thinking and behaviour,' says Dr Jim. 'Because if we can assist you to do this in relation to this issue, we can apply the same ideas to similar situations in the future.'

Challenging Sean's 'A'

'We could dispute or challenge your "A" – your interpretation of this assignment and the dangers you associated with it,' Dr Jim explains. 'I could probably dispute with you where your proof was that the dangers you laid out were really going to happen. What is much more effective, is to challenge the "B" and the "C". What I mean by this is challenge the irrational beliefs we have already uncovered, which are the real drivers of your anxiety, and also challenge the emotional and behavioural consequences of these beliefs.'

Challenging Sean's 'C'

Dr Jim starts by asking Sean the value of just trying to stop being anxious, and they both agree that this is neither useful nor realistic. It's better to simply accept our emotions as they are, Dr Jim says.

'What caused all of the physical symptoms that you experienced when you became anxious as a result of your demand that you had to present a perfect assignment to your tutor, on time?' Dr Jim asks.

When Sean suggests that his extreme anxiety was the cause, Dr Jim asks him what happened in his body during all this. Sean, based on the work they did on his panic attacks, suggests that his stress system was behind the physical symptoms.

Dr Jim then reminds him of their discussion about the amygdala: how it is in charge of his stress system, whose function is to seek out danger in the environment, and, if it perceives any, to fire; and how it is the amygdala that triggers the fight-freeze-or-flight response. It was this organ, he explains, that had triggered Sean's stress system to produce the physical symptoms he was feeling.

Dr Jim reminds Sean that these symptoms posed no actual danger, but stresses that he understands that they were extremely uncomfortable. He then explores again the idea of learning to accept that the more Sean demands his symptoms go away, the more they will increase; and the more he accepts and just goes with them, the more they will start to become background noise. He also explains how, when we are constantly anxious, we release our chronic-stress hormone, glucocorticol; it is this, Dr Jim says, that left Sean feeling fatigued, having difficulties with concentration and feeling tired-but-wired at night when he was trying to sleep.

Sean queries why he would experience these same physical symptoms at times when there was no obvious trigger for them. Dr Jim explains that this was probably because our amygdala is hypersensitive in GAD, and can trigger these symptoms of its own accord. He notes that the best way to manage these symptoms is a combination of physical exercise, mindfulness exercises, and treating them like background noise and just going with them.

'Now,' Dr Jim says, 'let's examine your behaviour when you became very anxious about the absolute demands you were placing on yourself in relation to this assignment. Was it useful, for example, to constantly procrastinate or to keep rechecking it, looking for perfection?'

Sean agrees that this behaviour was only creating problems. Dr Jim explains that a better approach would have been to break the assignments into small parts and do one small part each day until it was done. 'We also have to become more realistic: in real-life, perfection is a myth; the more we strive for it, the more anxious we will become,' he says.

Dr Jim and Sean also agree that not eating, using alcohol as a crutch and self-harming would only add to his distress, rather than relieving it. 'I need to find new techniques to cope with such situations,' Sean says.

Challenging Sean's 'B'

'We need now to examine and challenge your "B" – your irrational belief,' says Dr Jim.

He and Sean agree that this took the form of a few absolute demands: 'My assignment must be done perfectly and be in on time with my tutor. If this does not happen, then I am a failure. I must not fail this module or the whole year – if I do I am a failure. I must be certain that I do not get more anxious or have more panic attacks. If this happens, it will be awful and I am a failure for letting it happen.'

Dr Jim continues: 'When you look at these demands, Sean, do you think that they are irrational?'

Sean admits that when he looks at them on paper, using his common sense, he sees that they are irrational.

'But why?' asks Dr Jim.

Sean feels that they are absolute demands that are not achievable in real life. He agrees that thinking *I am a failure* is also quite irrational.

'This lies at the heart of the problem,' explains Dr Jim. 'When we are anxious, it is usually because we are making impossible demands on ourselves, and, when we can't achieve our goals, we rate ourselves as a failure.'

Dr Jim goes on to show Sean the big MACS, and explain how to use them to challenge his demands. He then challenges Sean's 'B'. He explains that people who suffer from anxiety live in the 'land of must'. 'So, returning to your absolute demand that your assignment had to be done perfectly and be in to your tutor in time, what would be a healthier demand?' he asks.

After some discussion, they agree that a more rational, healthier demand in this situation would be that he would prefer to do his assignment as well as he could, and get it in to his tutor in time, but whether this happens or not is out of his control.

That leads to a discussion on the importance of control in Sean's life. Dr Jim asks him what he can really control in his life. After a few attempts to try to answer this, Sean begins to realise that, in reality, he is able to control very little.

When we are seeking control, Dr Jim says, we are looking for one or more of the following: 100-percent certainty, order, security or perfection. After a good conversation about Sean's need for 100-percent certainty that, for example, he would be able to produce a perfect assignment for his tutor, Sean realises that that would be impossible to guarantee.

'Can we be 100-percent certain about anything in life other than death?' Dr Jim asks.

Sean has to agree that we can't.

'So we have to accept that in real life there is always a chance that what we fear might happen can actually occur, and we have to live with that possibility,' Dr Jim says.

They also agree that there is no such thing as 100-percent security, order or perfection, and that to demand any of those is unrealistic and doomed to make us anxious.

Dr Jim goes on to explain that the main reason we seek control in the 'big' areas of our lives is that we think we are in control of the little things, and points out how our domestic lives are a good example of this. He gives Sean the coin-toss and disorder exercises.

Many people who suffer from anxiety spend a lot of time imagining worst-case scenarios, where everything becomes a 'catastrophe', Dr Jim says. Sean says he can relate to this. 'I spend so much time imagining the worst,' he says.

They agree that Sean's assumption that if his assignment was not in time, he would automatically fail not only his module but also the whole year was an example of this type of thinking. Where was his proof that this would be the case? Sean has to agree that he had no proof – he was just imagining the worst.

Dr Jim goes on to explain that this tendency to visualise the worst, 'catastrophising', comes from our right PFC, and is really common in anxiety. The only way we can challenge these negative thoughts and visualisations is to write down what we think is going to happen, and then try to prove it on paper.

Dr Jim shares with Sean the spilt-milk analogy. 'If you can't prove on paper that what you are visualising is definitely going to happen, then it is only a drop of spilt milk, not a puddle,' he says.

Sean finds this concept really helpful. From now on, he will write down negative possibilities and challenge their accuracy on paper, rather than ruminate on them or catastrophise, he says.

Dr Jim explains that it is quite common for those who suffer from anxiety to assume that they will not be able to cope if their demands are not met and the resulting worst-case scenario unfolds. 'But in real life, is there really any alternative to coping?' he asks.

Dr Jim then challenges Sean on his habit of 'self-rating'. 'This lies at the heart of anxiety, and, indeed, depression,' Dr Jim says. 'This is where we not only judge ourselves but accept others' opinions of us as well.' He introduces Sean to the Raggy Doll Club, explaining that it is a highly exclusive club that he himself has been a member of for many years. 'There are three important criteria for membership: 1) we cannot rate ourselves; 2) we cannot accept other people's ratings of us; and 3) we can rate our behaviour, but not ourselves,' he says.

Dr Jim goes on to ask Sean what a 'failure' is. This leads to an animated discussion on what the difference is between being a failure as a person, and just failing in a specific task or in our behaviour. Dr Jim explains to Sean that we have this voice in our head called our 'pathological critic', which exists to make our lives as miserable as possible.

'In anxiety and depression, in particular, this inner voice is especially active,' Dr Jim says. 'It blurs the margins between who we are as people, and our behaviour. It is this part of our brain and emotional mind that convinces us we are failures, whilst in real life this is obviously completely untrue. In real life, nobody can be defined as a failure as a person – no such person exists.'

This is another light-bulb moment for Sean, who has spent his whole life living in the world of rating. He struggles to conceive of a world where this would no longer be relevant.

'So what you are really saying is that I have to learn to accept myself just for myself?' Sean asks.

'Yes,' says Dr Jim. 'Learning to accept ourselves unconditionally is the most important step we can ever take in our lives.'

They then begin to examine Sean's long-term quest for perfection, and the importance of the fact that anybody who is a member of the Raggy Doll Club accepts that they are not perfect and, indeed, have regularly messed up in terms of their actions in life.

'We have to understand that we can try to do our best in life, but will regularly fail and must accept that this is OK,' says Dr Jim.

Sean feels a huge weight falling away from him, and reflects on the years he has spent seeking perfection in so many ways, and how this search has made him so anxious.

Dr Jim then explains to Sean that the ABC example they have just worked through was a microcosm of what happens to us when we become anxious. If Sean can apply the lessons learnt, he can reshape his thoughts and feelings.

But he will have to work hard over a period of time if he wants to get better. They then decide that Sean will keep a notebook to document situations in which he becomes anxious, and write down the trigger and all the other information in the ABC manner they have worked on. Dr Jim also challenges Sean to regularly do the coin-toss and disorder exercises.

Sean follows this advice, and finally learns to accept that life is completely out of his control, and stop demanding that it should be any different. He also becomes a Raggy Doll, and, even though it is difficult, he put the concepts into action as often as he can.

After a series of sessions with Dr Jim, Sean is experiencing a lot less anxiety, and has become more realistic in the demands he places on himself. He has also learnt about the practice of mindfulness and begun to practise the three-minute breathing space every day. He is delighted to be able to report back to Dr Jim that his panic attacks are now a remnant of his past. He still suffers from GAD, and acute stressors still occasionally throw him off line, but, overall, he has reshaped his mind and brain pathways.

IV.
SOCIAL ANXIETY

10.
When People Make Us Anxious

Now that we have examined the worlds of panic attacks and general anxiety disorder, it's time for us to enter the world of those for whom anxiety is triggered by interactions with other people. We define those who struggle with significant anxiety in such situations as suffering from social anxiety, or, as some prefer, social phobia. This is one of the most common anxiety conditions, and can cause untold difficulties. It is also one which is eminently treatable with CBT techniques.

What Is Social Anxiety?

Social anxiety is a common, disabling condition, where the person suffers from intense anxiety in social situations for a period greater than six months. They experience a persistent fear of being judged harshly by others, and are embarrassed by their own actions in social situations. Their fears can be easily triggered by perceived or actual scrutiny from others, and may by accompanied not only by the normal symptoms of acute anxiety, but also by blushing, excessive sweating, stammering and their mind going blank. It is often these symptoms which are the presenting problem. The most famous sufferer was Charles Darwin, who described many of the symptoms. Unlike other phobias, continuous exposure to social situations does not seem to lead to lessen anxiety.

It is normal, particularly as teenagers and young adults, to become anxious in social situations. But for 7-8 percent of the population, this social anxiety persists. We can learn about the effects of this disorder in people's lives by examining their thoughts and behaviours in social and professional situations. The key behaviour pattern is social avoidance, which worsens and perpetuates the problem. They fear and avoid group interactions, dating, restaurants and meeting strangers, among many other things. Paradoxically, many present as socially quite sophisticated. They are intensively self-critical of their 'performances' in public situations.

Types of Social Anxiety

Generally, people with social anxiety disorder fear and avoid social situations. These fall into two broad categories:

- Performance situations, which involve performing in front of others or being observed by others.

- Social interaction situations, which involve engaging or interacting with one or more people.

Most people with social anxiety disorder fear both types of situations.

Performance situations that people with social anxiety disorder often fear include the following:

- Public speaking
- Talking in meetings/classes
- Participating in sports or working out in front of others
- Performing music or acting on stage
- Writing in front of others
- Eating or drinking in front of others
- Using public restrooms when other people are nearby

- Making mistakes in front of others
- Being in public areas, such as shopping malls or buses

Social interaction situations that people with social anxiety disorder often fear include the following:

- Going to a party
- Initiating or maintaining a conversation
- Talking to strangers
- Inviting friends over for dinner
- Talking on the phone
- Expressing personal opinions
- Being assertive – refusing to give in to unreasonable requests, or asking others to change their behaviour
- Being in intimate situations
- Talking to people in authority such as their employers, professors or doctors
- Returning items to stores, or sending food back in restaurants

Typical thoughts or beliefs of people with social anxiety might be:

- I have nothing interesting to say and I am boring.
- I will make a fool of myself. They will all notice and judge me to be wanting.
- I will be paralysed with fear.
- They will see me blushing or sweating.
- They will see in my eyes that I am anxious.
- They will see me fidgeting with my hands or feet.

- They will see that I am an anxious person and judge me as weak and socially inept.

- I will say the wrong thing in conversation.

- Or, even worse, I will not know what to say at all.

The list is endless, of course, as people can have so many negative thoughts and beliefs about themselves.

People with social anxiety disorder also learn safety behaviours that they use when exposed to social situations. Again, the list of possibilities is extensive. Here are a few examples:

- Trying to remain anonymous by saying nothing controversial

- Staying close to the exit door

- Trying to cover up blushing or excess sweating

- Avoiding eye contact

- Repeatedly checking whether they are coming across well – self-monitoring

- Gripping glasses or cups tightly

- Continuously rehearsing what they are going to say

- Rehearsing before they get to the social gathering, often in front of a mirror, to see how they will come across

- Constantly going to the ladies or gents to check in the mirror to make sure they are not blushing or in some other way obviously anxious

- Doing a post-mortem on how they did, when they get home from a social gathering

Why Does Social Anxiety Occur?

After much research into the cause of this disorder, there is general agreement that the typical mixture of genetic, environmental and epigenetic forces are at work. Those with an underlying genetic predisposition to social anxiety are then influenced by their upbringing and social environment. Resulting brain and mind pathways are set down by the late teens.

Personal experiences are thought to significantly influence the development of social anxiety disorder. Negative experiences in social situations, such as being teased or mocked in school, may later cause a person to fear and avoid social situations, if being around people becomes associated with the negative experience.

In addition, an individual who is exposed to others with extreme social anxiety – growing up with parents who themselves have social anxiety disorder – may learn, through observation, to fear the same situations. Messages that a child receives from parents, teachers, friends, and media – it is important to make a good impression, for example – may also affect the development of social anxiety disorder. However, negative social experiences alone are not enough to cause social anxiety disorder; only a small percentage of people who have such experiences develop the problem. There are other factors involved. In the modern world of the screenager, there are however numerous opportunities for young people to experience such negative social interactions.

There is another, more worrying cause of severe social anxiety, resulting in the phenomenon of the social isolate. We are starting to encounter, particularly with young men between the ages of sixteen and twenty-one, situations in which the individual becomes addicted to the Internet, social media or online gaming. Instead of real life, face-to-face interactions, that person lives in a virtual world, where all social interaction occurs through the medium of technology. They risk withdrawing further and becoming increasingly anxious if they have to face real-life encounters. Some end up struggling to even leave the house or attend school or college.

We have also started to see young girls beginning to spend long periods of time creating virtual, online identities and losing the natural skills of face-to-face, empathetic interaction.

The vast majority of cases probably have their primary cause in some early social experiences, where that person suffered significant embarrassment or shame, either at school or at home.

What Is Going on in the Brain?

We have already discussed the importance of the amygdala in social anxiety, where this part of the brain incorrectly misreads facial expressions in a negative manner, leading to many of the physical symptoms of this condition. We also know that the right PFC, which assesses non-verbal communication, plays a key role in misreading these signs and interpreting them as dangerous. It will also play a role in catastrophising before such social interaction or performance situations.

What most likely happens is that an early environmental negative interaction, in the presence, in some cases, of a genetic predisposition, reshapes the amygdala and PFC to misread and misinterpret social situations and learns to dread them. And since there is a strong link between the right PFC and amygdala when perceived dangers are present, it is not surprising that the final results are amygdala based secondary physical symptoms. We also know that on examining pathways between the amygdala and the various parts of the PFC, there is, in particular, reduced functional connectivity. So we end up with the amygdala misreading the situation and the normal oversight capacity of PFC reduced through this mechanism.

Any therapy that is going to successfully deal with this condition will have to reset these brain structures and pathways.

How to Manage Social Anxiety

Lifestyle Changes and Complimentary Therapies

The following have been shown to be of some benefit:

- Taking regular exercise – thirty minutes a day if possible. Any form of exercise is good. This reduces activity in our amygdala, and has other positive benefits.

- Avoiding alcohol as a crutch to ease the feelings of social anxiety. It will lower your mood, as well as increasing your risk of addiction.

- Alternative therapies such as yoga, meditation and mindfulness.

Drug therapies have no real place in the treatment of social anxiety. There is an argument that SSRIs may have a role in calming the amygdala, but the reality is that in the vast majority of cases they are simply not necessary. Talk therapy, and particularly CBT is such a powerful tool. Beware of using tranquillisers, as they dampen the ability of the amygdala to reform new memories.

Talk therapies should always be the treatment of choice. The options include:

- Counselling

- Behaviour therapy

- CBT therapy

One must be careful, when using routine counselling, to locate the source of the person's social anxiety. As previously discussed, the amygdala does not do routine talk therapy. While it is useful knowing where one's social anxiety is coming from, it may not be of much assistance when faced with the reality of an upcoming social event. Behaviour therapy can be effective at dealing with the behavioural consequences of social anxiety and exposure part of therapy, but does not change the thinking part of this condition.

CBT has become the treatment of choice, as it allows the therapist to deal with both the PFC- and amygdala-based anxiety and secondary physical symptoms created by social anxiety. It does this by challenging the thinking and behaviour of the person.

Christopher's Story

Christopher, a twenty-six-year-old graduate, visited his doctor, complaining of a plethora of physical symptoms. Following investigations, he was diagnosed with anxiety. He admitted to having significant difficulties in social situations and to misusing alcohol on a regular basis, as a coping mechanism.

On further questioning, he said he suffered through periods of extreme anxiety in social gatherings since his late teens. He had grown to dread meeting strangers, attending big family events, going to the theatre (which he loves) and work meetings. He mentioned one episode of depression at the age of twenty-one, but said he had 'dealt with it himself'. He was highly critical of himself and his perceived social incompetence.

He had hoped that his GP would prescribe medication to ease his anxiety, and was disappointed to be refused antidepressants, as he was not suffering from depression. His GP also refused to prescribe tranquillisers, saying they would not address the problem. She explained that the real problem was social anxiety, referring him to Dr Jim for CBT therapy.

Dr Jim is in agreement with the GP's diagnosis, and gives Christopher some information on social anxiety. They discuss some lifestyle changes, particularly those relating to his tendency to use alcohol as a crutch. The doctor mentions the risk of addiction. He also recommends daily exercise, as it is beneficial for both anxiety and stress, and that Christopher attend a mindfulness course. He explains the role of the amygdala and the PFC, and how lifestyle changes and therapies can assist with anxiety.

Christopher then asks Dr Jim where his social anxiety comes from. Dr Jim discusses the possibility that, given his history, it may be rooted in some event in his childhood or adolescence, when he felt publicly ashamed or embarrassed. Christopher immediately remembers an instance in which he was humiliated in front of his class by a teacher, who told him he was stupid, because of mistakes he made in his homework.

He shares this insight with Dr Jim, who feels that this may have been the initial triggering episode. In practice, however, it does not much matter, Dr

Jim says. His concern is how these issues are impacting Christopher's life now, and how he can learn to deal with them. 'We are going to discuss some CBT techniques, so that you can learn new ways of dealing with your anxiety in social situations,' Dr Jim says.

He then explains the importance of distinguishing between rational and irrational beliefs, which form the lens through which we view our lives. This is particularly the case with anxiety, he says. 'We pick up irrational beliefs like viruses, in our childhood, adolescence or adult life,' Dr Jim says. 'In your case, the virus may have been planted by your experiences with that particular teacher.'

Dr Jim goes on to explain the ABC concept, and how it will help to locate and manage Christopher's irrational beliefs. He asks Christopher for a recent example of something that triggered a bout of social anxiety for him, so they will have something concrete to work on. Christopher talks about meeting his friends in a pub the previous Saturday.

'I was anxious for hours before even getting there,' he exclaims. 'How was I going to interact with them? What made it worse was that I knew that two of them were inviting their new girlfriends, neither of whom I had met before. It was going to be so embarrassing.'

'Now we have the trigger and the emotions that followed,' says Dr Jim. He asks Christopher to write this information down in their ABC.

A   Activating Event:

    o   Trigger: meeting friends in a pub, and two girls he had never met before

    o   Inference/danger:

B   Belief/Demands:

C   Consequences:

    o   Emotions: anxiety, embarrassment and shame

    o   Physical reactions:

C   Behaviour:

Dr Jim asks what Christopher's physical responses were, both before he went to the pub and then upon entering. Christopher lists the physical symptoms he felt at his apartment before going to the pub.

'My muscles were all tensed up, my heart was beating fast, my mouth was dry and my stomach was churning,' he says. 'The closer it got to the time I needed to leave, the worse I felt. When I walked into the pub, I felt sweaty, shaky and weak. My muscles were even tenser, and I was convinced that my face was scarlet. My heart was really thumping, and my breath came faster. And that was before I even reached the group of friends.'

'These are the typical physical symptoms experienced when we become anxious in social situations,' Dr Jim says. 'We will examine why they happen.'

Christopher adds the information about his symptoms to their ABC.

A   Activating Event:

- o   Trigger: meeting friends in a pub, and two girls he had never met before

- o   Inference/danger:

B   Belief/Demands:

C   Consequences:

- o   Emotions: anxiety, embarrassment and shame

- o   Physical reactions: dry mouth, shaking, sweating, blushing, heart thumping, breathing faster, stomach in knots and general weakness

- o   Behaviour:

Dr Jim asks how Christopher behaved in response to his feelings of anxiety about meeting his friends in the pub, and what he did once he arrived.

'While I was in my apartment, I kept checking my appearance, something I do all the time before outings like this,' Christopher says.

'And what was the purpose of this behaviour?' Dr Jim asks.

'It was to ensure that my general appearance, including my clothes and hair, would stand up to public scrutiny,' Christopher says. 'In particular, I wanted to ensure that I was not obviously sweating or blushing, and that I was presenting a confident image of myself. I also found myself rehearsing everything I would say to the two new girls. I hoped this would make me less anxious, but found that it actually stressed me out more.'

'And when you got to the pub, what did you do?' asks Dr Jim.

Christopher reflects on this for a while. 'Well, the first thing I did was to go straight to the bar and order a drink,' he says. 'I downed a pint in a very short space of time. I also kept my jacket on to ensure nobody would see me sweating.'

When he did meet his friends and the two girls, he remained at the edge of the group, he says. 'I did my absolute best not to start any conversation unless somebody asked me something,' Christopher says. 'In fact, one of my friends wondered if everything was all right, as I was so quiet. I felt more relaxed after a few pints, but I was still rehearsing what I would say in my head before contributing to the conversation, in case I said something inappropriate and looked stupid.'

He became anxious when one of the girls started to talk to him, as he felt like his face had gone scarlet. He then rushed out to the gents to check how red his it had become. Even though it did not look very red, it remained on his mind for the rest of the night. He excused himself from the group as early as possible. They continued on to a nightclub without him, and he went to his apartment exhausted from the ordeal.

On returning home, he spent hours going over the night in his head, trying to decide how well he had done. He wondered how he had come across to his friends and, in particular, to the new girls. He wondered whether they had noticed how red his face had become and what they had thought about him.

Dr Jim explains that much of this behaviour is common with social anxiety.

Christopher adds the information about his behaviour to their ABC.

A   Activating Event:

    o   Trigger: meeting friends in a pub, and two girls he had never met before

   o Inference/danger:

B Belief/Demands:

C Consequences:

   o Emotions: anxiety, embarrassment and shame

   o Physical reactions: dry mouth, shaking, sweating, blushing, heart thumping, breathing faster, stomach in knots and general weakness

   o Behaviour: rehearsed what he would say before arriving at the pub; checked himself constantly in the mirror before leaving the apartment; went straight to the bar for a drink to reduce his anxiety; kept his jacket on to make sure nobody would notice that he might be sweating; stayed at the edge of his group and avoided starting a conversation; rehearsed what he might say before contributing to any conversation; went to check himself in the mirror when he thought he might be blushing; left the gathering early; did a post-mortem when he got back to his apartment on how well he had done, and anyone had noticed his blushing.

'What was it about meeting your friends and their new girlfriends that made you so anxious?' Dr Jim asked. 'When we are anxious about something it means that we are applying some danger to the trigger. So what danger were you applying to this upcoming meeting in the pub? What did you imagine would happen?'

'I suppose the main danger was that they would notice that I was different,' Christopher answers.

'And what was it about you that they would consider different?' Dr Jim asks.

'They would see that I was tense, quiet and, in particular, that I was sweating and blushing,' Christopher says.

'And why would you be anxious if they saw this?' Dr Jim asks.

'Maybe then they would think that I was an anxious person,' Christopher says.

'So what you are saying is that if they see you as quiet, tense, sweating or blushing, they might think that you suffer from anxiety?' asks Dr Jim.

Christopher agrees.

'Is there anything else you think might lead them to this conclusion?' Dr Jim asks.

'They might see it in my face, even my eyes,' answers Christopher. 'It might be in my posture, or my difficulties with conversation. It would be obvious to everyone present.'

'And why would it bother you if your friends or either of the two girls thought you were an anxious person?' Dr Jim asks.

'Because only weak people get anxious,' says Christopher. 'They would end up making judgments about me, assuming I was unable to handle social situations and that I was best avoided.'

'So what you are saying is if they thought you were anxious, people would judge you as weak and unable to cope with social situations?' Dr Jim asks.

Christopher agrees.

'And why would it bother you if people thought you were weak?' Dr Jim asks.

'Maybe they are right, and I am a weak person. After all, strong confident people do not get anxious in normal social situations like this – only weak, socially inadequate people like me,' says Christopher. 'It is so shameful and embarrassing that they would think of me like that, and that is why I get so anxious when exposed to such situations.'

'Was there anything else that bothered you about the meeting?' Dr Jim asks. 'Any other dangers?'

Christopher admits that one of his big dangers in such situations is that he lacks the necessary social skills to talk to people. He is convinced that people think he is a boring person.

'And why do you think that is the case?' asks Dr Jim.

'Because they observe that I am so quiet,' says Christopher. 'I clearly have nothing interesting to say. In my own mind, if I do say something I always feel that it is uninteresting. So if I talk, the other person is going to assume that I am boring, and not worth talking to. Or, even worse, they will see that I am struggling with conversation because I am anxious, and decide that I am an anxious, boring person.'

Dr Jim asks him to add this information to their ABC, which he does.

A   Activating Event:

- o   Trigger: meeting friends in a pub, and two girls he had never met before

- o   Inference/danger: people would see he was tense, quiet, sweating, blushing and not interacting with the group; they would then assume that he was an anxious person; as a result, they would assume he was a weak person, as only weak people get anxious, and he would agree with their opinion; people might also think he was a boring person, an assessment he would again agree with.

B   Belief/Demands:

C   Consequences:

- o   Emotions: anxiety, embarrassment and shame

- o   Physical reactions: dry mouth, shaking, sweating, blushing, heart thumping, breathing faster, stomach in knots and general weakness

- o   Behaviour: rehearsed what he would say before arriving at the pub; checked himself constantly in the mirror before leaving the apartment; went straight to the bar for a drink to reduce his anxiety; kept his jacket on to make sure nobody would notice that he might be sweating; stayed at the edge of his group and avoided starting a conversation; rehearsed what he might say before contributing to any conversation; went to check himself in the mirror when he thought he might be blushing; left the gathering early; did a post-mortem when he got back to his apartment on how well he had done, and anyone had noticed his blushing.

'Now let's examine what irrational beliefs were triggered by this situation, and the danger you assigned to it,' says Dr Jim. 'This usually takes the form of some absolute demand you are making about the trigger. What demands were you making in relation to this meeting that ended with you feeling so anxious?'

'I suppose my main demand was that I must not become very anxious when I met my friends in the pub,' says Christopher.

'And how would you have felt about yourself if you did become anxious?' asks Dr Jim.

Christopher says would have felt like a failure. He also demanded of himself that he must not blush, and felt that if he did it would have been awful.

'Were you making any further demands that were leading you to feel embarrassed or ashamed?' asks Dr Jim.

'I suppose I was demanding that my friends, and, in particular, the two new girls, would not end up judging me as a weak person,' replies Christopher.

'And supposing they did, would you have had to accept their judgment?'

'Yes, I would have felt that it was true.'

'So, your perception is that you must accept their judgment?'

'Yes, I guess it is,' Christopher says.

'What lies at the heart of shame or embarrassment is the belief that people will discover something secret about us,' says Dr Jim. 'In your case, it is that you get anxious. After learning this secret, the fear is that we would be judged negatively, a pronouncement that we would be forced to accept.'

Christopher adds this final piece of information to their ABC.

A   Activating Event:

   o   Trigger: meeting friends in a pub, and two girls he had never met before

o   Inference/danger: people would see he was tense, quiet, sweating, blushing and not interacting with the group; they would then assume that he was an anxious person; as a result, they would assume he was a weak person, as only weak people get anxious, and he would agree with their opinion; on the other hand, people might think that he was a boring person, an assessment he would again agree with.

B   Belief/Demands: he must not be exposed to any social situation where he gets anxious; if he does get anxious he will have been a failure for letting it happen; he must not blush; people will judge him, and he must accept their judgment.

C   Consequences:

o   Emotions: anxiety, embarrassment and shame

o   Physical reactions: dry mouth, shaking, sweating, blushing, heart thumping, breathing faster, stomach in knots and general weakness

o   Behaviour: rehearsed what he would say before arriving at the pub; checked himself constantly in the mirror before leaving the apartment; went straight to the bar for a drink to reduce his anxiety; kept his jacket on to make sure nobody would notice that he might be sweating; stayed at the edge of his group and avoided starting a conversation; rehearsed what he might say before contributing to any conversation; went to check himself in the mirror when he thought he might be blushing; left the gathering early; did a post-mortem when he got back to his apartment on how well he had done, and anyone had noticed his blushing.

'This is what lies at the heart of social anxiety. We demand that we must never get anxious in social situations, because if this happens other people will judge us. We then feel we must accept their judgment,' says Dr Jim. 'When we cannot meet these impossible demands and satisfy our irrational beliefs, we become incredibly anxious and ashamed. We then use avoidance and complicated safety behaviour, which ends up increasing our anxiety and resulting in uncomfortable physical symptoms. This is why you became so anxious about a seemingly routine meeting in a pub with your friends. It also explains your behaviour. Let's see if we can assist you in reshaping your thinking and behaviour. If you are able to succeed in relation to this issue, we can apply the same concepts to similar future social situations.'

Challenging Christopher's 'A'

'We could challenge the "A" of your interpretation – the activating triggers and inferences – of this meeting with your friends. This approach has limited scope, though, in that it will only address this specific situation in which you became very anxious. What happens tomorrow or the next day, when the next social gathering arrives? Will the pattern not just repeat itself?' Dr Jim asks.

Christopher agrees that that this is what keeps happening to him.

'What is much more effective,' Dr Jim, goes on, 'is to challenge the "B" and the "C". What we mean by this is to challenge the irrational beliefs – the real drivers of your anxiety – and to also challenge the emotional and behavioural consequences of this belief.'

Challenging Christopher's 'C'

'Let's challenge "C": the consequences,' Dr Jim says. He begins by asking Christopher the value of simply trying to stem his anxiety, and not become embarrassed or ashamed when in such situations. They both agree that this is neither useful nor realistic.

'Christopher, what caused the physical symptoms you experienced when you become anxious before and during the meeting with your friends in the pub?' Dr Jim asks.

Christopher suggests that his extreme anxiety was the cause, and Dr Jim agrees. Dr Jim goes on to explain how his stress system is behind these physical symptoms.

'Whenever our emotional brain senses a danger, whether real or perceived, it immediately activates our acute stress system, which prepares us to fight, freeze or flee,' Dr Jim says. 'It does so by activating our internal nervous system, as well as by releasing our fear hormone, adrenaline.'

Dr Jim and Christopher discuss adrenaline, and how it is our do-a-runner hormone, and that the symptoms it causes are uncomfortable but not dangerous. It is this discomfort that so many with social anxiety struggle most to deal with. The more Christopher tries to make these feelings go away, the more intense the symptoms will become, Dr Jim explains. Conversely, the more he accepts them, the more they will become background noise.

'It is very important to make a detailed examination of your behaviour at the moment that you became anxious about meeting your friends,' says Dr Jim.

This leads to a discussion of the unhealthy behaviours Christopher has fallen into as a result of his demands about not getting anxious.

'Does it help to constantly check your appearance before leaving the apartment, or to rehearse what one will say?' Dr Jim asks.

Christopher agrees that these behaviours are unhelpful, only making him more anxious. They also agree that heading for the bar as quickly as possible is not the answer, nor is staying at the edges of groups and not engaging in conversation unless asked; these actions just increase the pressure.

'And what about leaving your jacket on to avoid anyone seeing that you might be sweating, or heading to the gents to check if you were blushing or not?' Dr Jim asks. 'Were these behaviours going to make you calmer or more anxious?'

Christopher is forced to accept that these behaviours were actually making matters worse. It wasn't helpful to leave the social gathering early or to perform a long post-mortem after the event, either. All of these behaviours were unhealthy and only perpetuated the problem.

'We will return to these behaviours later, to discuss better options,' promises Dr Jim.

Challenging Christopher's 'B'

'Now we need to challenge "B", that is, your set of irrational beliefs. These took the form of some absolute demands: that you must not expose yourself to any social situation, such as meeting your friends in the pub, where you might become anxious, and that if you do so you are a failure for letting it happen; that you must not blush; and that people will judge you and that you must accept their judgment,' says Dr Jim. 'So do you think these beliefs and demands upon yourself are rational or irrational?'

Christopher accepts that they were irrational, and, after some consideration, that they can be identified as irrational because of the word 'must', and the idea that he could be 'a failure'. They also agree that Christopher's demand that he 'must' accept other people's opinions of himself was irrational.

Dr Jim then challenges Christopher's 'B'.

'Returning to your absolute demand that you must not be exposed to any social situation, such as meeting your friends in the pub, that might lead to you becoming anxious, what might be a healthier demand?' Dr Jim asks.

After some discussion, they agree that, in this situation, a more rational and healthier demand to make would be: 'I would prefer not to be exposed to a social situation where I might get anxious, but in real life, this is an impossible demand.'

They spend most of the time disputing Christopher's irrational belief that others would see him as weak, and that this was a judgment he must accept.

'Why is this belief irrational?' Dr Jim asks.

'I am not really sure. I do believe I am weak, because I cannot stop being anxious in social situations. I also believe that, when people in such circumstances view and judge me to be this way, they are correct,' says Christopher.

'I can see that we are going to have to make you a member of the Raggy Doll Club,' Dr Jim says. 'I'll explain what I mean. Between one and a hundred, where do you rate yourself as a person?'

Christopher replies that, in general, he would rate himself around fifty. Dr Jim draws a scale and marks in his estimate.

'And where do you feel others rate you?' Dr Jim asks.

'Around the same,' Christopher says.

Dr Jim adds this to the scale.

'And if you became very anxious on meeting some friends in a social situation, where would you then rate yourself?' Dr Jim asks.

Christopher drops his rating down to twenty.

'And others, such as your friends or the girls with them, where would they would rate you?' asks Dr Jim. Here, the rating goes down to five.

Christopher is beginning to see that his rating changes depending on the circumstances.

'And now for the most important question of the day,' Dr Jim says. 'Can we rate a human being? Where is the measuring tool with which to do this?'

On reflection, Christopher says he feels that it is really impossible to rate a person, as we are too complex.

Dr Jim asks him if he would like to join the Raggy Doll Club. Christopher looks puzzled. Dr Jim explained that this is a highly exclusive club, of which he himself has been a member for many years. 'There are three important criteria for membership: 1) we cannot rate ourselves; 2) we cannot accept other peoples' ratings of us; and 3) we can rate our behaviour, but not ourselves,' Dr Jim says. 'So, to join the Raggy Doll Club, you have to decide to meet these three criteria.'

Dr Jim explains that as a member of the Raggy Doll Club, he accepts that he is just a normal, fallible human being. He accepts that he will make mistakes on some occasions, get it right on others, and always accept that he can't judge or rate himself, no matter what happens. He also will not accept others' ratings. He explains that in life we can rate our behaviour and even our skills, but not ourselves.

'Let's return to your concern that you and others could judge you as a weak person, and a failure,' Dr Jim says. 'Can anyone be described as weak? Can anyone be described as a failure?'

He explains how the pathological critic in our emotional mind, which we discussed earlier, can try to bully us into such erroneous beliefs. But if we are true Raggy Dolls, then we can dismiss such ideas.

'We can be weak at doing something, or fail at something in life. But, as human beings, we can never define ourselves as weak or as failures,' Dr Jim says. 'No such person exists.'

This is truly a life-changing moment for Christopher. He now sees that he has been playing the rating game for years. He vows from then on to try to challenge this pattern, and practise becoming a Raggy Doll. 'But I am still unsure as to how to deal with my anxiety in these social situations, and what I should be doing to improve my behaviour,' he says.

'OK, we'll get to that, but first, can we challenge some common misconceptions that people who suffer from social anxiety often have?' Dr Jim says. 'Can you see anxiety in a person in a social situation?'

'Of course you can,' Christopher replies. 'Can't people see that you are tense, sweating or blushing? They must be able to see that you are anxious.'

'But how observant are people in real life?' asks Dr Jim. 'Do you seriously believe that people take in the physical and emotional details of what others, as individuals, are like? Are people normally not so self-obsessed as to be completely oblivious to what is going on around them?'

This is the first time Christopher has ever really considered this possibility. 'Are you saying that people in social situations don't pick up on these signs of anxiety?'

'If I asked you, for example, to put on a scarlet shirt and a gaudy tie, and then, at the end of the night, in a busy pub, asked people whether anyone had seen somebody attired in this way, almost nobody would have noticed,' Dr Jim says. 'Everyone is too busy, either in their own little bubbles of conversation and thoughts, or in watching sport on the pub's TV.'

Christopher struggles to accept that people cannot see his symptoms of anxiety. Dr Jim then gives him the following exercise. He is to become the 'anxiety inspector' at the next social gathering he encounters.

'I want you to systematically go around the crowd like a ticket inspector on the bus,' Dr Jim jokes. 'Instead of checking who has no ticket, you must find the people who are anxious, and be able to explain to me, on your next visit, why you felt this to be the case.'

Christopher is beginning to feel a touch like Alice in Wonderland, as his entire world is being turned upside down. But he decides to try it out.

'People are simply not aware of our composure in most social situations, never mind what our clothes or hair colour is like, or whether we are happy or sad or anxious,' Dr Jim says. 'Even friends are usually too preoccupied with themselves and their own lives, interests and activities to notice whether you are anxious, sweating, blushing or tense. They may notice you are quiet, but will usually assume you have something on your mind. They will certainly not be deciding whether you are anxious, or making other judgments about you as a result. That belief is not a reality, it is only a visualisation created in our own minds.'

With a smile, Dr Jim adds: 'Even if others were making such judgments, as a new Raggy Doll Club member, you would not be allowed to accept them.'

He continues: 'The most important message today is one that you might be surprised to hear: we are not as important as we think we are. We easily fall into the trap of assigning more importance to ourselves than others actually do. It is this misconception that lies at the heart of social anxiety. Once we begin to realise that, in social situations, people are usually blissfully unaware of what you are feeling, which, in this case, includes the symptoms of anxiety, you relax. Soon, you will cease being anxious about such symptoms. To really grasp this concept, not just in your logical mind but in your emotional mind, in your gut, you need to do some shame/embarrassment exercises.'

The first exercise involves a busy local supermarket. Dr Jim asks Christopher to do a few things that might make people look at him strangely. When Christopher hears what he is being asked to do, he blanches. 'But I will get so anxious doing that!' he exclaims. 'And I will also be so embarrassed.'

Dr Jim reassures Christopher that the simple things he will be doing will not harm him or interfere with the other people in the supermarket. This is merely an opportunity for Christopher to put the messages he has been given into practice, in a safe environment. 'The main point of this exercise is for you to be the observer as you perform, and then come back to me to report what you experienced,' Dr Jim says.

Dr Jim then gives Christopher another exercise. He is to go to a local coffee shop and sit on his own for one hour with a pot of coffee. He is not allowed any props: no phone, no paper, no book. 'You must sit there for one hour, doing nothing but observing,' Dr Jim says.

Once again, Christopher feels panicky at the thought of this exercise. Dr Jim reassures him that it has a real point.

'If you want to get over social anxiety,' Dr Jim explains, 'in addition to understanding what is going on cognitively, you have to experience, on an emotional level, the feelings of anxiety and embarrassment, and learn how to deal with them. These simple exercises will facilitate this process. This is because one part of our brain – the PFC or logical mind – can come to grips with the concepts we have discussed. But another, the amygdala, which is contains our ability to recognise danger, has, in the case of anxiety, built up negative memories of such social situations. It needs to experience these emotions, recognise that there really is no associated danger and learn how to readjust to them.'

Christopher leaves to carry out the anxiety inspector and embarrassment exercises. He returns a few weeks later, and says he found the exercises very stressful, particularly the one focussing on shame, but that he learnt a lot.

He started with the anxiety inspector exercise, he says. 'It was truly amazing. I expected that it would be easy picking up the signs of anxiety in others, but when I went looking, I really struggled to find them. On a few occasions, if I really focused on somebody, I could almost convince myself that they looked anxious or stressed. But there were no obvious signs.'

'So what did you learn from this exercise?' asks Dr Jim.

'The most important message I learnt was that, when a person is anxious, we cannot see the external signs. It is more of an internal feeling,' Christopher says. 'I also began to examine my own fears of others noticing I was anxious. I eventually realised that if I cannot see any signs of anxiety in others, neither should they be able to see them in me.'

'Most people could not tell if somebody was anxious if they were there forever,' says Dr Jim. 'Now what about the two shame exercises?'

'I initially felt apprehensive about this exercise, and postponed it for a week,' Christopher says. 'I felt very anxious going into the supermarket, when I was about to carry out the task. I also found myself obsessively examining the faces of those around me while I carried it out. But, just as you predicted, to my great surprise nobody batted an eyelid. I actually left the supermarket slightly deflated at just how invisible I seemed to be.'

Christopher continued: 'Sitting in the coffee shop for an hour was a real learning experience for me. I initially felt very self-conscious. I was both anxious and embarrassed, and felt like everyone would be looking at me, making some judgment about this strange man, just sitting there, drinking coffee and looking around him. After a while, I realised that nobody was in the slightest bit interested in what I was doing. It was a sobering experience. Perhaps you are right. Maybe we are not as important as we think we are. By the end of the hour any symptoms of anxiety were long gone, and boredom had stepped in.'

Dr Jim is delighted that Christopher grasped the concepts on an emotional level. He called this 'emotional insight'. 'Let's now return to the behaviour patterns that you developed. What have these exercises shown you?' Dr Jim asked.

'For starter,' Christopher says, 'I now realise that spending lots of time rehearsing or doing post-mortems on social interactions is a waste of time. There is no reason for me to run in and out of the gents, as it is impossible to detect any real signs of anxiety. I also know that trying to dampen the physical symptoms of my anxiety with alcohol is not going to work. I have to accept that these symptoms are normal and uncomfortable, but not dangerous. I have started just going with them, and they are becoming less intense. I would, however, like some help on how best to converse with people in social situations. I wanted to ask you for some advice on this today.'

'This skill, starting and continuing conversations, particularly with new people, is easy,' says Dr Jim. He brings Christopher back to their previous visit, when Christopher described himself as a boring person. 'Can a person be described as boring and, if so, what is it about the person that makes them boring?'

Having practised being a Raggy Doll for the previous few weeks, Christopher replies that he now accepts that there is probably no such thing as a boring person.

'If that is the case,' asked Dr Jim 'then what can we describe as boring?'

Christopher is flummoxed by this.

'Let's suppose,' Dr Jim says, 'that you talk to me for five minutes about horse racing, something which I have no interest in, and that I talk to you about golf, which you, similarly, have no interest in. Are we both boring people?'

'Of course not,' answers Christopher.

'Then,' asks Dr Jim, 'what is boring?'

Christopher is beginning to see where this is going. 'I assume you mean that it is the topic of conversation that is boring, and not us,' he says.

'What topic of conversation does almost everybody show immediate interest in?' Dr Jim asks.

Christopher thinks about the usual topics – weather, sport and politics – and mentions some of these, but Dr Jim says some people might have no interest in any of them.

'You mean that people like to talk about themselves, and what is going on in their own lives?' asks Christopher.

'Yes, most people love to talk about themselves,' says Dr Jim, who then gives Christopher a conversation exercise. 'On meeting anyone between now and your next visit, immediately ask them some question about themselves. Continue to ask further questions, based on the answers they give, to draw out the other person. For example, if you know the person has an interest in GAA or a particular soccer team, or if they have a particular hobby, then ask them some question relating to their interest. Continue asking them questions based on the answers you get. In most cases, the other person will chat away, and you can just stay for the conversational ride. By the time the conversation finishes, they will think they have had a most interesting conversation with a most interesting person.' Christopher says he can definitely work on this.

Over the next few visits, following further shame exercises, and, in particular, practising the conversation exercise, Christopher is in a new space. He is getting much more comfortable in social situations. He is gradually becoming a real Raggy Doll. He no longer worries about people seeing that he is anxious, and accepts that if he does get anxious, these feelings of anxiety and the physical sensations they produce are normal. He isgetting to be an expert at chatting to people, and has a new girlfriend. Within a few months, his social anxiety is a thing of the past.

Oliver's story

Oliver, a thirty-year-old businessman, arrives to see Dr Jim. He has been referred by his GP. The GP conducted extensive investigations for numerous physical symptoms, particularly persistent fatigue. Oliver told his doctor he suffered from significant social anxiety, and that he had noticed increasing levels of anxiety following a recent promotion that had led to him having to present data on a fortnightly basis to various groups within the company, and to some outside agencies.

'It is really embarrassing,' Oliver explains to Dr Jim. 'My job involves meeting people, often strangers. Even though, on the outside, I appear to cope well, in practice I am exhausted from persistent feelings of anxiety. Since I have started presenting data to differing groups at work, my anxiety levels have gone through the roof. I give these talks every second Tuesday of the month, and spend the preceding Monday nights in a sweat.'

Oliver asked his GP for some tranquillisers to get through the meetings with new customers, and, in particular, for the days when he had to give presentations. His GP reluctantly prescribed him some. Oliver found that they made him drowsy, and stopped taking them.

He had always been a shy man, and found social interaction difficult. In this, he said that he was 'just like his father'. He had found public speaking especially difficult, after a particularly embarrassing experience in a school debate.

Dr Jim listens carefully to his story, and to his admission that he is increasingly using alcohol to self-medicate his anxiety.

'It is the only thing that calms down these symptoms,' says Oliver.

Dr Jim feels that Oliver's symptoms are due to social anxiety, and explains what this is and how it can affect us. 'In your case, Oliver, you are suffering from both types of social anxiety: social interaction anxiety and performance anxiety,' he says.

Dr Jim discusses the importance of lifestyle changes with Oliver. In particular, they talked about his tendency to use alcohol as a crutch, and the risk of addiction he would face if this continued. He also recommends daily exercise, and that Oliver attend a mindfulness course. 'However, my task is to show you some CBT techniques to assist you in dealing with anxiety in social situations,' says Dr Jim.

They decide to tackle his performance anxiety first, as this is causing him the most difficulties. 'Later, if you wish, I can work with you on how to deal with social interactions,' says Dr Jim.

Dr Jim then explains the rational and irrational beliefs through which we see our lives, as well as the ABC concept. They will use this system to try to locate Oliver's irrational beliefs, and show him how to deal with them, Dr Jim says. He then asks for a recent example of a workplace presentation during which Oliver had become anxious, as this will give them a concrete example to work on.

'I only have to go back to last Tuesday morning,' Oliver begins, 'when I had to give a presentation to a large group, including the managing director, on an important project we are working on. I felt very anxious all of Monday, particularly Monday night, and especially anxious on Tuesday morning. I ended up not sleeping on Monday night, and could not eat my breakfast on the Tuesday. When I arrived, I felt increasingly anxious, and sure that I was going to mess up the presentation.'

'We now have the trigger and the emotion, so we have the beginnings of our ABC,' Dr Jim replies. He asks Oliver to write them down.

A   Activating Event:

     o   Trigger: having to give an important company presentation at which his managing director will be present

     o   Inference/danger:

B   Belief/Demands:

C   Consequences:

     o   Emotional reactions: anxiety, slight panic

     o   Physical reactions:

o   Behaviour:

'Now,' continues Dr Jim, 'what were your physical responses when you became extremely anxious, on both the Monday night and Tuesday morning before you arrived in the office, and then before the presentation itself?'

Oliver explains that, on the Monday, he felt like his stomach was in knots, he was sighing all the time, his heart was beating faster, his muscles were tense, he developed a tension headache towards the end of the night and he noticed significant levels of fatigue. Just before the presentation on Tuesday, all of these symptoms were present and getting worse, and his mouth was very dry.

'These are typical physical symptoms we feel when we get anxious,' Dr Jim says. 'We will go on to examine why they happen. What was your behaviour like when you became anxious about this upcoming presentation, both on the night before and on the day of the meeting?'

'I spent the night before checking and rechecking the presentation. I must have gone over it at least ten times,' Oliver says. 'My eyes and brain were exhausted by this, but I had to be sure that I would present it as well as I could. I also found that I was using whiskey to calm me down. I practised in front of the mirror on a few occasions to see how I was coming across. I kept seeking reassurance from my wife that I would not make a mess of it. I also struggled to eat my evening meal and, more so, my breakfast on the morning of the presentation. I found sleeping impossible; I tossed and turned all night. I couldn't take my mind off the image of me making a complete hash of the presentation.'

Oliver continues: 'As for the morning of the meeting, I was there for an hour before everybody else, checking and rechecking the equipment. I went through my presentation over and over, trying to rehearse and memorise every detail of the talk. I was exhausted before we even started. On giving the presentation, I found myself constantly checking the faces in front of me to see whether I was making a mess of it or not, particularly observing the managing director.'

'If you had a choice not to do the presentation, would you have taken it?' asks Dr Jim.

'If there was a way I could have got out of it, I would have grabbed it with both hands,' answers Oliver. 'On a few occasions, I have been so anxious on the morning of a presentation that I considered asking my wife to ring in to say I was sick, but so far I have not yielded to this temptation.'

Dr Jim explains that many of these behaviours are quite common in performance social anxiety, and are in fact a large part of the problem. Dr Jim and Oliver will come back to these behaviours, to see how they can be exchanged for healthier ones.

For now, they add the information they have gathered to their ABC.

A   Activating Event:

- o   Trigger: having to give an important company presentation at which his managing director will be present

- o   Inference/danger:

B   Belief/Demands:

C   Consequences:

- o   Emotional reactions:

- o   Physical reactions: physical reactions – stomach in knots, heart beating faster, sighing, fatigue, muscles tense, tension headache, and dry mouth

- o   Behaviour: checked and rechecked his presentation, both on the night before and on the day of the meeting; used alcohol as a crutch; practised in front of the mirror; sought reassurance from wife; struggled to eat or sleep; catastrophised when awake at night and before meeting as to how badly the presentation would go; arrived at the venue an hour before, to check and recheck the equipment; rehearsed over and over right before the talk; would have avoided the talk if at all possible, and was on occasion tempted to ring in sick.

'When we are anxious about something, Oliver, it usually means that we are applying some danger to the trigger. So, what danger were you applying to this presentation? What did you see happening?' Dr Jim asks.

Oliver has to think about this question. 'I suppose the main danger I saw was that I would make a mess of the presentation,' he answers.

'And what did you think was going to happen to cause this to occur?'

'I always worry that I am going to get so anxious during the presentation that I will make a mess of it.'

'And what is it about being anxious that would make this happen?'

'I suppose the main potentiality I am most bothered about,' replies Oliver, 'is that my mind will become so anxious I will draw a blank. Yes, that's what I am most afraid will happen. I am afraid that I will lose track of where I am in the presentation, and struggle to continue on.'

'And what would happen if this did occur?' asks Dr Jim.

'I would simply end up standing there in silence in front of everybody.'

'And why would you be bothered if this happened?'

'I would seem weak and incompetent,' answers Oliver, 'and they would think I was anxious, unable to give a simple presentation and above all not really in charge of my brief.'

'So, to summarise,' says Dr Jim, 'your main danger is that you would become very anxious, your mind would go blank and you would clam up, unable to pick up the thread of the presentation. If this happened, your work-mates would see you as incompetent and not in charge of your brief.'

'That is exactly what I am afraid will happen. I am afraid that I will clam up and end up looking like a fool.'

'And how would you feel about yourself if this happened?'

'I would feel like a complete and total failure.'

Dr Jim explains to Oliver that these dangers are quite common in per-formance anxiety, and that they will return to them later.

For now, Oliver adds them to their ABC.

A   Activating Event:

- o Trigger: having to give an important company presentation at which his managing director will be present

- o Inference/danger: that he would become very anxious when giving his presentation; that, as a result, he would find his mind going blank; that if this happened he would eventually stop talking, standing in silence in front of his colleagues; that he would be unable to pick up the thread of his presentation, if he were to clam up in this manner; that if he did clam up, his colleagues would think he was unable to even give a simple presentation; that if this happened they would assume he was incompetent, and not *au fait* with his brief.

B   Belief/Demands:

C   Consequences:

- o Emotional reactions:

- o Physical reactions: physical reactions – stomach in knots, heart beating faster, sighing, fatigue, muscles tense, tension headache, and dry mouth

- o Behaviour: checked and rechecked his presentation, both on the night before and on the day of the meeting; used alcohol as a crutch; practised in front of the mirror; sought reassurance from wife; struggled to eat or sleep; catastrophised when awake at night and before meeting as to how badly the presentation would go; arrived at the venue an hour before, to check and recheck the equipment; rehearsed over and over right before the talk; would have avoided the talk if at all possible, and was on occasion tempted to ring in sick.

'Now let us examine what irrational beliefs were triggered by this situation, and the danger you assigned to it,' says Dr Jim. 'This usually takes the form of some absolute demand you are making about the trigger. So, what demands were you making about this presentation that ended up with you feeling so anxious?'

'Based on what we have just discussed, I assume I am demanding of myself that I must not make a mess of my presentation, or clam up,' says Oliver.

'How would you feel about yourself if this happened?' Dr Jim asks.

'I would feel as if I was a failure,' Oliver answers.

Dr Jim asks Oliver to add this final piece of information to their ABC, which he does.

A   Activating Event:

-   o   Trigger: having to give an important company presentation at which his managing director will be present

-   o   Inference/danger: that he would become very anxious when giving his presentation; that, as a result, he would find his mind going blank; that if this happened he would eventually stop talking, standing in silence in front of his colleagues; that he would be unable to pick up the thread of his presentation, if he were to clam up in this manner; that if he did clam up, his colleagues would think he was unable to even give a simple presentation; that if this happened they would assume he was incompetent, and not *au fait* with his brief.

B   Belief/Demands: that he must not clam up because, if this happened, it would be awful and he would be a failure for letting it happen; that he must not be seen as incompetent, as if this happened he would be a failure for letting it happen.

C   Consequences:

-   o   Emotional reactions:

-   o   Physical reactions: physical reactions – stomach in knots, heart beating faster, sighing, fatigue, muscles tense, tension headache, and dry mouth

-   o   Behaviour: checked and rechecked his presentation, both on the night before and on the day of the meeting; used alcohol as a crutch; practised in front of the mirror; sought reassurance from wife; struggled to eat or sleep; catastrophised when awake at night and before meeting as to how badly the presentation would go; arrived at the venue an hour before, to check and recheck the equipment; rehearsed over and over right before the talk; would have avoided the talk if at all possible, and was on occasion tempted to ring in sick.

'Let's see if we can now reshape your thinking, and your behaviour in relation to this,' says Dr Jim. 'If we can assist you to do this in relation to this episode, we can apply the same concepts to future meetings and other situations where you will have to speak at public events.'

Challenging Oliver's 'A'

'We could dispute or challenge your "A", your interpretation of having to give this presentation to colleagues and the dangers you associated with it,' Dr Jim explains. 'But what is much more effective is to challenge the "B" and the "C". What we mean by this is to challenge the irrational beliefs that we have already uncovered which are the real driver of your social anxiety and also challenge the emotional and behavioural consequences of this belief.'

Challenging Oliver's 'C'

'Let's start by challenging the "C", the consequences,' Dr Jim says. He asks Oliver the value of trying to stop being anxious when faced with having to give such a presentation to colleagues at work. They agree that this would not be useful or realistic.

'Oliver what caused all of the physical symptoms you experienced when you became anxious about giving this presentation?' Dr Jim asks.

When Oliver suggests that it was his anxiety that was the cause, Dr Jim reveals how his stress system lay behind the physical symptom.

'Whenever our emotional brain senses a danger, whether real or perceived, it immediately activates our acute stress system, which prepares us to fight or flee. It does so by activating our internal nervous system and also by releasing our fear hormone, adrenaline,' says Dr Jim.

They discuss adrenaline, and, using the leopard example, help Oliver to see that this was simply our do-a-runner hormone, and that the symptoms it causes are uncomfortable but not dangerous. There is no actual danger from these physical symptoms, even though they are extremely uncomfortable, he explains. He then explores with Oliver the idea of simply learning to accept that the more he demands they go away, the more the symptoms will increase, but the more he accepts and just goes with them, the more they will start to fade into the background.

'Let's examine in detail everything you did,' says Dr Jim. 'What was your behaviour when you became anxious that you must not clam up during your presentation?'

This leads to a discussion of the unhealthy behaviours that Oliver has embarked upon as a result of these demands.

'Was it really helpful to check and recheck your presentation ten times the night before, for instance?' Dr Jim asks.

'I guess not,' Oliver replies. 'In fact, it led to me getting increasingly anxious.'

Standing in front of a mirror to practise, checking over and over with his wife, not eating his evening meal and dipping into the whiskey were really safety behaviours – and not particularly useful.

'Was spending an hour before the talk, rechecking the equipment and then rehearsing the talk in your mind over and over helping you achieve your goal?' Dr Jim asks.

'It actually stressed me out even more,' Oliver says.

'There were two other behaviours that are worth examining,' says Dr Jim. 'Was avoiding the presentation by ringing in sick going to help you learn to deal with your anxiety?'

'I knew deep down that that was only running away, and I was happy that I didn't go there,' Oliver says.

'Avoidance is usually our first port of call when we are anxious,' Dr Jim says, 'but it usually makes the situation worse.'

Dr Jim goes on to discuss the catastrophising that Oliver engaged in on the night before the presentation. Whilst it was also unhealthy, it was not possible for him to stop unless he developed some skills to deal with these thoughts, he said.

They agreed to return to this later.

Challenging Oliver's 'B'

'Now we need to examine and challenge your "B", that is, your set of irrational beliefs. Do you think these beliefs and demands are rational or irrational?' Dr Jim asks.

'Irrational,' Oliver admits. He says it is probably the 'must not' and possibly the idea that he could be 'a failure' that are the irrational parts of his demands.

'Yes, it is your absolute demand that you must not clam up that is really at the heart of the whole issue. Is this possible in real life?' Dr Jim asks.

Oliver agrees that it probably is not.

'And can anyone really be described as a failure?' asks Dr Jim.

Oliver is not so sure. 'I feel I am a failure if something like the presentation goes wrong,' he says.

'Just what does a failure look like in real life?' Dr Jim asks.

After some sparring about this, they eventually agree that it is actually impossible to define what a failure really is.

They then discuss the big MACS, and how they will use them to challenge Oliver's demand. Together, they then challenge Oliver's 'B'.

'Returning to your absolute demand that you must not clam up during the presentation, what might be a healthier demand?' Dr Jim asks.

He suggests that a more rational, healthier demand in this situation would be that Oliver would prefer not to clam up during his presentation, but this was out of his control.

That leads to a brief discussion on the importance of control in Oliver's life. 'What can you really control in your life?' Dr Jim asks.

Oliver begins to realise that he is able to control very little.

'Is it really possible to ever achieve 100-percent certainty that you or anyone else will never clam up during a talk or presentation?' Dr Jim asks.

Oliver has to agree that this is not possible. Anything could go wrong, from the equipment going down, to a sudden sore throat, to Oliver actually having a blank. It was his absolute demand that he must have complete 100-percent certainty that the latter would not happen that was causing him to be so anxious. In real life, having such a blank is very common.

'So many people who get really anxious due to this demand don't realise,' Dr Jim says, 'that almost every single person who has given talks or presentations, or who has had to give speeches or weddings, has at some stage in their lives had a blank. And that includes me.'

Oliver is quite relieved to hear this. 'You mean it has happened to you?' he asks. 'That must have been awful.'

'It could have been an uncomfortable experience, but I coped with it for two reasons. First, I accept that I am not perfect, and, if it happens me, it has also happened to loads of other people and it doesn't define me as a person,' Dr Jim says. 'Also, I often make a joke, at my own expense, at the start of such a presentation, making it clear that I do not take myself too seriously. This often puts the audience in your pocket before you start and takes the pressure immediately off yourself. In certain situations, I might say to the audience, "If I do lose my train of thought, just give me a minute, as I am sure it has happened to everyone here." This gets the audience on my side, as they put themselves in my position and internally empathise. The next time it could be them. After that the pressure is off, and it doesn't matter if you clam up, as they are expecting it and happy to give you a moment to get your thoughts in order.'

Dr Jim goes on to challenge Oliver's catastrophising in relation to the situation. He asks for proof that Oliver's visualisation of what might happen would in fact occur, and he shares the spilt-milk analogy discussed earlier. He also challenges Oliver's assumption that if he did clam up, he would not be able to cope. They agree that he would cope, because there was really no other option. They also spend a lot of time disputing his irrational belief that if he did clam up, he would be a failure for letting it happen. They continue the earlier discussion on what a failure is.

'I can see that we are going to have to make you a member of the Raggy Doll Club,' says Dr Jim. 'Where do you rate yourself as a person, between one and one hundred?'

Oliver replies that, in general, he would rate himself around seventy. Dr Jim draws a scale, and marked in Oliver's estimate. 'And others? Where do you feel others rate you?' he asks.

'Around the same,' Oliver says.

Dr Jim adds this to the the the scale. 'And if you did clam up during your presentation? Where would you rate yourself then?' he asks.

Oliver drops his rating down to thirty.

'And others, such as your work colleagues – where would they would rate you?'

Oliver reduces the rating to twenty.

Oliver could now see that his rating changed depending on the circumstances. 'The most important question is, can we rate a human being? Where's the measuring tool?' Dr Jim asks.

'I suppose not – we are too complex,' Oliver says.

Then Dr Jim asks him if he would like to join the Raggy Doll Club. Oliver is puzzled.

Dr Jim explains that this was a highly exclusive club, of which he himself had been a member for many years. 'There are three important criteria for membership: 1) we cannot rate ourselves; 2) we cannot accept other people's rating of us; and 3) we can rate our behaviour but not ourselves as human beings. To join the Raggy Doll Club, you have to decide to meet these three criteria.'

Dr Jim explains that he is a member: a normal, fallible human being. He accepts that he will make mistakes, getting it right on some occasions and wrong on others, all the time accepting that he can't judge or rate himself, no matter what happens. He also doesn't accept others' ratings of him. In life, we can rate our behaviour, he says, but not ourselves; and it's the same with others.

Oliver is blown away by this simple but very profound insight. 'I wish I had registered this much earlier in my life,' he says. 'It would have made things so much easier.'

'We discussed the idea of failure earlier,' says Dr Jim, 'but can you or anybody else really be described as a failure?'

'Are you trying to say that we can fail at something, but we can't be regarded as a failure?' Oliver asks.

Dr Jim explains how our emotional mind, and particularly our internal pathological critic, can try to bully us into accepting erroneous beliefs. But if we are real Raggy Dolls, we can dismiss this.

'We can be weak at doing something or fail at something in life,' Dr Jim says, 'but we can never define ourselves as weak or failures, for no such person actually exists.'

Oliver suddenly sees how, through the years, he has been playing this rating game. He vows to try to challenge this pattern. He leaves to try to put some of these concepts into action.

Three weeks later, Oliver returns and is elated that he has for the first time given a presentation without symptoms of severe anxiety. He felt some normal anxiety, but due to a radical change in his behaviour, coped without any difficulty.

'I only allowed myself to check my presentation once the night before, avoided the whiskey, made sure I had my dinner, and even went for a walk,' Oliver tells Dr Jim. 'On the day of the presentation, I arrived fifteen minutes early, checked the equipment once and then went straight into the presentation. And finally,' he chuckled, 'I made some good humoured comments about myself, which went down really well, and felt immediately relaxed for the rest of the presentation. But I still find myself getting very anxious in social interactions, particularly with strangers.'

So Dr Jim and Oliver proceed to tackle this.

Dr Jim asks for a recent example of something that has triggered in Oliver a bout of this form of anxiety. This will give them a concrete example to work on.

Oliver gives a recent example where he was asked to travel with a colleague to meet four new potential customers in a busy city-centre hotel, to discuss informally a possible project. He found himself becoming increasingly anxious as the day of the meeting approached. He now knew that the physical symptoms were simply the body's response to him being anxious about the meeting. He found that he was able to let them go a bit more. But he could not get around the catastrophic thought in his head that he would end up making a fool of himself in front of these new clients.

Dr Jim and Oliver now had the trigger, which was the upcoming meeting, and the emotions, which were anxiety and shame. Following the same routines as with his performance-anxiety, they came up with the following ABC:

A   Activating Event:

  o   Trigger: going to meet new customer in city-centre hotel

  o   Inference/danger: The new people he would be meeting would see he was tense, quiet, sweating, blushing and not interacting with the group. They would then assume he was an anxious person. As a result, they would assume he was a weak person, as only weak people get anxious. He would have to accept their opinion of him. They would think that he was a boring person and he also would agree with this assessment of himself.

B   Belief/Demands: He must not be exposed to any social situation where he gets anxious. He must not get anxious on meeting these new customers. If this occurs, it would be awful, and he would be a failure for letting it happen. They would judge him as weak, and he would have to accept their judgment.

C   Consequences:

  o   Emotional reactions: anxiety, embarrassment/shame

  o   Physical reactions: stomach in knots, heart beating faster, sighing, fatigue, muscles tense, tension headache and dry mouth o Behaviour: checking himself constantly in the mirror before leaving the office, rehearsing what he would say before arriving at the hotel, keeping on his jacket to make sure nobody would notice he might be sweating, trying to avoid starting a conversation, rehearsing mentally what he might say before contributing to the conversation, checking in the hotel toilet mirror to see whether he was 'looking anxious' and sweating, doing a post-mortem when he got back to his office.

'Now that you have an idea what was making you so anxious about this meeting and your resulting behaviour, Oliver, let's see if we can assist you to reshape your thinking and your behaviour,' says Dr Jim. 'If we can assist you to do this in relation to this issue, we can apply the same concepts to future similar social interactions.'

Challenging Oliver's 'A'

'As before, we could dispute or challenge your "A", your interpretation of this meeting with these new customers and the dangers you associated with it,' Dr Jim explains. 'I could probably dispute with you where your proof was that the dangers you laid out were really going to happen. What is much more effective, however, is to challenge the "B" and the "C". We will challenge the irrational beliefs that we have already uncovered, which are the real driver of your anxiety, and also the emotional and behavioural consequences of these beliefs.'

Challenging Oliver's 'C'

Dr Jim asks Oliver whether it would be possible to simply stop being anxious when faced with such a social event, or to just not become embarrassed or ashamed when in such situations. They agree that this would be neither useful nor realistic.

They also revisit the cause of his physical symptoms, and how they are uncomfortable but not dangerous. Dr Jim again explores the idea of learning to accept that the more Oliver demands that the symptoms go away, the more they will increase – and vice versa.

Together, they examine how, again, Oliver's behaviour was a large part of the problem. Constantly checking himself in mirrors before leaving the office, constantly rehearsing the upcoming conversations in his mind before the meeting, keeping his jacket on and checking himself in the toilet to see if he was sweating – none of these were diminishing his anxiety. The post-mortems were not helpful either.

Challenging Oliver's 'B'

'Now we need to examine and challenge your "B", that is, your set of irrational beliefs,' Dr Jim says. 'These took the form of an absolute demand that you must not be exposed to any situation, such as meeting new customers, in which you might become anxious – plus your belief that people such as these customers would judge you and that you must accept their judgment. Do you think these beliefs and demands are rational or irrational?'

Oliver says he sees that the 'must', the idea that he could be a failure, and his belief that he has to accept other people's opinions of him are irrational.

Dr Jim revisits the big MACS, and how they will use them to challenge Oliver's demand. He then challenges Oliver's 'B'.

'Returning to your absolute demand that you must not get anxious if you meet up with strangers such as these customers in a hotel, what would be a healthier demand?' Dr Jim asks.

They eventually agree that a more rational, healthier demand in this situation would be that he would prefer not to get extremely anxious in such social situations, but in real life it was out of his control. That leads to a further discussion on the importance of control in Oliver's life, and Oliver has to agree that control is impossible to achieve.

Dr Jim also challenges Oliver's catastrophising in relation to the situation. He asks Oliver if he has any proof that his visualisation of what might happen would in fact occur. He also mentions the spilt-milk analogy discussed earlier.

Then Dr Jim challenges Oliver's assumption that if he did get very anxious in such a social situation, he would not be able to cope. Eventually, they agree that he would cope, because there really was no other option.

Together, Dr Jim and Oliver revisit the idea of the Raggy Doll Club to dispute his irrational beliefs that if he did become anxious he would be a failure for letting it happen, and that others would judge him as being weak and he would have to accept their judgment.

'If we are real Raggy Dolls, we do not rate ourselves and will not allow other people to rate us,' Dr Jim reminds Oliver.

They have a further discussion on the importance of applying this to all situations in our lives. Oliver can see he fell back into the trap of rating again, and vows to work even harder at becoming a Raggy Doll.

'We have now put the framework in place for you to really take on board the changes we have to make,' says Dr Jim. 'But firstly let's look at some common misconceptions that people with social anxiety often have.'

He challenges whether one can see anxiety in a person in social situations and gives Oliver the 'anxiety inspector' exercise. He challenges how observant others are in real life and gives Oliver some shame exercises similar to the ones given to earlier. They also discuss his conversation skills, as dealt with already.

Three months later, Oliver is a changed man. He has found that the various exercises Dr Jim gave him revolutionised how he looked at social situations. He still got normal symptoms of anxiety when going into new social situations, but no longer became extremely anxious and had really developed his conversation skills. He was still doing his presentations, but was now comfortable with this. His social anxiety was almost a thing of the past.

V.
PHOBIAS, PTSD AND OCD

11.
The World of Phobias

Phobias are one of the most common psychological conditions affecting human beings. A phobia can be defined as an excessive and persistent fear of a particular object or situation, where exposure to the latter provokes an immediate anxiety response, leading to a tendency to avoid it.

Common objects of simple phobias include animals or insects, such as cats, dogs, mice, spiders or snakes. A large percentage of the population suffers from such phobias. This is an evolutionary remnant of earlier times, when spiders, snakes and large cats were things to fear and avoid. Most of the time, such phobias are just nuisances, and do not require intervention.

People also commonly have phobias of situations such as being in confined spaces, at heights, on planes, on motorways, or in contact with blood. Many people fear heights and enclosed spaces, and one of the most common modern simple phobias is the fear of flying, which can keep people/families from travelling abroad.

Generalised phobias include social phobia/social anxiety disorder, and also agoraphobia, a fear of open spaces (*agora* is Greek for a public open space). This phobia is often present in those who suffer from panic disorder. At any given time, up to 20,000 people in Ireland might be suffering from this condition. Like social phobia, agoraphobia leads to significant difficulties in the lives of sufferers.

Agoraphobia also refers to situations in which people dread leaving the house and entering public areas like churches, supermarkets, cinemas and shopping centres. In severe cases, the sufferer might have difficulty leaving their own room. Agoraphobia can be an isolating, paralysing condition. It can also prompt safety-seeking behaviour such as demanding to be accompanied by family members or friends, and avoidant behaviours, such as finding excuses not to leave the house or go to public areas.

At the heart of this phobia is the fear that if they encounter the situation, the result may be a panic attack, or at the very least extreme anxiety with very uncomfortable physical symptoms. It is this fear which makes them avoid the situation. In severe cases, the resulting isolation can trigger a bout of depression.

Because we have examined panic attacks in detail earlier, we will not review this condition much more, other than adding that it is the avoidant or safety behaviour which often becomes the main problem. If, for example, I refuse to leave my house for fear of developing panic attacks, then it is this behaviour that is causing my problem.

Learning to deal with panic attacks through the approach I explained earlier, and graded exposure to the trigger – leaving the house in stages, for example – are the keys to dealing with this form of chronic anxiety. I have been contacted on many occasions about people who have ended up trapped in their homes. This is one phobia where you will need the services of a CBT therapist to assist you in making the first step.

Later, we will visit two people with this condition and see how they managed to turn their lives around.

General Management of Phobias

We know that general stress- and anxiety-reducing measures like exercise, yoga, moderation in relation to alcohol, relaxation exercises, meditation and mindfulness are all useful but do not deal with the core underlying problem.

We also know that apart from severe cases of agoraphobia, drug therapy is, in general, of very limited assistance. As is often the case with anxiety, talk therapy is the therapy of choice, with a particular emphasis on measures to challenge the significant amygdala influences at play.

Let's examine two common phobias – fear of blood and fear of the motorway – and see how they affected the lives of two sufferers, and how they subsequently learnt how to deal with them. The lessons learnt from these cases can then be applied to all other phobias of this type.

Tony's Story

'I just can't enter the hospital,' Tony explains to Dr Jim on their first visit. 'I get as far as the front gates and simply can't progress any further.'

He has been referred by his GP to deal with the fact that Tony's brother is terminally ill in hospital, but Tony feels he can't enter the grounds, due to a longstanding phobia. He desperately wants to visit his brother, but cannot get beyond his phobia of blood, which he now associates with the hospital.

Tony tells Dr Jim about his lifelong phobia of blood, which he says started with a bad experience when he had to give blood as a child.

'Even hearing the word makes me so anxious that I feel I am going to faint, or something worse,' Tony says. 'I can't visit people I know when they are in hospital. Even when my mother was dying in the nursing home, I struggled to visit her there, but now I have a crisis. My brother, who I am very close to, is seriously ill in hospital. I can't get in to see him due to this phobia, which is distressing both him and my family – not to mention myself.'

Dr Jim explains a little about CBT, and, in particular the ABC system, and how they would use it analyse the problem. He explains that Tony will write down information on the ABC sheet as they go along, and why this is such a powerful exercise. They decide to take his last attempt to enter the hospital as an example.

'So your trigger was entering the hospital to see your brother. What was your emotional response to this?' Dr Jim asks.

'Becoming extremely anxious, almost panicky,' Tony replies.

'And how did you feel, physically, when you experienced this severe anxiety at the hospital gate?' Dr Jim asks.

Tony describes the symptoms: his heart was thumping, he was having difficulty breathing, his mouth was dry, he was sweating, his muscles were tense, he was shaking all over and he felt like his stomach was in his chest. His instinctive behaviour was to avoid, at all costs, going into the hospital.

Dr Jim asks Tony to write up these initial findings on their ABC.

A   Activating Event:

    o   Trigger: arriving at the gates of hospital on way to visit ill brother

    o   Inference/danger:

B   Belief/Demands:

C   Consequences:

    o   Emotional reactions: panic

    o   Physical reactions: heart thumping, difficulty breathing, dry mouth, sweating, muscle tension, bodily shaking, stomach 'in chest'

    o   Behaviour: avoided going into the hospital

'In almost every case of anxiety, we are assigning some danger to the trigger,' says Dr Jim. 'So, in this case, what danger were you assigning to going into the hospital? What did you visualise was going to happen?'

'The real danger for me,' Tony replies, 'was that I would see some blood, or hear someone mention blood. Even the thought of it as I am talking to you is making me feel anxious.'

'What is it about hearing the word "blood" or seeing somebody either giving or receiving blood that bothers you? What do you think is going to happen if this situation occurs?' Dr Jim asks.

Tony is flummoxed by this question, as he has never really considered it. 'I am not really sure. I just know it would be awful,' he says.

'But what would be awful?' enquires Dr Jim. 'Is it the blood itself, or the word or is it how it would affect you if you encountered it?'

'I think it is how it would affect me,' Tony says.

'But how would it affect you?' asks Dr Jim.

'I would just get so shaky, my stomach would be in knots, my heart pounding, my mouth dry, my breathing laboured. It would be awful. I can't even imagine how awful it would get if I got as far as the hospital ward where my brother is,' Tony says.

'And why are you so anxious about these physical symptoms?' asks Dr Jim. 'What dangers do you associate with them'?

'Well, they would be so uncomfortable, and then there is a risk they would get so severe that I would just lose it, and run amok in the hospital,' says Tony. 'It would be awful. I can almost see the security in the hospital coming to restrain me and remove me from the building.'

'So what you are really saying, Tony, is that it is not so much seeing or hearing about blood that really bothers you, it is the way you might react if you were exposed to it,' Dr Jim says. 'So what were you demanding in relation to this trigger and danger?'

'I suppose my big demand was not to be exposed to blood,' Tony says.

Tony put all of this information down on the ABC.

A Activating Event:

- o Trigger: arriving at the gates of hospital on way to visit ill brother

- o Inference/danger: 'If I go into the hospital, I may see or hear about blood. If this happens, I will get significant physical symptoms, which will be extremely uncomfortable. I may lose control and run amok. I may have to be escorted out of the hospital by security.'

B Belief/Demands: 'I must not be exposed to any situation, such as encountering blood, in which I will become extremely anxious.'

C   Consequences:

   o   Emotional reactions: panic

   o   Physical reactions: heart thumping, difficulty breathing, dry mouth, sweating, muscle tension, bodily shaking, stomach 'in chest'

   o   Behaviour: avoided going into the hospital

So, says Dr Jim, putting this altogether:

- It was not the hospital, but the possibility of seeing blood or hearing someone talk about it that was making Tony anxious.

- It was also not even the sight of blood, or the sound of the word 'blood', that was making him anxious, but how he would feel and react.

- It was actually fear of the discomfort of the physical symptoms he would suffer if he were exposed to the mention or sight of blood, and the possibility that he might run amok as a result of them – or do something even worse – that were the real dangers.

- This was making him demand that he must not be exposed to any situation, such as coming into contact with blood, in which he might become extremely anxious.

- This resulted in avoidant behaviour, such as not visiting the hospital or even his GP, for fear of exposure to the sight or mention of blood.

'Most phobias are red herrings or false trails, as my friend and colleague Enda Murphy often says,' Dr Jim explains. 'It is not the trigger that is really the cause of the phobia, but our reactions to it. What we are really afraid will happen is that if we are exposed to the trigger, we will become very anxious, and possibly even have a panic attack. We often also visualise that something terrible is going to happen, such as running amok, or some other unknown catastrophe. Now, what caused the physical symptoms you experienced?'

'It was the feelings of anxiety or panic that triggered them,' says Tony.

'What happened in your body to cause these symptoms?' Dr Jim asks.

Tony struggles with this question. 'It must be my brain that was the cause of these symptoms,' he suggest.

Dr Jim explains that Tony's stress system was behind these physical symptoms. 'Whenever our emotional brain senses a danger, whether real or perceived, it immediately activates our acute stress system, which prepares us to fight, freeze or flee,' he says. 'It does so by activating our internal nervous system, and also by releasing our fear hormone, adrenaline.'

They discuss what adrenaline is. Using the leopard example from previous chapters, Dr Jim helps Tony to see that it is simply our do-a-runner hormone, and that the symptoms it causes are uncomfortable but not dangerous. There is, in fact, no actual danger from these physical symptoms, Dr Jim says, stressing that they are extremely uncomfortable, and that it is this discomfort that so many people with phobias struggled most to deal with.

Dr Jim then explores with Tony the idea of learning to accept that the more he demands that the symptoms go away, the more they will increase, but the more he accepts them and just goes with them, the more they will start to fade into the background. He talks about the role of the amygdala in creating strong emotions of fear or panic, and the physical symptoms they lead to. He details how this organ can only be faced head on, if Tony wants to beat this phobia. And that means accepting and absorbing the physical symptoms. He also mentions the role of Tony's right PFC, and how it is this part of his brain that is catastrophising about how awful it will be if he is exposed to blood.

Both Tony's amygdala and his right PFC will have to be challenged, Dr Jim says.

This leads them back to discussing the danger that Tony assigned to going into the hospital and being exposed to blood. Tony begins to accept that it was actually the physical symptoms of anxiety that he was most afraid of. They discuss whether people actually run amok when they become anxious. Tony agrees that in real life such things do not happen.

They also discuss the way in which our emotional brain, in the form of our right PFC, is capable of creating catastrophic possibilities with no basis in reality. They start to challenge this. Dr Jim gives Tony the spilt-milk analogy. Does Tony have any proof that any of the scenarios he visualises were going to happen? Dr Jim asks. Or were they just a drop of spilt milk, and of no real significance?

Tony finds it extremely helpful to have a picture of what is going on in his brain and mind. But now comes the crux of the matter: his behaviour.

'Is not going into the hospital going to assist you in learning how best to deal with the physical symptoms of anxiety?' asks Dr Jim.

'It won't,' says Tony, 'but how do I deal with the extreme discomfort of these symptoms in the hospital?'

'Well, we now know that with amygdala-based anxiety symptoms like these, the only way is to let them happen and let them wash over you,' says Dr Jim. 'You now know that they are not dangerous, only uncomfortable. If you go with them, then very quickly your amygdala or emotional brain realises there is actually no danger. When this happens, the amygdala starts to shut them down and they diminish quite quickly. It is only when you are afraid of them and try to stop them, or prevent them from happening, that the difficulties begin.'

Dr Jim continued: 'You also have to ask yourself which is the greater discomfort – running from these physical symptoms for the rest of your life and not being able to visit loved ones in hospital, or learning to face and accept these uncomfortable physical symptoms in the short term. There can only be one winner here, and you must choose.'

'So what you are saying,' said Tony, 'is that it is in my interest to learn how to deal with these uncomfortable physical symptoms once and for all by exposing myself to the hospital and the potential of seeing or hearing about blood whilst there?'

'There is no other way to eliminate this phobia, except to challenge your amygdala,' says Dr Jim. 'Once it realises that the danger it has been ascribing to blood is actually not a serious one, it will quickly calm down about future exposure.'

Dr Jim continues: 'Modern research has shown that the amygdala has to be exposed to both the trigger and the perceived danger at the same time, which will trigger all of the usual physical symptoms. Then, when it quickly realises nothing dangerous is actually happening, it will reset its responses to that trigger from then on. In your case, Tony, this means exposing yourself to the trigger – the hospital, blood and the visualised dangers we have already discussed – and the uncomfortable physical symptoms which will accompany this process. Because you now know what to do with these physical symptoms, and because your amygdala will soon see that there is no actual danger, you will find it calming down very quickly and resetting itself for the long term. There is no other way of defeating this phobia.'

Tony agrees to put this into practice. Two weeks later, he returns, relieved.

'It was so wonderful to be able to go in and embrace my brother, who is dying,' he says.

He explains that he got very anxious before he went to the hospital for the first time, and, in particular, when he went inside it. He found that his physical symptoms came to a head when one of the nurses mentioned that his brother's blood count was down.

'But I stood my ground, let the symptoms wash over me and, quite quickly, they began to lessen and then disappear. It was a watershed moment for me. For the first time, I realised that it was my emotional mind just playing tricks with me. I now know, in my gut, that it is not blood that was causing my problems, but my mind's irrational reactions, and that it was the resulting uncomfortable physical symptoms that were my enemy.'

Tony was able to go in and out of the hospital on a daily basis for the next four weeks, to be with his brother on his final journey. He still got some symptoms of anxiety, but found that they gradually disappeared with his regular visits. Never again would the sight or mention of blood be an issue for him, for he had reset his amygdala's response. He had also put his PFC back in its box. His phobia was gone for good.

Maria's Story

'I had to take every back road to get to see you,' Maria explains to Dr Jim on her first visit. 'There was just no way that I could drive the motorway.'

Maria has had a phobia of travelling on the motorway for the previous five years. She is thirty-three and has two children and a very busy life as an accountant and mother. She can't really pin down when her phobia first began, she says.

'I just started to feel increasingly anxious at the thought of going on to the motorway, and this anxiety grew until I just couldn't travel on it any longer,' she tells Dr Jim.

She describes how difficult this is making her work, and also how difficult it is making journeys to visit her mother. 'I have to either wait until my husband Peter is around to drive me, or else take the back roads,' she says. 'Have you any idea how long that takes?'

Dr Jim empathises with her difficulties, and suggests that some CBT techniques could help her deal with her phobia. Maria is quite happy to try anything which can get her back driving the motorways like everyone else.

Dr Jim then explains CBT, and, in particular, the ABC system, and how they will use it to lay out the problem. He emphasises the importance of Maria writing down all the information they gather.

They decide to use the example of her recent attempt at overcoming her fear. She drove up near the motorway entrance, but then she became anxious, turned around and went home by the back roads.

'So we know that your trigger was the thought of driving on the motorway, and your emotion was anxiety,' says Dr Jim. 'But how did you feel physically when you began to think about getting on the motorway?'

Maria describes a thumping heart, difficulty breathing, sweating, tense muscles, her stomach in knots, weakness, a dry mouth and bodily shaking. 'I just felt terrible.'

'And what was your behaviour when you became very anxious about the thought of driving on the motorway?' Dr Jim asks.

Maria describes how she turned back when she got close to the motorway. She includes this information in their ABC.

A   Activating Event:

   o   Trigger: the thought of driving on the motorway

   o   Inference/danger:

B   Belief/Demands:

C   Consequences:

   o   Emotional reactions: anxiety

   o   Physical reactions: heart thumping, difficulty breathing, sweating, muscle tension, stomach in knots, weakness, dry mouth and shaking

   o   Behaviour: avoided driving on the motorway

'In almost every case of anxiety, we are assigning some danger to the trigger,' says Dr Jim. 'In this case, what danger were you assigning to entering on to the motorway? What did you visualise was going to happen?'

'I am not really sure,' Maria replies. 'I am a good driver and have no problem driving on the back roads. But I just feel that something terrible is going to happen the minute I get on the motorway.'

'And what terrible occurrence do you visualise happening?' Dr Jim asks.

'It is not really a fear that I am going to crash,' she replies. 'I know that this could just as easily happen on the back roads. It is something else, but I don't really know what it is.'

'Well that is one of the main dangers out of the way,' says Dr Jim. 'Some people's danger is that they might crash. But if it is not the fear of having a crash, what else could you be visualising might happen when you get on the motorway?'

'I just think that I will feel crowded in, and I don't really like that feeling,' Maria says.

'And what will your reaction be if you feel crowded in on the motorway?' Dr Jim asks.

'I know I will feel incredibly tense, that my heart will be in my mouth, that I will find my breathing disturbed and my stomach churning,' Maria replies.

'And what is it about these feelings that would bother you?' Dr Jim asks. 'What danger are you associating with them?'

'I just feel they are going to get overwhelming and something terrible is going to happen,' Maria replies. 'My biggest fear is that I will lose control as a result of these feelings, and do something stupid.'

'What do you visualise happening then?' Dr Jim asks.

'My fear is that I might end up being the cause of an accident, and somebody else might get hurt,' Maria replies.

'So now we know that it was not the motorway that was really the danger, but the physical sensations that being on the motorway would bring on, and the potential consequences you visualised happening if these occurred,' Dr Jim says.

Maria agrees.

'And what do you feel causes these physical sensations?' Dr Jim asks.

Maria says she thinks that they are most likely due to anxiety. Dr Jim agrees.

'Most phobias are red herrings or false trails,' he says. 'It is often not the trigger that is really the cause of the phobia, but our reactions to it. What we are really afraid of is that we are going to get very anxious when exposed to the trigger, which in your case is the motorway. So what demand were you making in relation to this danger?'

'I suppose I was demanding not to be put into the situation where it might happen,' Maria says.

Dr Jim asks her to write this information on their ABC.

A   Activating Event:

- o   Trigger: the thought of driving on the motorway
- o   Inference/danger: if she drives on the motorway, she will end up becoming anxious, she will suffer significant physical symptoms, she will end up losing control, something terrible will happen and somebody else will get injured.

B   Belief/Demands: 'I must not be exposed to a situation (e.g. driving on a motorway) in which I will become extremely anxious.'

C   Consequences:

o   Emotional reactions: anxiety

o   Physical reactions: heart thumping, difficulty breathing, sweating, muscle tension, stomach in knots, weakness, dry mouth and shaking

o   Behaviour: avoided driving on the motorway

Challenging Maria's Phobia

'When you became very anxious, what do you think caused the physical symptoms you described so well?' Dr Jim asks.

Maria says she is not sure.

Dr Jim explains how her stress system is behind these physical symptoms.

'Whenever our emotional brain senses a danger, whether real or perceived, it immediately activates our acute stress system, which prepares us to fight or flee,' says Dr Jim. It does so by activating our internal nervous system, and also by releasing our fear hormone, adrenaline.'

They discuss adrenaline, and, using the leopard example, Dr Jim helps Maria to see that it is simply our do-a-runner hormone, and that the symptoms it causes are uncomfortable but not dangerous. There is no actual danger from these physical symptoms, Dr Jim says, but they are extremely uncomfortable and it is with this discomfort that people with phobias struggle.

Dr Jim explores with Maria the role of her amygdala in creating strong emotions of fear or panic, and the resulting physical symptoms. This organ must be faced head on if Maria wanted to learn to beat this phobia, he says. That means accepting and absorbing the physical symptoms. He also discusses with her the right PFC, and its role in her catastrophising about what might happen. Both of these organs will have to be challenged, he says.

'Let's now move on to examine the danger that you will become extremely anxious, and suffer from all of the physical symptoms you described,' Dr Jim says. 'Is it the job of our stress system to kill us or to protect us?'

'I assume,' answers Maria, 'that its job is to protect us.'

'So if you were on the motorway, is its job to protect you or to potentially injure or kill you or somebody else by causing a crash?' Dr Jim asks.

Maria says she has never really examined this question. 'What you are really saying is that if there was any potential danger on the motorway, my stress system would kick in to protect me,' she says.

Dr Jim acknowledges this to be the case. 'No matter how uncomfortable the physical symptoms of anxiety might be, the reality is that our stress system is designed to assist us to make the right decisions if something potentially dangerous happens,' he says. 'But let's go further. When was the last time you heard of somebody causing an accident on the motorway simply because they became anxious?'

Maria has to agree that she has never heard of this happening.

'And why do you think that is?' Dr Jim asks.

Maria is beginning to understand. 'What you are saying is that the physical symptoms are simply uncomfortable, but not dangerous. That not only will they not end up causing me to crash and hurt somebody else, but they will actually protect me if anything untoward were to happen,' she says.

'So if we assume that these physical symptoms are not going to cause you to crash and hurt somebody, why else would you be bothered about them?' Dr Jim asks.

'I think it is really the discomfort of the sensations,' Maria replies.

'And is it in your interest to learn to accept this discomfort?' Dr Jim asks.

Maria agrees that it is. 'I guess that there is no real danger from these physical sensations,' she says. 'So, yes, if it got me able to travel on the motorway, it would be very much in my interest to learn to accept this discomfort.'

They then decide that Maria will begin taking short journeys on the motorway, to put these ideas into practice.

'We can understand it in our head,' explains Dr Jim, 'but we still need to feel it in our gut to fully grasp that the physical symptoms of anxiety are uncomfortable but never dangerous.'

A month later, Maria returns to see Dr Jim and is proud to announce that she has come via the motorway. Following Dr Jim's advice, she had begun with short trips on the motorway. She became anxious, and experienced the physical symptoms, but just went with them and found that they settled much more quickly than she had expected. Eventually, she travelled on the motorway all the way down to see her mother.

What Have We Learned?

These two stories reveal the typical pattern present in almost all simple phobias. So let's review the lessons we have learnt, and how they can be applied to most simple phobias.

- The first key point is that it is never the trigger that is the cause of our phobias, but rather the danger we assign to that trigger. So whether we are talking about a phobia of spiders or a phobia of getting on a plane, it is not these things that are causing the person to get anxious, but rather the danger they assign to them.

- The second key point is that the danger assigned is always a combination of physical symptoms of anxiety that will be extremely uncomfortable, and distressing visualisations that something terrible will happen if we are exposed to the trigger. Usually, the latter entails elements of losing control or some other unknown catastrophic outcome.

- In all cases, the pattern will be the same. The person will assign the danger to an object or situations, demand that they must not be exposed to this object or situation, become anxious if they are exposed to the trigger, and develop the typical physical symptoms of anxiety detailed so often in this book.

- They will either try to avoid the situation or engage in some safety behaviours to reduce their anxiety.

- The key is to understand the roles of our amygdala and our right

PFC in the above process, and how both need to be challenged, in order to defeat the phobia in question.

Dr Jim will always challenge the sufferer's danger, which is usually that they will develop the physical symptoms of anxiety, which will be very uncomfortable, and also the catastrophic visualisation that something terrible will happen, often involving losing control and running amok. To do this, he tries to help the sufferer understand two vital pieces of information:

- The role of the stress system, which creates all of these physical symptoms, is to protect us, not harm us.

- Our danger that something terrible will happen is actually not a real danger, just a visualisation in our minds.

Dr Jim will then encourage the person to challenge their avoidant and safety behaviours, while accepting that when they do, they will become anxious and experience uncomfortable physical symptoms. If they can learn to accept this, and to believe that it is the job of our stress system to protect us and not to harm us, that is the real key to beating the phobia.

★

There is a separate group of phobias that are more like GAD. Some common examples of this are airplane phobias, where the danger is more to do with a fear that the plane will crash, and motorway phobias in which the danger is not that the person will get the physical symptoms of anxiety, but that the car will crash.

Once again, the phobia is not really about the plane or the car – it's more about the danger they will end up crashing. In both cases, the emotion will be anxiety, which will come with the usual secondary physical symptoms, and the behaviour is either avoidant or safety in type.

These phobias are common in people with GAD-type symptoms, for whom the absolute demand for 100-percent control is the issue. The earlier section on GAD explains how this should be tackled.

Jennifer's Story

Jennifer comes to see Dr Jim with her brother, who has, after months of urging, finally persuaded her to make the visit.

She says she has been having increasing difficulty leaving her house over the previous twelve months, and has become very isolated. She lost contact with her friends, making up excuses as to why she can't see them. She developed feelings of anxiety about going mad, and of shame about her behaviour. Her family became increasingly frustrated with her – she was letting them down.

Jennifer tells Dr Jim that she has a history of panic attacks. She is adamant that she does not want any form of drug therapy. Dr Jim offers to show her some CBT techniques, and explained the ABC system to her. They come up with the following ABC analysis of her problem:

A   Activating Event:

  o   Trigger: leaving the house

  o   Inference/danger: she may get anxious or experience a panic attack if she leaves the house, and if she does, she might have a heart attack, die or go mad.

B   Belief/Demands: she must not get anxious or have a panic attack if she leaves her house.

C   Consequences:

  o   Emotional reactions: anxiety

  o   Physical reactions: stomach in knots, tension headache, heart palpations, difficulty sleeping, difficulty breathing

  o   Behaviour: avoids leaving the house, makes excuses to friends and family about why she can't meet them, has somebody with her as a safety measure

Dr Jim explains to Jennifer that it is not possible to prevent her from feeling anxious and developing the associated physical symptoms. Then they discuss what causes such symptoms, and how to accept them as uncomfortable but not dangerous.

They explore the role of the amygdala in creating strong emotions of fear or panic and the physical symptoms that they lead to. Dr Jim explains how this organ must be faced head on if Jennifer wants to beat her phobia, and that that would mean accepting and absorbing the physical symptoms.

Dr Jim then challenges Jennifer's behaviour, explaining how it was making the situation worse. He also challenges her danger that she might have a panic attack and go mad or die if she leaves her house, and her demand that she must not get anxious.

Dr Jim explains the mechanisms underlying panic attacks, and how to cope with panic attacks if they occur. Jennifer begins to understand that the physical symptoms of anxiety are uncomfortable but not dangerous.

Dr Jim introduces the idea of an initial behavioural exercise in which she leaves the house and, on reaching grade seven out of ten in terms of anxiety, returns – gradually increasing the distance she travels. He encourages the flooding-exposure technique of allowing the physical symptoms to just wash over her.

Losing her fear of anxiety, Jennifer stops demanding that it must not happen if she leaves the house. With Dr Jim's support, she ends up investigating what actually happens when she leaves the house, and, as a result, soon loses her fear.

Josephine's Story

Josephine, a mother of three, comes to see Dr Jim, complaining of difficulty visiting her local shopping centre.

Recently, the issue came to a head when Josephine felt herself becoming weak within minutes of entering the centre to visit her favourite store. She made excuses to the friend she was with, and returned home. Since then, Josephine has not been in the centre, and she becomes anxious if somebody proposes meeting her there.

Dr Jim suggests that they try some CBT techniques, and, when she agrees, explains the ABC system to her. They come up with the following ABC analysis of her problem:

A   Activating Event:

 o Trigger: entering her local shopping centre

 o Inference/danger: she will become very anxious and develop distressing physical symptoms, which will get progressively worse until something terrible happens. She is not sure what will happen – but thinks she may lose control and run amok.

B   Belief/Demands: she must not get anxious if she enters the centre, and if she does it would be just awful.

C   Consequences:

 o Emotional reactions: anxiety

 o Physical reactions: stomach in knots, tension headache, palpations, difficulties sleeping, difficulties breathing

 o Behaviour: she leaves the centre immediately and avoids returning, making excuses as to why she cannot go there.

Dr Jim explains to Josephine that there is no way to prevent this anxiety, or the physical symptoms it brings about. They discuss what causes such symptoms, and how there is little we can do when they occur except learn to accept them as uncomfortable but not dangerous.

He explores the role of the amygdala in creating these strong emotions of fear or panic, and the physical symptoms they lead to. He also details how she must face this organ head on if she wants to learn to beat her phobia. And that that means accepting and absorbing the physical symptoms.

Dr Jim challenges her behaviour, and how it is consolidating her fears. He then challenges her danger – that she will get very anxious if she enters the centre – and her demand that she must not get anxious. He explains what the symptoms of anxiety are, that they are uncomfortable but not dangerous, and how to cope with them if they occur. They agree that people do not really run amok, and that terrible things don't happen to us just because we have normal symptoms of anxiety. This will help Josephine to cease demanding that she must not get anxious if she enters the centre, as she no longer fears the resulting physical symptoms. Instead, she now knows she must accept them as due to a simple adrenaline rush, which will pass.

Josephine goes away to put all this into practice, and decides to make an effort to visit the centre on a daily basis. Although she experiences the uncomfortable symptoms of anxiety, she learns to accept them as normal. She now no longer demands that she should not become anxious when she enters the centre. When she returns to see Dr Jim four weeks later, she has made major inroads into eliminating her phobia.

We can see with these two cases just how consistent the pattern is in most phobias. The danger is, almost all the time, the fear of developing the uncomfortable physical symptoms of anxiety, or a panic attack, and the demand is that this must not happen. It is usually the avoidant or safety behaviour that is doing most of the damage to the person's life, so it is often this that leads them to come for help.

Before leaving the world of phobias, it is worth stressing again that most phobias are a mixture of amygdala-based and PFC-based anxiety. It is the amygdala that gives rise to the often extremely uncomfortable physical symptoms that sufferers are so determined to avoid. It is the PFC – and particularly the right PFC – that causes the catastrophic visualisations. Since there is a strong link between the right PFC and the amygdala, they feed on one another.

That is why we need to challenge both of these in the manner shown above. In particular, exposing the amygdala to the danger and physical symptoms helps it to reshape its negative emotional memory bank, making it easier to really beat these phobias in the long run.

12.
Post-Traumatic Stress Disorder

All of us will experience traumatic stressful periods in our lives and manage them healthily. But following particularly traumatic occurrences, some will develop a type of chronic persistent anxiety called post-traumatic stress disorder (PTSD). This is most likely to occur following severe accidents, assaults, rapes and war incidents, when there has been a definite threat to the life of the sufferer or their family. A diagnosis is made only when symptoms are present for more than six months.

Following such events, the sufferer complains of constant flashbacks and nightmares relating to the event, a tendency to avoid thinking or dealing with the matter and many of the typical physical symptoms of anxiety: muscle pain, headaches, panicky feelings. Some may feel down, ashamed or guilty they have survived the event. Many find themselves feeling on-guard all the time, constantly scanning their environment for danger. Many have difficulties with sleep and use alcohol to blot out how they feel. Following a trauma, PTSD can affect a sufferer for the rest of their life.

In terms of treatment, PTSD has always been seen as a particularly difficult anxiety condition, especially when there has been extreme trauma. This makes a lot of sense, since trauma creates powerful amygdala memories of the emotions experienced at the time. It also has marked effects on our PFC.

In terms of general management, we know that lifestyle changes like regular exercise, good nutrition and moderation in alcohol are extremely helpful. Yoga (with or without meditation) and mindfulness can reduce the symptoms of anxiety, but on their own will not deal with the problem. Drug therapy using SSRIs is useful if depression or very severe bouts of PTSD are present. But various forms of talk therapy, and particularly CBT, are the primary method of addressing PTSD.

One of the biggest dangers in PTSD is the tendency to self-medicate to try to deal with the extremely uncomfortable physical and psychological symptoms of this form of anxiety. This will most often take the form of alcohol misuse or abuse, but it can also involve illegal and legal substances to which the sufferer may become in some situations addicted.

Here in Ireland, there are still many survivors of the Troubles who suffer symptoms of PTSD. There is an increasing number of victims of violent urban and rural crime, who can end up very traumatised – particularly our elderly. We are also likely to see PTSD in the refugees coming our way from war-torn parts of the world such as Syria. Many of these will have been through horrific experiences, and will be at risk of PTSD.

Although they vary significantly in terms of severity, the symptoms of PTSD, and the way it develops a life of its own, are fairly similar, irrespective of the cause.

This can be a life-threatening condition, as the high suicide rate amongst American veterans returning from wars in the Middle East and Afghanistan in the past few years can testify to. There is a recent concern that more soldiers are felt to be dying by suicide from PTSD and related problems, than from hostile actions in the war zones themselves.

Whilst war is the most obvious trigger for this condition in other countries, here in Ireland road-traffic accidents are one of the most common causes. We are going to meet Ciaran, who had such an experience, and see how he learnt to deal with it. The lessons we can learn from his story are almost universal to all victims of trauma who develop PTSD.

In terms of the brain, in PTSD sufferers, there is mounting evidence of functional difficulties in and between the amygdala and the PFC – common in many anxiety conditions. We know that the amygdala is particularly irritable and hypersensitive, and the capacity of the PFC to dampen down its activities seems to be significantly impaired.

Ciaran's Story

Ciaran attends Dr Jim with his wife. He has tried every form of conventional and alternative remedy over the previous three years. It has become clear that his problems relate to a bad car crash three and a half years ago. He had just left his wife and children off at the swimming pool when he was hit by a truck, which had suddenly gone out of control. He managed to steer the car out of a head-on collision, but ended up spending six weeks in hospital with multiple injuries and everyone telling him how lucky he was to be alive.

Dr Jim sees the typical symptoms of PTSD. Ciaran has constant flashbacks of the incident, nightmares, panicky-type physical symptoms, sudden drops in mood, intermittent bursts of unexplained anger for which he later feels ashamed, and periods where he feels guilty for upsetting everybody around him. On occasions when he has become extremely anxious or his mood has dropped suddenly for short periods, he has developed thoughts of self-harm. The most common flashbacks relate to seeing the truck coming straight at him. He constantly agonises over how close the whole family unit was to being wiped out. What would have happened if they had been with him?

Ciaran says he tried drug treatment, but found it unhelpful. He admits to self-medicating with alcohol on a regular basis. He says he had some counselling sessions, which, although helpful, did little to diminish the constant feelings of anxiety and the associated physical symptoms, which were messing up his life. There was a legal case, which has been settled, but his PTSD symptoms continue unabated.

Dr Jim starts by explaining just what PTSD is, and then he lays out the usual lifestyle changes, such as exercise, yoga and mindfulness classes and moderation of alcohol intake. But the best approach, Dr Jim says, is to learn some CBT techniques. He then explains the ABC system, and the importance of rational and irrational beliefs in our lives.

Dr Jim asks Ciaran to give an example of a recent situation which triggered his anxiety.

'I only have to go back to yesterday,' says Ciaran. 'I was driving down the country with my family to see my parents, and I found myself feeling incredibly anxious.'

'Now we have the trigger, which was you driving your family to your parents' house, and your emotion, which was anxiety,' says Dr Jim. 'But how did you feel physically when you became very anxious?'

Ciaran says his heart started to pound, his stomach was in knots, he had difficulty breathing, he began sweating, his muscles all tightened up and his mouth went dry.

Dr Jim asks Ciaran to begin their ABC by writing down this information.

A   Activating Event:

   o   Trigger: driving his family down to see parents

   o   Inference/danger:

B   Belief/Demands:

C   Consequences:

   o   Emotional reactions: panic

   o   Physical reactions: heart thumping, difficulty breathing, sweating, muscle tension, stomach in knots and dry mouth

   o   Behaviour:

'When we are anxious about something we are applying some danger to the trigger,' Dr Jim says. 'So what dangers were you applying to this journey? What did you visualise was going to happen?'

'My mind was filled with images of another car or truck going out of control,' says Ciaran.

'And what do you visualise will happen then?' asks Dr Jim.

'That the vehicle will crash headlong into us with terrible consequences,' Ciaran replies.

'And what would you visualise those consequences to be?' asks Dr Jim. 'That some or all of us would be severely injured or die,' says Ciaran. Ciaran adds this to their ABC.

A   Activating Event:

  o   Trigger: driving his family down to see parents

  o   Inference/danger: another vehicle will go out of control and crash headlong into his car, and some or all of his family will be severely injured or killed.

B   Belief/Demands:

C   Consequences:

  o   Emotional reactions: panic

  o   Physical reactions: heart thumping, difficulty breathing, sweating, muscle tension, stomach in knots and dry mouth

  o   Behaviour:

'Let's see what irrational beliefs were triggered by this situation and the danger you assigned to it,' says Dr Jim. 'This usually takes the form of some absolute demand you are making about the trigger and associated danger. So what demands were you making of these?'

Ciaran has to think about this 'I think that I am demanding that what happened before must not happen again,' he says.

'This is typical of the demands we make in this condition,' says Dr Jim. 'The irrational belief or demand in PTSD is that we must not be exposed to any situation which might put us or loved ones at risk of serious injury or death. And that is what you are demanding here. What was your behaviour when you became very anxious in this situation?'

'It was the same as usual,' Ciaran replies. 'I am constantly on high alert, looking for any potential danger as I am driving. I took the back roads, as usual, feeling that there was less chance of meeting a large truck there. I find myself driving slowly to try to minimise any potential collision. If I do see any larger vehicles or any car driving fast, I find myself slamming on the brakes to prepare for any eventuality.'

Dr Jim asks Ciaran to add this information to their ABC.

A   Activating Event:

- o   Trigger: driving his family down to see parents

- o   Inference/danger: another vehicle will go out of control and crash headlong into his car, and some or all of his family will be severely injured or killed.

B   Belief/Demands: 'I must be certain that what happened the last time will not happen again. I must be certain that my family and I will not be exposed to a situation where we would be at risk of serious injury or death.'

C   Consequences:

- o   Emotional reactions: panic

- o   Physical reactions: heart thumping, difficulty breathing, sweating, muscle tension, stomach in knots and dry mouth

- o   Behaviour: remaining in a hypervigilant state when driving, avoiding driving on busy main roads, scanning the environment for possible danger, driving slowly to make sure he has time to react if something happens, slamming on brakes if he encounters a truck or fast car

'Now that we have some understanding, Ciaran, of what made you so anxious about driving your family to see your parents, and your resulting behaviour, let's see if we can reshape both your thinking and your behaviour in relation to this situation,' Dr Jim says. 'If we can assist you to do this, then we can apply the same concepts to future situations.'

Challenging Ciaran's 'A'

'We could dispute or challenge your "A", your interpretation of this journey and the dangers you associated with it,' says Dr Jim. 'We could probably dispute where your proof was that the dangers you laid out were really going to happen. The difficulty with that is that it would only deal with this one situation in which you became very anxious. But what would happen tomorrow or the next day – isn't the whole pattern just going to repeat itself?'

Ciaran agrees that it probably would.

"What is much more effective,' says Dr Jim, 'is to challenge the "B" and the "C". What I mean by this is to challenge the irrational beliefs we have already uncovered as the real drivers of your anxiety, and also the emotional and behavioural consequences of these.'

Challenging Ciaran's 'C'

They begin by having a long conversation about the physical symptoms Ciaran experiences when he gets anxious. They discuss the role of the stress system, and how its function is to protect us, not kill us; they also discuss the role of adrenaline. Dr Jim goes on to explain that there is no actual danger from these physical symptoms, but that they are extremely uncomfortable – and that it is this discomfort that so many people with PTSD struggle the most to deal with. They then explore the idea of learning to accept that the more he demands that the symptoms go away, the more they will increase, but the more he accepts and just goes with them, the more they will start to fade into the background.

Dr Jim explores with Ciaran the critical role of the amygdala in creating these strong emotions of anxiety and the physical symptoms that they lead to. He also details how this organ must be faced head on if Ciaran wants to learn to beat his PTSD. And that that means accepting and absorbing the physical symptoms. Dr Jim also mentions the role of his right PFC, and how it is this part of his brain that is catastrophising about how awful it would be if he or his family were exposed to the risk of major injury or death.

'In PTSD,' Dr Jim says, 'your emotional brain has suffered a major trauma and has laid down some very unhelpful emotional memories in your amygdala and your right PFC, in particular. Your amygdala is now completely hypersensitive, and will fire for the most minor of triggers – and sometimes for no reason at all. This is why you are getting so many physical symptoms of anxiety, and sometimes low mood. Your right PFC is now flooded with all kinds of catastrophic possibilities, as it too took a big hit following the trauma. Since its job is to calm down the amygdala, you can see why you are experiencing so many difficulties.'

Dr Jim continued: 'To help you deal with your PTSD, we are going to have to challenge both your amygdala and your right PFC. The best way to deal with the amygdala is to learn how to deal with the physical symptoms by going with them. Eventually, it will begin to reset itself, and, in time, these symptoms will diminish. We will also challenge the catastrophising of the PFC. If we are successful, it can exert more control over the amygdala in the future.'

Dr Jim moves on to challenge Ciaran's behaviour. 'Do you feel that constantly scanning the environment, taking quieter back roads or braking every time you see a truck or fast car is actually helping you to deal with your anxiety?' he asks.

'No,' says Ciaran. 'It is just making me more hyped up and anxious.'

Dr Jim explains that as a result of the changes to their amygdala and PFC, almost everybody with PTSD ends up being hypervigilant.

'My colleague Enda Murphy often describes it as being like living in a watchtower,' Dr Jim explains. 'It means you are like a sentry in wartime – on high alert in his watchtower, looking for any evidence of danger in his environment. It can become exhausting trying to stay constantly on high alert. The other behaviours are all part of an overall strategy of trying to eliminate any potential danger that might arise.'

Ciaran can definitely relate to this. 'It has been like that since the accident,' he says. 'I never really thought about what the function of this behaviour was. But I can now see that it is only making me more anxious and exhausted.'

They agree that Ciaran will try to challenge this behaviour from now on.

'You may initially find yourself becoming more anxious,' warns Dr Jim, 'and the physical symptoms may be uncomfortable. But if you challenge your behaviour in this manner, these physical symptoms will begin to reduce, and you will find yourself becoming less anxious.'

Challenging Ciaran's 'B'

Dr Jim then moves on to challenging Ciaran's 'B', his set of irrational beliefs. These take the form of two absolute demands:

- He must be certain that what happened the last time will not happen again.

- He must be certain that neither he nor any of his family will be placed at risk of serious injury or death.

Dr Jim goes on to show Ciaran the big MACS, and explain how they can be used to challenge these demands. They decide that it is his demand that he 'must be certain' that is irrational and unhelpful, and is leading to his constant anxiety. So together they challenge Ciaran's need for 100-percent certainty that he must never have a car crash again.

'Is there anything in life that is 100-percent certain?' Dr Jim asks Ciaran. 'Is 100-percent certainty possible in any area of our lives? Is there a car that comes with a crash-free-guarantee sticker on its bonnet?'

They decide that instead of the word 'must', Ciaran should use the word 'prefer', implying there was always going to be a chance – however small – that he could crash again.

Dr Jim also challenges the idea that it is possible to prevent Ciaran and his family from being exposed, through circumstances beyond their control, to potentially life-threatening situations such as illnesses and traumas. He then moves on to examine other areas of Ciaran's life where he is demanding 100-percent certainty. He gives Ciaran the coin-toss exercise, which we discussed in the section on GAD. This is designed to help him experience the reality of not being in control in everyday life.

Then Dr Jim and Ciaran have a discussion about his tendency to catastrophise and how his right PFC is driving this. To try to give Ciaran a visual image of how to challenge this, Dr Jim gives him the spilt-milk analogy: unless he can prove on paper that his visualisation is true, then it is only a drop of spilt milk, and not a puddle. Ciaran finds this analogy extremely helpful and promises to try to put the idea it into action.

★

Ciaran now has a mental image of why he has felt and behaved the way he has. He is determined to put his misfiring amygdala and PFC in their box. He now has a clear enemy to face down, and this assists him greatly in his journey back to full recovery.

Following a number of visits over the next six months, and with the assistance of multiple coin-toss exercises, Ciaran learns to cease looking for 100-percent certainty in relation to driving – and, indeed, other areas of his life. He he is also challenging his catastrophic visualisations on paper, and finds that he is winning the battle.

Ciaran has become much more aware of the emotions and physical symptoms that are created by his amygdala's hypersensitivity. He has learned to roll with these sensations rather than fight them; he finds exercise and mindfulness extremely helpful in reducing their impact on his life. He ceases scanning his environment for danger, and stops many of his other safety behaviours too.

In time, the image of the truck bearing down on him diminishes, and he becomes more relaxed on the road. Thankfully, the queues behind him also disappear.

What Can We Learn from Ciaran's Story?

There are a number of important lessons to be gleaned from Ciaran's story.

- Whenever we, or somebody close to us, is exposed to a life-endangering trauma, it leaves a profound mark on our emotional brain, particularly the amygdala and the right PFC.

- This may lead us to start assigning constant danger to similar situations that arise in our lives.

- We end up searching for absolute control in our lives, and fear the possibility of a similar life-endangering experience occurring again.

- We become incredibly anxious, which brings the usual amygdala-based physical symptoms.

- We then develop a host of avoidant and safety behaviours. The main behaviour is that we become hypervigilant and live in our watchtower, constantly scanning our environment for danger.

- To deal with this scenario, we need first to challenge our behaviour – in particular, our scanning of the environment.

- This means challenging the uncomfortable physical symptoms of anxiety, which challenging our behaviour will bring on.

- We then need to challenge our demand for total control in relation to this or anything else in our life.

- Together with the lifestyle changes already detailed, approaching PTSD in this manner will help us to downplay the amygdala-based negative emotional memories that have become embedded as a result of the trauma. In severe cases, drug therapy, using SSRIs, also may be necessary as part of this treatment plan.

- This will help us to reshape the PFC to downplay the catastrophic visualisations and the tendency to constantly scan the environment that plays such a role in this condition.

13.
Obsessive-Compulsive Disorder

OCD is a distressing anxiety disorder, causing immense difficulties to sufferers and their families and loved ones. Many of us have periodic obsessive thoughts, and, on occasion, behave compulsively – particularly those suffering from other forms of anxiety. OCD is different, in that it literally takes over the life of the sufferer. It is characterised by persistent obsessions, with or without compulsions. This latter point is important, as OCD may remain undiagnosed for long periods due to the absence of obvious compulsions. This is even more stressful for the sufferer.

Obsessions are intrusive, anxiety-provoking thoughts, ideas or images. Compulsions are repetitive rituals or mental actions performed in response to obsessions, in order to decrease anxiety; they aim to remove contaminants. Eventually, those suffering from OCD build into their lives a complex series of avoidant and safety behaviours, which create their own set of problems.

People with OCD experience their disturbing thoughts and images as intrusive and troublesome, but recognise them as products of their own minds. Although patients report a range of different kinds of obsessions and compulsions, there is a notable consistency of themes. A modern view of the compulsive nature of this illness is to regard it as a form of 'behaviour addiction', similar to other common addictions.

Incessant thoughts and compulsions, which the person tries to suppress or avoid, cause major interference with their family and working relationships, not to mention their own psychological state. These thoughts are not simple worries about everyday difficulties. Obsessive thoughts use up the person's mental energy by causing extreme feelings of anxiety. The tension is only relieved by doing what the thoughts demand. This is incredibly tiring, as the thoughts are never-ending.

These obsessive thoughts may relate to:

- Fears over health, and particularly personal health

- Fear of contamination by dirt, germs, sticky materials and bodily fluids like blood, faeces or urine – and overestimation of the risk of such contamination

- Fear of harming themselves, or, more distressingly, those close to them – a mother may worry she will harm her children

- Fear of hurting others, which may compete with fear they may already have done something awful in the past

- Sexual obsessions, such as fear of being gay or being a paedophile

- Religious obsessions, such as fear of offending God

- Fear that something terrible is going to happen

- Fear of having failed to perform some task adequately, and that dire consequences will follow as a result

Examples of compulsive actions are:

- Cleaning – includes excessive hand-washing or home-cleaning

- Checking repeatedly – might involve light switches or door locks

- Counting

- Repeating – words, images or numbers, in mind

- Arranging – making sure everything in the room is in exactly the right place, as a means of remaining in control

- Making lists
- Hoarding – usually items of no intrinsic value

Compulsions persist. In the short term, they seem to reduce anxiety. Over time, this becomes less effective, so the compulsive behaviour has to increase – eventually becoming the problem. This is typical of what happens in routine addictions. In OCD, however, this behaviour pattern is not associated with feelings of enjoyment or satisfaction. Rather, it is associated with a sense of relief, even if short-term, that the anxiety associated with the obsessive thoughts has been relieved.

A typical example of compulsive behaviour is the ritual of hand-washing. Most of us finish washing our hands when they are clean. Those with OCD will only cease when they feel certain their hands are completely free of any possible contaminants, which can often take a considerable period of time.

Obsessions and compulsions go hand in hand.

Washing compulsions are commonly associated with contamination obsessions. For example, a person concerned about contamination from the outside may shower and launder all their clothing immediately upon coming home. A compulsion may be triggered by direct contact with a feared object. In many cases, being in its general vicinity may stir up intense anxiety and a strong need to engage in a washing compulsion.

Other common patterns are worrying about turning out lights or locking doors and then having to check and recheck that it has been done. Or a fear of hurting loved ones leading to an avoidance of using knives while cooking. Or an obsession with order prompting someone to constantly arrange things in a precise, rigid way. A person's feeling that they may have hurt somebody might may lead to compulsions to constantly check and to confess – causing them to admit to things they had no part in, a phenomenon familiar to law enforcement agencies, following highly publicised crimes.

The more a person engages in compulsive behaviour to counteract the anxiety caused by their obsession, the more embedded the obsession becomes.

In terms of safety behaviours, simple examples would be using tissues to avoid touching door handles, and only touching people or things if assured it is safe.

Avoidant behaviours might involve avoiding contact with toilet seats, door handles or taps, to name but a few examples. A person whose main obsession is a fear of germs or dirt may avoid leaving their home or allowing visitors to come inside it. People with such contamination obsessions may wear gloves, coats or even masks if they have to leave their home for some reason.

OCD can affect both adults and children as young as ten. The typical age of onset is late adolescence to early adulthood, and women are slightly more likely to be affected than men. Women have more contamination obsessions and cleaning rituals, while men have more symmetry, ordering and sexual obsessions. Men usually start earlier in their teens, and women may present much later. It is estimated that 2 percent or more of the population may be affected by OCD, but it is still a disorder that may not be diagnosed for up to ten years.

People who suffer from OCD are often deeply ashamed, going to great lengths to hide their ritualistic behaviours. It may be diagnosed when family members get tired of the impact of the person's behaviours on their lives, and force them to consult a doctor. In other cases, the person may go for help themselves. Sometimes the patient will present with depression, a commonly associated illness; 65 percent of OCD sufferers develop depression at some stage in their lives.

There has been an extraordinary amount of interest in the causes and brain pathways underlying OCD. It is now recognised as a classic example of what can happen when key brain pathways become disrupted. The person with OCD knows that their thoughts and actions are not logical, but still can't stop them. So, as is usual in the area of mental-health distress, the problem lies in the inability of the logical brain to put manners on the more unruly emotional brain.

Much work has been done through neuroimaging and other research studies to understand this condition. I will not go into detail here, other than to say that the PFC and the amygdala are once again part of the dysfunctional neurocircuitry behind this condition. The critical point is this: it seems to be a functional neurocircuitry problem rather than a structural one, and this means that it is open to neuroplastic change. We know that successful treatment will normalise the dysfunctional neurocircuitry pathways.

Once again, it is the amygdala which gives rise to the intense physical symptoms of anxiety created when the sufferer tries to challenge the obsession by not giving in to the compulsion. It is the other parts of the brain, such as the PFC, which give rise to the obsessional thoughts and compulsive behaviour.

For further, more detailed information, please refer to my earlier books or to relevant articles in the bibliography.

There appear to be genetic factors involved in OCD. The relatives of people who are diagnosed with it have a greater risk of OCD than the general population. Childhood-onset OCD appears to run in families more than adult-onset OCD, and studies indicate that identical twins are more likely to share the disorder than fraternal twins. Even identical twins do not always share the disorder, however, which suggests that the occurrence of OCD is affected by environmental as well as genetic factors. In addition, it is the general nature of OCD that seems to run in families, rather than the specific symptoms. Thus, one family member who is affected by the disorder may have a compulsion about washing and cleaning, while another is a compulsive counter.

If a person has OCD, there is a 25-percent chance that one of their immediate family members has the condition too. It also appears that stress and psychological factors may worsen symptoms, which usually begin during adolescence or early adulthood. A lot of work has been done to elucidate the genes involved, but no specific gene has been found, so we are probably looking at a polygenetic predisposition. Family upbringing plays a part in how such predispositions develop and prosper.

OCD is a chronic disease that, if untreated, can last for decades, fluctuating from mild to severe and worsening with age.

How to Manage OCD

When treated with a combination of drugs and talk therapy, some patients go into complete remission, and the vast majority experience significant alleviation of their symptoms, allowing them to lead normal lives.

Unfortunately, not all patients have such a good response. About 20 percent of people cannot find significant relief with either type of therapy. Hospitalisation may be required. Despite the crippling nature of the symptoms, many successful doctors, lawyers, business people, performers and entertainers function well in society with the condition. However, the emotional and financial cost can be quite high.

In terms of general management, we know that lifestyle changes like increasing exercise, improving nutrition and moderating alcohol intake are extremely helpful. Yoga (with or without meditation) and mindfulness can reduce the symptoms of anxiety, but on their own may not be sufficient to deal with the problem. We will have an example later where mindfulness ends up playing an important backup role to CBT.

OCD is one of the few anxiety conditions where drug therapy plays a really important role, in association with talk therapy. If somebody feels they may have OCD, it is usually advisable for them to have at least one full assessment by a psychiatrist, to verify the diagnosis and possibly initiate drug therapy.

Some drugs, particularly the SSRIs normally used to treat depression, may be helpful in treating the distressing symptoms of OCD. This requires high doses, and is probably only effective in 50-60 percent of cases. When SSRIs are used to treat anxiety, their effects take a minimum of eight to ten weeks to kick in – longer than with depression. Some feel the eight-week lead-in is due to delayed activity in the PFC.

Small amounts of major tranquillisers like Seroquel, if used in conjunction with the SSRIs, increase the chances of drug therapy being effective. These are quite different from the more addictive sedative tranquillisers that were mentioned earlier in the sections on GAD and panic attacks.

Psychotherapy can be helpful to some patients concerned about the relationship between their upbringing and specific features of their OCD symptoms. Counselling can be helpful to some patients concerned about the consequences of OCD on their personal and social lives.

Behavioural treatments using the technique of exposure and response-prevention are particularly effective in treating OCD. In this form of therapy, the patient and therapist draw up a list or hierarchy of the patient's obsessive and compulsive symptoms. The symptoms are arranged in order from least to most upsetting. The patient is systematically exposed to the anxiety-producing thoughts or behaviours, beginning with the least upsetting. They are then asked to endure the feared event or image without engaging in the compulsion normally used to lower anxiety about it.

For example, a person with a contamination obsession might be asked to touch a series of increasingly dirty objects without washing their hands. In this way, the patient learns to tolerate the feared objects, reducing both worrisome obsessions and anxiety-reducing compulsions. A substantial number of patients respond well to exposure and response-prevention, with very significant reductions in symptoms. But it is a long, difficult road for both patient and therapist.

CBT is also quite effective in the management of OCD, and we will see later how Andrew learned to deal with his condition.

By challenging the thoughts, dangers, demands, and behaviours of the sufferer, the therapist can often help them to achieve a better quality of life. CBT teaches patients how to confront their fears and obsessive thoughts by making the effort to endure or wait out the activities that usually cause them anxiety, without compulsively performing the calming rituals.

From a CBT perspective, there are similarities between phobias and OCD. In both, sufferers will get anxious if exposed to a trigger – a door handle, for example – and will engage in safety and avoidant behaviours to prevent this from happening. It is this pattern that CBT hopes to alter. Because of the complexity of the condition, only a therapist who is highly skilled in CBT should really be involved in managing OCD.

Apart from the need for behavioural changes, which are the essence of any

CBT approach to OCD, there is a need to understand the cognitive dynamics which give rise to so much of the anxiety and frustration underlying this condition, and the resulting compulsive behaviours.

In the following case, let's see how Dr Jim helped Andrew deal with both of these emotions.

Andrew's Story

Andrew is referred to Dr Jim by his GP, with a diagnosis of OCD. Initially he had presented with a history of recurrent dermatitis of the hands. Eventually, however, he admitted he was living in a nightmare world of obsessive thoughts that his hands and body were never fully clean, and was compulsively washing both. This is what had led to his skin problems.

It had been going on for more than ten years, but he had been ashamed to reveal his inner world for fear of ridicule.

Andrew's GP referred him to a specialist, who agreed with the diagnosis of OCD and put him on an SSRI and a small dose of a major tranquilliser. He also noted that Andrew had had two prior incidents of depression associated with his OCD, but had not presented to anybody for assistance. He had also recommended that Andrew would benefit from CBT, which is why Andrew came to see Dr Jim.

Dr Jim empathises with Andrew's story. After some discussion, it becomes clear that Andrew's father, although never diagnosed with the condition, had all of the behaviours typical of OCD. Andrew is still a little unsure of just what OCD is and how best to deal with it, so Dr Jim fills him in on many of the important facets of the condition.

'The most important point is that we now know, from neuroimaging, that we can reshape many of the brain pathways causing the condition, through a mixture of drug therapy and CBT or behaviour therapy,' says Dr Jim.

Dr Jim explains what CBT is, how it works and the importance of rational and irrational beliefs in our lives. He also elaborates on the ABC system, and then asks Andrew for a typical situation that would make him anxious.

Andrew gives him one that he faces every day: going to the toilet.

'Now we have the trigger and the emotion,' says Dr Jim.

Dr Jim asks Andrew to write this down on their ABC, which he does.

A Activating Event:

  o Trigger: going to the toilet

  o Inference/danger:

B Belief/Demands:

C Consequences:

  o Emotional reactions: anxiety

  o Physical reactions:

  o Behaviour:

'Let's now examine what was it about visiting the toilet that was making you so anxious,' says Dr Jim. 'When we are anxious about something, it usually means we are applying some danger to the trigger. So what danger were you applying to your visit to the toilet – what did you visualise was going to happen?'

Andrew explains that his visualised danger was that as a result of going to the toilet, his hands would be unclean and covered with germs.

'And what is it about your hands being unclean and covered with germs that was making you so anxious?' asks Dr Jim.

'If my hands were unclean, I could pass the germs on to somebody else, particularly my children, at home – or even my colleagues, at work,' Andrew says. 'And it wouldn't matter if I washed my hands. They would still be unclean, and I could still pass on the germs.'

'And why would it bother you if your children were to pick up these germs?' asks Dr Jim.

'Because they would end up ill as a result, and it would be my fault for letting it happen,' Andrew says.

'So your danger is that if you go to the toilet, your hands will end up unclean, despite normal hygiene measures. If this happens, you will store germs and then pass them on to others such as your children, who will end up very ill,' says Dr Jim.

Andrew agrees that this is the case.

'So how did you feel physically when you got very anxious about your hands not being clean?' Dr Jim asks.

'Just terrible,' Andrew replies. 'My stomach was in knots, my muscles were all tensed up, my heart was racing, I was having difficulty breathing and I was just plain exhausted.'

Dr Jim asks Andrew to add this information to their ABC.

A   Activating Event:

    o   Trigger: going to the toilet

    o   Inference/danger: 'If I go to the toilet, my hands will end up unclean, covered with germs, which I will pass on to others, such as my children, who might get very ill – and I would be responsible.'

B   Belief/Demands:

C   Consequences:

    o   Emotional reactions: anxiety

    o   Physical reactions: stomach in knots, muscle tension, palpations, difficulties sleeping, difficulties breathing and fatigue

    o   Behaviour:

'Let's now see what irrational beliefs were triggered by this situation and the danger you assigned to it,' says Dr Jim. 'This usually takes the form of some absolute demand you are making about the trigger. So what demands were you making about the danger that your hands might not be clean?'

'My hands must be clean,' says Andrew.

'And what was your behaviour when you became anxious?' asks Dr Jim.

'I just kept scrubbing and scrubbing my hands until they were raw. I knew deep down they were clean, but just couldn't stop myself doing it. If I didn't do it, my anxiety levels would climb through the roof,' says Andrew.

Dr Jim explained that this was completely normal in OCD. 'We know that the compulsive actions are unhealthy, but just can't stop doing them,' he says. 'This is due to functional obstructions in key pathways in the brain.'

Dr Jim asks Andrew to add this information to their ABC.

A   Activating Event:
  o   Trigger: going to the toilet
  o   Inference/danger: 'If I go to the toilet, my hands will end up unclean, covered with germs, which I will pass on to others, such as my children, who might get very ill – and I would be responsible.'

B   Belief/Demands: 'My hands must be clean.'

C   Consequences:
  o   Emotional reactions: anxiety
  o   Physical reactions: stomach in knots, muscle tension, palpations, difficulties sleeping, difficulties breathing and fatigue
  o   Behaviour: ritualistic washing of hands until raw

'Now we have some understanding, Andrew,' says Dr Jim, 'of what made you so anxious about visiting the toilet, and your ensuing behaviour. Let's see if we can help you to reshape your thinking and behaviour in relation to this. If we can assist you to do this in relation to this situation, we can apply the same concepts to future, similar ones.'

Challenging Andrew's 'A'

'We could dispute or challenge your "A", your interpretation of this visit to the toilet and the dangers you associated with it,' Dr Jim explains. 'We could probably dispute where your proof was that the dangers you laid out were really going to happen. What is much more effective is to challenge the "B" and the "C". What I mean by this is to challenge the irrational beliefs that we have already uncovered, which are the real driver of your anxiety, and the behavioural consequences of these beliefs.'

Challenging Andrew's 'C'

They begin by having a long conversation about the physical symptoms Andrew experiences when he is anxious. They discuss the role of the stress system, and how its function is to protect us, not kill us – and also the role of adrenaline. Dr Jim explains that there is no actual danger from these physical symptoms, while stressing that they are extremely uncomfortable, and that it is this discomfort that so many people with OCD struggled most to deal with. He explores the idea of learning to accept that the more Andrew demands that they go away, the more the symptoms will increase, but the more he accepts them and just goes with them, the more they will start to fade into the background.

Dr Jim explores the critical role of the amygdala in creating these strong emotions of anxiety, and the secondary physical symptoms. He also details how this organ must be faced head on, and how that means accepting and absorbing the physical symptoms. He gently challenges Andrew's behaviour.

'Do you feel that constantly washing your hands is actually helping you to deal with your anxiety that your hands must be clean?' Dr Jim asks.

Andrew says it isn't. They agree that trying to reduce his strong tendency to continuously wash his hands in such circumstances would be much healthier.

'But what do I do when this compulsion to do it comes into my mind?' Andrew asks.

'We will deal with this later, but first let's challenge your "B",' Dr Jim suggests.

Challenging Andrew's 'B'

Dr Jim introduces Andrew to the big MACS, and then starts challenging

Andrew's 'B'.

'We need to examine and challenge your "B", that is, the set of irrational beliefs which took the form of your absolute demand that your hands must be clean,' Dr Jim says.

They agree that the demand is completely irrational. The rational belief would be that Andrew prefers his hands to be clean, but whether they are is out of his control. Dr Jim asks Andrew if there is any area of his life where he looks for 100-percent certainty or control and usually succeeds in getting it. Andrew says he constantly arranges the dishes at home in an exact manner, and feels less anxious when he has done so.

This leads to a long discussion on the nature of control, and particularly on whether there is any such thing as 100-percent certainty or order. Andrew accepts that in real life there is not. Dr Jim gives him the coin-toss and disorder exercises, which we discussed in earlier chapters. He puts particular emphasis on the latter, with instructions for Andrew's wife to start changing little things in areas of the house where Andrew most seeks order. He has to learn to live with and absorb the physical feelings of anxiety this engenders.

Dr Jim also disputes with Andrew his catastrophic visualisations that his children could get very ill from germs on his hands. Where was his proof for this? Dr Jim asks.

'I know deep down that this is not actually going to happen,' Andrew says. 'But I just can't stop the thought itself.'

Dr Jim shares the spilt milk analogy, and introduces Andrew to the Raggy Doll Club – which Andrew finds especially helpful.

Several months later, Andrew's condition has improved greatly, with the help of medication from the psychiatrist, and following many visits to Dr Jim and a lot of hard work on his thinking and behaviour, including many coin-toss and disorder exercise. He has drastically reduced his ritualistic hand-washing and his need for complete order at home.

However, Andrew admits to Dr Jim, six months later, on a review visit, that although he now understands that the content of the thoughts is not true, and is no longer seeking as much control, he is still getting very distressed at having the thoughts at all. Dr Jim explains to him that this is very common in OCD.

'There are two parts to these thoughts,' Dr Jim says. 'The first relates to the content of the thoughts, which is what we have dealt with to date. The second relates to just having the thoughts, and many with OCD struggle to understand the difference.'

To illustrate this, Dr Jim decides to do an ABC on a different thought that has started to creep into Andrew's mind: that he might have AIDS.

'I know that this is completely impossible, but the more I try to push away this thought, the stronger it gets,' says Andrew.

It is quite clear that there is nothing in his lifestyle to suggest any possible risk of Andrew having acquired the condition, so it is back to his OCD again. Andrew is spending hours online when the thought comes into his mind, trying to relieve his high level of anxiety and all of the physical symptoms that come with it. He is becoming increasingly frustrated at having this thought.

'It just won't go away,' Andrew tells Dr Jim.

Dr Jim does an ABC on the content of the thought, using the same principles they had used for previous obsessive thoughts, such as that his hands were not clean, and reinforced the messages already detailed above. Then he moved on to do a second ABC, based on the thought itself.

'So the trigger is the thought,' says Dr Jim. 'What are your emotions about this?'

'Anxiety and frustration,' says Andrew.

His behaviour was that he was ruminating a lot about this thought, as well as constantly checking online for information about AIDS.

Dr Jim asks him to write this information on their ABC.

A   Activating Event:

    o   Trigger: the thought that he might have AIDS

    o   Inference/danger:

B   Belief/Demands:

C   Consequences:

    o   Emotional reactions: anxiety and frustration

o Physical reactions: stomach in knots, muscle tension, palpations, difficulties sleeping, difficulties breathing and fatigue

o Behaviour: ruminating, constantly checking online for reassurance that he does not have AIDS

'What is it about having the thought that makes you feel anxious?' asks Dr
Jim.

Andrew explains that he understands that the content is untrue, but his
danger is that maybe the thought will never go away.

'And what is it about the thought that is causing you to feel frustrated?'
asks Dr Jim.

'It is very uncomfortable, and I can't make the thought go away,' says
Andrew. 'I keep asking myself why I should have to put up with the discomfort of this condition. None of my friends or family complain of these difficulties.'

Dr Jim explains that many people with OCD are anxious that the thoughts
will just keep on coming. In particular, they are frustrated at being unable to
control or get rid of the thought itself, and the discomfort it creates.

Following further discussion, they end up with this final ABC:

A   Activating Event:

o Trigger: the thought that he might have AIDS

o Inference/danger: 'This thought will never go away. Having
these thoughts is uncomfortable. Why can't I get rid of this
thought myself? Why do I have to put up with the discomfort
of this condition? Why am I not like my friends and colleagues, who do not suffer from this condition?'

B   Belief/Demands: 'This thought must go away. I should not have to
put up with this discomfort.'

C   Consequences:

o Emotional reactions: anxiety and frustration

o   Physical reactions: stomach in knots, muscle tension, palpa- tions, difficulties sleeping, difficulties breathing and fatigue

o   Behaviour: ruminating, constantly checking online for reas- surance that he does not have AIDS

'Is it rational to demand that a particular thought must go away?' Dr Jim asks Andrew.

Andrew agrees that it is irrational.

'Are all thoughts true?' Dr Jim asks.

Andrew agrees that, in reality, most are not.

This leads to a discussion of the way all kinds of thoughts are flying through our mind at any given time.

'Many of these are being generated by our emotional mind, and often do not make any real, logical sense,' Dr Jim explains. 'Most of the time, we are only vaguely aware of our thoughts as they flit around like butterflies through our mind. Trying to stop a particular thought is like trying to stop the tide coming in. It is pointless. In OCD, it is particularly challenging, as our brain is struggling to move our thoughts on, due to functional blocks in our neuro- circuitry. It's better to accept that a thought is just a thought.'

This leads to a discussion of mindfulness, which Dr Jim recommends Andrew take up. 'If you can learn to just accept the thought, and stop trying to block it out, the thought loses its power over you. Mindfulness will help you learn this skill,' he says.

Finally, they looked at the demand behind Andrew's frustration: that he should not have to suffer the discomfort of the condition. 'Is there any law in the universe that states that you, or indeed any of us, as human beings, should not suffer discomfort?' asks Dr Jim.

This leads to a fruitful discussion, and Andrew begins to accept that although the thoughts produced by his OCD are uncomfortable, and he would prefer not to have them, he, like every other person, has to accept that discomfort is part of the human condition. He has to accept that every person will suffer some form of discomfort in life, and he is no different.

If he wants the long-term gain of learning how to cope with such thoughts, Dr Jim says, then he will have to accept the short-term pain of learning and practising the skill of mindfulness. This is how he will learn to eliminate his frustration.

One year later, Andrew is in a much better space. He is still getting bouts of obsessive thoughts, and he still feels the compulsive urges, but their power has greatly diminished. He accepts that he might continue to need drug therapy in the long term. He will have to continue applying what he has learnt, and practising mindfulness; he practises this daily, and has noticed that his thoughts are no longer bothering him as much. He has learnt to accept the physical symptoms associated with the times when he becomes anxious. He keeps a close eye on his behaviour. He accepts that discomfort is a part of life. He still has OCD, but feels that he is able to live a fruitful and rewarding life despite it.

Now that we have explored how to reshape the anxious mind, let's see how we can reshape our anxious brain.

PART THREE
Reshaping the Anxious Brain

VI.
THE ANXIOUS BRAIN AND ITS POTENTIAL FOR CHANGE

14.
Reshaping the Brain Structures and Pathways Involved in Anxiety

The approaches to treating anxiety that I have explained and recommended throughout this book are based on a foundation of neuroscience. I have touched on this with my explanations of the roles of the amygdala, the PFC, the stress system and adrenaline. But now I'd like to dive further into the world of neuroscience to give you a deeper understanding of why I have been advocating the CBT approaches I introduced in earlier chapters, and how they can reshape our anxious brains.

We will begin by examining in detail the two main departments of the brain relevant to our discussion: the PFC, which is our logical brain, and the limbic system, our emotional brain, which includes the amygdala, which has played such an important role in our previous discussions.

Let's now examine what is going on in the anxious brain and learn how we can reshape it. We will begin by examining in detail the two main departments of the brain that are relevant to our discussion: the prefrontal cortex (PFC), which is our logical brain, and the limbic system, which is our emotional brain.

Let's think of these as two departments of a company, each with a different function. The prefrontal cortex is like the head office. Within the head office, each section is in charge of particular areas. The limbic system is a second department of the company, which is in charge of looking after our emotional world. It too has different sections with particular functions, and we will examine these further on. There is a constant flow of information and data between these two major departments of the company, and there is also a lot of tension, with emotion often winning out. Not every worker in a company is in agreement with the head office, and it is the same in the brain.

With this in mind, let's explore further.

The Prefrontal Cortex (Logical Brain)

The PFC makes up 29 percent of the modern brain, and has connections to every other part of the brain – particularly the emotional brain. It has four divisions: the logic box, the emotional control box, the social behaviour box and the attention box (see Figure 9).

The Logic Box (Dorsal Pre-Frontal Cortex or DPFC)

This division is the 'boss'. This is the part of your brain that is buzzing when you are logically analysing situations, planning strategies, focusing your conscious attention on thoughts, emotions or behaviours, deciding on options, meditating, problem-solving or reasoning. The right logic box is associated with creativity and visual imagery; the left is associated with the hard-nosed decision making of everyday lives, and is more activated by concepts involving language and planning. Power failure in the left logic box is one of the most important findings in depression. This is the part of the brain used when writing down and analysing information in CBT, as its function is to rationalise situations.

The Emotional Control Box (Ventromedial Pre-Frontal Cortex or VMPFC)

This division monitors emotions, deciding if, when and how they should be 'modified', and the appropriate emotional behavioural responses. The

VMPFC is in constant communication with the amygdala, keeping it in check through connections with the intercalated neurons. When we are well, this dialogue ensures that negative emotions don't take over our lives. This section of the PFC is now seen as one of the most important players in anxiety.

The Social Behaviour Box (Orbitofrontal Cortex or OFC)

This division is considered the most likely neural source of empathy. It helps us to defer immediate gratification, suppressing emotions for long-term gain. It makes sense of our social world, making lightning-fast assessments of people we encounter, deciding whether we face or withdraw from particular social situations. It may control our unique capacity to sense where people we meet are, from an emotional point of view.

This box is also in constant communication with the amygdala, dampening down emotional surges and impulses. There has been considerable interest in assessing its role in behaviour. When it is malfunctioning, we lack motivation and behavioural control. Some regard it as the main link between our thinking (DPFC and VMPFC), our emotions (amygdala) and our automatic behavioural/physical responses (brain stem). It is therefore no surprise that it is another important PFC player in anxiety.

The Attention Box (Anterior Cingulate Cortex or ACC)

This division links our logical and emotional worlds. Some regard it as the meeting point between the information flowing up from our unconscious, emotional limbic system and the conscious, logical, more rational areas of the pre-frontal cortex. Its known functions – some of which are central to 'intelligent behaviour' – include information processing, attention, focused problem-solving, error-recognition, and the expression and modulation of emotion (emotional self-control).

When well, the ACC makes sense of our inner emotional world, ensuring a healthy analysis of how an emotion is affecting us, and ensuring that our rational mind can assess whether such emotions are appropriate. The more activated our ACC is, the calmer and more sensible our emotional responses will be. It may also be involved in the maturation of self-control as we progress from infancy, through childhood to adulthood. Its functioning is increased in individuals with greater social insight and maturity, and higher levels of social awareness.

★

Before leaving our discussion on the various sections of the PFC, it is worth adding a few notes of caution:

- The areas mentioned above and the functions assigned to them are considered by some as being too broad and too vague. Purists prefer to use localised numbered areas called Brodmann's areas. Others, however, find that the descriptions above are a useful way of grouping particular structures and functions. The above approach has the advantage of being simple, and it gives us a flavour of what these sections of the PFC do.

- There is a wide variety of opinions as to what areas of the PFC are actually included under these headings.

- It is useful to keep in mind the advice of some neuroscientists, such as the great Joseph LeDoux, that we have to be cautious about claiming that any one function can be simply assigned to one particular section of the brain. The reality is that the brain is a computer-like organ that gathers and shares information. So it is likely that any one function involves several sections passing information back and forth.

- There is a clear, hierarchical chain of command here (see Figure 10). The DPFC is clearly the boss – the cold, rational, problem-solving officer-in-charge. It, like any top executive, doesn't do emotions. It does, however, pass on and receive back information from the VMPFC and OFC, who are its managerial underlings, looking after our emotional and social worlds.

- Despite the DPFC being in charge, it is often sidelined or over-ruled by our emotional brain. The amygdala is the chief culprit, as we will see later.

Limbic System (Emotional Brain)

This department, in the heart of the ancient brain, has extensive connections with the PFC. There are three important divisions relevant to our discussion: the amygdala (stress box), the hippocampus (memory box) and the insular cortex, also known as the insula (the island) (see Figure 11).

Amygdala (Stress Box)

The amygdala controls responses to perceived threats from within the body and from the external environment. It is the main processor of the primary emotions of fear, hate, love and anger. It helps the brain store emotions related to unpleasant memories, which may or may not be consciously accessible. It plays a role in our assessment of facial expressions. In depression, for example, by misreading other people's facial expressions, it can unleash a stream of negative emotional thoughts and behaviors. It is larger in men. It is also in charge of our stress system. We will examine its role in anxiety further on in this chapter.

Hippocampus (Memory Box)

This is where memory is manufactured, filtered and retrieved. It also puts these recalled memories into context. This box becomes extremely active when we are dreaming, which is when memories are consolidated. Even when the stress box generates negative emotions such as fear, it requires this box to store the contextual memory of the event in question. Every time we retrieve a memory from this box and use it, that memory is subtly altered. A good analogy is retrieving a computer file, opening, reading it, adding some data to the file, saving the file and returning it to its original storage area. The next time the file – or memory – is recalled, the alterations are present. The same process occurs when we access emotional memories with the help of the amygdala. The hippocampus is larger in women.

Nucleus Acumens (Pleasure Box)

This is activated when we are participating in rewarding activities – eating, drinking, sex, etc. It is part of the pleasure/reward circuit. It has important connections with the amygdala, and is the link between panic attacks and addiction.

The Island (Insula)

This part of the limbic system has leapt to prominence after years of being regarded of little consequence. It was known to be important for our perception of pain, and the unusual emotion of disgust. But research has gradually uncovered a different picture. This tiny structure deep in our limbic mood department is now felt to be important in social emotions like pride, guilt, humiliation, lust, disgust and, particularly, empathy. It is also involved in anticipating and feeling pain, and the ability to share another person's pain.

The insula receives information from the skin and the internal organs. It registers heat, cold, pain, hunger and thirst, along with information from the heart, lungs and gut. There is a crucial part at the front of this organ that reinterprets these sensations, turning them into social emotions. A bad odour is translated into disgust, a caress into a feeling of loving warmth, and so on; the right insula is more active in this transformation.

The insula is where we sense love, hate, resentment, embarrassment, trust, distrust, pride, humiliation, guilt and deception. It also liaises closely with the amygdala and is a major player in our world of emotions. It has particularly strong connections with the OFC (social behaviour box), forming the basis of emotions. It seems to be an important player in some phobias. It is also felt to be of great importance in eating disorders and in the feelings of emotional pain.

The Amygdala and PFC: the Key Players in Anxiety

Before leaving this discussion, it is important to elaborate further on the role of our amygdala and prefrontal cortex (PFC) in anxiety, as understanding this is essential if we want to understand the condition. There are some new findings which are relevant to our discussion.

In researching and putting together this section, I have looked at extensive research carried out by leading neuroscientists in the field, including Joseph LeDoux, Elizabeth Phelps, Helen Mayberg, Mauricio Delgado, Richard Davidson, Wayne Drevets, Dennis Charney and Catherine Harmer, a friend and colleague from Oxford. Some of these have devoted years of research to studying anxiety pathways in the brain, and, in some cases, how therapies can influence them. I also found Catherine Pittman and Elizabeth Karle's book *Rewire Your Anxious Brain* particularly insightful. Those who would like to examine in more detail the research underlying the sections to follow can review the relevant articles and books detailed in the bibliography.

There are also some important points to be made about our current knowledge of the neuroscience of anxiety:

- Despite the extraordinary body of work on the subject that exists, we remain at the early stages of understanding the complexities of the neural basis of anxiety.

- Much of this work has been achieved by a synthesis of animal studies and human functional neuroimaging.

- It is not just about the activity of one particular part of the brain, but also about the functional neurocircuitry between sections involved in creating and maintaining anxiety.

- This is by no means an exact science. The complexity of the brain is staggering. We are only capable of making some reasonable conclusions based on the evidence garnered to date.

- As we will see later, much of the evidence shows functional rather than structural changes in the brain. This is particularly exciting, as we will see in the next chapter how the brain is neuroplastic: such functional changes can be reshaped.

With these provisos, and based on the evidence to date, let's review what we know. It will reveal a fascinating picture of what happens in our brain when we are anxious.

Why Is Our Amygdala So Important in Anxiety?

The amygdala plays such an important role in our emotional life and in all forms of anxiety, that it is important to explain it further. We have two amygdalae, one on each side of the brain. The amygdala is very old, from an evolutionary point of view, and its primary role since inception has been to seek out danger and protect us.

But it has a much wider role than this. Many neuroscientists think it assigns emotions – both positive and negative – to every aspect of our lives. Critically, it is also the source of our emotional memory. So not only does it assign the emotion to what happens to us, it also retains a memory of it.

The first thousand days of a child's life are of great importance to their future mental health and well-being. We now know that from the second the baby is born the amygdala is in overdrive, absorbing all kinds of emotions from the world it finds itself in and the people it encounters. However, the part of the brain called the hippocampus or memory box, which gives context to our memories, is not really mature until we are three. So it is the emotional memory built up in our amygdala during this first thousand days that most influences us in the future. This emotional memory is often built up independently of our more logical brain, the PFC. So the amygdala can influence our lives without the latter's input. This is particularly the case where the emotion is strongly negative and associated with some significant danger, such as fear or panic.

Even though the amygdala has many other functions involving our emotional world, it is its role in protecting us from perceived danger that overrides all others. It is the commander-in-chief of our stress system, our body's 'security service'. Its job is to instantly pick up danger signals and fire our innate stress system's fight-freeze-or-flight response, long before our more logical PFC has time to assess the danger. Just like when there's a major terrorist attack on a city and the security services commandeer and lock down all of the critical services, so too during risky periods will the amygdala temporarily take over complete control. It will, for example, temporarily block out any information from the PFC or logical brain, if it decides there is a potentially life-threatening danger. Once the immediate danger has passed, then the PFC will be allowed back in to make a more in-depth analysis of the situation. All this happens at lightning speed in the brain.

Already, readers who suffer from panic attacks will begin to see where this is going. Trying to use logic in the middle of a panic attack is doomed to failure, as the amygdala has activated the stress system's flight response and locked down the PFC, or more logical brain.

All sensory information – sight, sound, smell, touch – comes into an area of the brain called the thalamus, which is, like the GPO in Dublin, a central sorting agency whose job is to distribute these physical sensations to appropriate sections in the brain. It achieves this task by sending the information through a 'short loop', to a section of the amygdala called the lateral amygdala, and through a 'long loop' to various parts of the PFC.

Critically, information gets to the lateral amygdala via the 'short loop' much faster than to the PFC through the 'long loop'. This is no coincidence, as the brain is set up first and foremost to keep us alive, safe and well. It is the job of the lateral amygdala to rapidly analyse all sensory information coming in, to see if there is any imminent danger. If it picks up such a threat, it rapidly passes the information on to another section of the amygdala, called the central amygdala. This acts like the command-control for emergency services in our local area, whose job it is to send, or not, fire engines or ambulances thundering down our streets with klaxons blaring.

The central amygdala has a direct connection with our acute-stress system, and particularly our SNS. If activated in the presence of a significant danger, the SNS fires and leads to the discharge of a huge burst of our fear hormone, adrenaline, into the bloodstream from the adrenal gland.

Adrenaline in such situations acts as the 'fire engine' of our stress system. If this burst of adrenaline occurs, we may experience the typical physical symptoms: a pounding heart, difficulty breathing, a stomach in knots, shaking, sweating, a dry mouth, our throat closing in, weakness and dizziness. It will therefore come as no surprise, when dealing with panic attacks later, that the amygdala turns out to be the main player. It is the central nucleus of the amygdala firing that gives rise to the very same physical symptoms which we experience in a panic attack.

The short loop getting the information to the lateral amygdala first makes evolutionary sense, as the lightning-fast responses it may trigger can save our lives. If we waited for the sensory information to travel the more leisurely long loop to our PFC, which has the job of analysing the data in more depth, we might be dead before we acted.

The degree to which the lateral amygdala will respond to the sensory information is, of course, proportional to the level of danger it assigns to it. If it believes the danger is life-threatening, it will instantly inform the central amygdala that all the stops are to be pulled out. This may result in us experiencing the uncomfortable physical symptoms that a typical adrenaline rush produces.

Interestingly, all sensory information coming in through the lateral amygdala is not only reaching the central amygdala, but also being distributed to other parts of the amygdala, particularly the basal amygdaloid nuclei. Here it will be compared to memories, and to what is going on within the body at that moment. The connections from the lateral amygdala to the basal amygdaloid nuclei are also important for forming long-lasting memories of fear. In addition, this area has significant links with the PFC and back to the central amygdala; it is thus well placed to modulate the activity of both the amygdala and the PFC. So the amygdala is a far more complex organ than it seems at first glance, and one which plays a major role in our lives, particularly in anxiety.

There are critical links between the PFC and the central amygdala. The PFC, if sensing a real or, in some cases, visualised danger, can stimulate the central amygdala to also activate our SNS, giving rise to all of the same physical symptoms. The strength of this activation is dependent on how significant a danger the PFC feels it is reacting to. So we can get the full gamut of physical symptoms, from feeling mildly uneasy to being significantly distressed. This is the mechanism that gives rise to many of the symptoms prevalent in more chronic forms of anxiety.

In general and social anxiety, we often experience levels of physical discomfort similar to the symptoms of panic attacks. They are much milder, but they last much longer and are extremely uncomfortable. We call these 'panicky feelings', and they are endemic to GAD. The central nucleus is once again the control centre in these situations for activating our SNS, in varying degrees, to produce these symptoms. We will be examining the effects of this later.

The amygdala is not a very 'smart' organ. Unlike the PFC, it is not always that effective in deciding whether particular situations are genuinely dangerous or not. The motto 'act first and think later' could easily be applied. It leaves the task of working out the real relevance of situations to higher structures in the brain, like the PFC. Whilst this makes a lot of sense in the presence of serious, immediate or life-threatening danger, it is of less assistance when the danger is either vaguer or, on occasions, not truly present at all.

The amygdala also has a long memory for situations that it perceived as potentially dangerous. It is not concerned about context, only about the emotions of fear the event created. For example, if you were stung by a wasp when very young, and have no contextual memory of the event, you may still find your amygdala making you very uneasy every time you hear the buzzing of an insect. It makes us uneasy by just giving us some mild physical symptoms. We may not really understand that it is the buzzing of the insect that is creating these sensations, but we will feel them anyway.

A more serious example of this might be where a woman is sexually abused as a child but does not remember the specific details of what happened. This can happen because the high glucocorisol level caused by the stress at the time prevents our hippocampus or memory box from creating contextual memories of the event. But one day, when in a shopping mall, the same person suddenly experiences an unexplained sense of dread and accompanying physical symptoms of fear. This occurs, although she does not realise it, because she just passed a man whose face her amygdala incorrectly misread as similar to the man who abused her.

Another common example is social anxiety, where, as a result of previous negative experiences in social situations, our amygdala also ends up busy negatively misreading the facial expressions of people we meet, with the usual ensuing physical symptoms.

So the amygdala is remembering the danger and the emotions of fear it sensed at the time, but not the context, as that is not its function. If it encounters anything from our environment that is similar to that event, it will trigger the usual amygdala response to danger. The amygdala's association of a trigger with danger is performed particularly by the lateral nucleus. This idea of matching a trigger with a danger interestingly correlates with CBT.

A trigger can be any sensation or object or occurrence. On its own, it may not be of any significance: blood, a particular noise or sound or smell, a particular place. It is only when the trigger is linked with some negative event – possibly shortly after that event – that the lateral amygdala associates the two and fires, producing the usual uncomfortable physical consequences. Most phobias, as we will see later, link triggers – such as blood or confined spaces – with danger; and the amygdala is once again the source of all of the physical symptoms of fear that we experience as a result.

Another example of this is in PTSD, where a soldier who has been injured by a bomb blast unconsciously associates a particular sound with it. The amygdala associates this sound with danger from then on. So if a car misfires or a firework goes off, the sound triggers the amygdala to completely overact. The sufferer may get incredibly anxious or even experience a panic attack, even though the trigger was actually quite innocent.

Another example of this is when we get scratched by a cat when we are very young, and have no contextual memory of the event. Later in life, we find our amygdala firing every time we see a cat, and we can't understand why we are experiencing the emotion of fear, and the amygdala-driven physical symptoms.

The Amygdala: the 'Gunslinger' of the Stress System

The amygdala has a tendency to 'go off' on its own. This can give rise to prob-lems for many who suffer from anxiety, particularly in GAD and PTSD.

People with these conditions are often extremely confused when, in the absence of a definite trigger, they suddenly develop the acute physical symp-toms of anxiety described above. Some think they are going mad. It can be very reassuring for them to realise that it is just the result of an oversensitive amygdala. The amygdala is not particularly smart, and as a result of constant stimulation through anxiety, it can become trigger-happy. We have to remember that the amygdala is the gunslinger of our stress system. It tends to draw and fire, often with little provocation, bypassing the more sensible PFC.

This latter is of great importance in how we manage the amygdala-based physical symptoms of anxiety. It will be quite different to how we will manage the PFC-based cognitive symptoms of worry and catastrophising.

The amygdala has an extremely close relationship with the hippocampus, which is in charge of organising our contextual memories. There is a contin-uous flow of information between the two, day and night. During the day, when we encounter situations and people, the hippocampus is drawing on its contextual memory, whilst the amygdala is focusing on its emotional mem-ory. We end up with a synthesis of both.

When we are sleeping, the two organs work together to strengthen our emotional and contextual memories. This is what happens to us when we dream or have nightmares.

The amygdala is in regular contact with some sections of our PFC, which plays an important role in increasing or modifying much of its activity. We use this capacity for modification of the amygdala when applying therapies such as CBT to general anxiety, social anxiety and PTSD.

The good news is that the amygdala, although not as smart as other parts of the brain, is neuroplastic, so it is capable of change. Just as we can end up reinforcing negative emotional memories, we can also – with the right approach – teach the amygdala to dampen down the effects of such negative memories. This capacity for neuroplasticity is critical.

There is an increasing body of opinion that maintains that the role of the amygdala in anxiety needs to be given much greater weight. For too long, we have been trying to use cognitive approaches to put manners on this unruly organ, particularly in more acute anxiety conditions, like panic attacks and phobias. It responds much better to different approaches, such as exposure-flooding techniques and mindfulness.

The Amygdala: A Word of Caution

It's worth noting that Joseph LeDoux, one of the world's leading experts on the subject, has begun to question whether we are correct in assuming that the amygdala is where we create the feeling of fear. He questions whether it is more likely that the amygdala just fires when it senses danger, whether real or not. He describes this process as the non-conscious aspect of fear. By this, he is referring to the detection of threats and the control of body responses that help to cope with the threat.

The higher centres in the brain, particularly the PFC, then pick up on the visceral sensations that ensue when, as a result of the amygdala firing, the stress system floods the body with chemicals and hormones. He postulates that these higher centres seek out the environmental cause for the amygdala firing, and check this information with previous emotional and contextual memories. If this conversation ends up with recognition of a known danger from the environment, the higher centres convert this information into a conscious feeling of fear. At present, this is just a postulation. If you would like to learn more, see LeDoux's latest book, *Anxious: Using the Brain to Understand and Treat Fear and Anxiety.*

In any case, the amygdala remains the gun-slinging organ of our stress system, which leads to the uncomfortably physical symptoms of anxiety.

Why Is Our Prefrontal Cortex So Important in Anxiety?

In my discussion on the amygdala, I mentioned that sensory information – sights, sounds, smells – passes through the central sorting agency, the thalamus, and splits into two loops, the shorter of which goes to the amygdala. The longer loop ends up in our PFC, where the information is analysed; the resulting decisions are fed back to the amygdala.

If, for example, the PFC feels the amygdala is overreacting, which is quite common, it can send down information through this process to tell it to calm down, so everything will go back to normal. It does this by connecting to an important group of cells in the amygdala called intercalated neurons. They lie between the lateral and central amygdala sections and are therefore in the ideal place to modulate the latter, in particular. If this happens, the SNS-driven symptoms will subside.

In this way, our brain has created a fairly sensible twin-track approach. When it receives sensory information that suggests we may be in serious danger, the amygdala instantly takes total control, bypasses the PFC and fires our stress system into immediate action. If the danger does not materialise, then the PFC, which receives the same information after a slight delay, can determine what is really going on. If the PFC feels the amygdala has been too quick off the mark, then it – through its connections back to the intercalated neurons – can calm down the amygdala's activity. But if the PFC decides there is a potential danger, it can alert the central amygdala to fire. If this happens, the latter will activate our SNS. The strength of this activation will depend on just how much significance the PFC assigns to the danger.

Separate to the above normal activities, the PFC can also end up triggering anxiety on its own volition. Although the PFC is much smarter than our gun-slinging amygdala, it is important to note that not all thoughts emerging from our PFC are necessarily correct or rational.

In general there are two ways in which our PFC can generate anxiety:

1. When it misinterprets the sensory information coming in from the body as dangerous, even though clearly it is not. In such situations it will activate the amygdala to fire, creating the usual physical symptoms associated with this, even though there is no actual danger present at all.

2. When the PFC has not received any sensory information that would imply danger, but it goes ahead and creates worrying thoughts – catastrophising about something that might happen in

the future. It can encourage distressing ruminations, which also
end up triggering the amygdala to fire.

Both of these paths into anxiety can affect people with the condition, to varying degrees. It is important to stress that when either of the above two scenarios occurs, the central amygdala eventually becomes secondarily involved.
This, in turn, triggers uncomfortable physical sensations: panicky feelings.
This is the mechanism for some of the more chronic anxiety conditions, such
as GAD and social anxiety.

There are differences between the right and left PFCs in the production of
cognitive symptoms such as worry and rumination. We know that the left
PFC is the more rational, problem-solving, analytical side of the brain, which
very much deals with the small print and makes many of the key decisions in
our lives. It is also more important in the area of language. The right PFC is
the more creative, artistic side of the brain and helps us see the bigger picture.
It is also important in facial recognition and in emotional expression. Each
has the capacity to cause anxiety by producing different but equally bother-
some scenarios.

The Left PFC in Anxiety: 'The Worrier'

The left PFC is associated with apprehension or worry about what might happen. This usually leads us to envisage negative outcomes. It is also the source
of rumination. This is where we constantly and repetitively reflect, in a negative manner, on particular difficulties in our lives in great detail. It is the
'washing machine' in our heads. Both worry and rumination, instead of helping us to solve problems, prevent us from finding solutions. But, more importantly, due to the links between the PFC and the amygdala, they can end up
giving rise to yet more unwanted physical symptoms of anxiety. Ruminations
are also extremely common in depression.

The left PFC is also important in our capacity to predict the possible outcomes of actions. This unique gift allows humans to plan ahead. It also gives
us the dubious potential to see only the potentially negative outcomes of our
actions. So we end up worrying and ruminating about such possible situa-

tions, which leads to mental distress, and, through secondary activation of our amygdala, unpleasant physical symptoms.

Many with general anxiety or depression will identify with some of these worrying thoughts and ruminations, and may find it interesting to know where they are coming from.

The Right PFC in Anxiety: 'The Catastrophiser'

The right PFC is more associated with anxiety based on imagination, visualisation and catastrophising. If, for example, we are visualising something frightening that might happen to us in the future, then this is emanating more from our right PFC. Those who get intensely anxious when visualising and imagining all kinds of catastrophic situations are operating from this side of their PFC.

The right PFC is where we assimilate data from nonverbal forms of communication such as facial expressions, tone of voice, body posture and so on. It is not surprising, therefore, that it can create intense anxiety symptoms when it misreads situations. The classic example of this is social anxiety, where these nonverbal forms of communication are often completely misread.

The right PFC is very closely linked to the central amygdala, so, when aroused, it is inclined to produce more severe amygdala-driven physical symptoms than the left PFC. Many phobias will involve the right PFC: for example, the person who visualises how awful it will be when the plane door closes and they can't get off. They will create in their emotional minds frightening images of getting incredibly anxious, losing control and running amok through the plane. This will often lead to intense amygdala-driven physical symptoms of anxiety.

In panic disorder, the right PFC is also heavily involved in our fear of getting panic attacks. The more we visualise having a panic attack, the more we trigger the amygdala to produce the usual low- to medium-grade physical symptoms of anxiety. These can then trigger the next panic attack.

The right PFC is involved in situations where we become hypervigilant and constantly scan the environment for trouble. This is commonly seen in a form of anxiety called post-traumatic stress disorder. It is more likely to occur following severe traumas – major road traffic accidents, assaults, rapes, war-related incidents – and when there has been a definite threat to the life of the sufferer or their family. Due to the right PFCs close links with the amygdala, this can produce intense physical symptoms when something, however small or seemingly innocent, in the environment, triggers concern.

Although most people with anxiety will be biased towards either their right PFC or their left PFC, some will involve both. This makes sense as the two PFC are strongly bonded together in the brain to create a synthesis of their differing views of the world.

When the PFC is creating persistent anxious thoughts and visualisations, it is also reinforcing pathways to our amygdala. This often means that it takes fewer and fewer PFC-driven anxious thoughts to trigger the amygdala-driven circuits. The good news is that the PFC and these connecting pathways to the amygdala are neuroplastic, so they can be modified. We will review in next chapter which specific pathways are involved and how they can be changed.

Summary of the Role of the Amygdala and PFC in Anxiety

- The amygdala is the part of the brain which causes the extremely uncomfortable physical symptoms of anxiety. The most obvious examples are panic attacks and phobias. That is not to say that the PFC is not indirectly involved in some phobias or in panic attacks. It is rather that the amygdala, in these conditions, is the bigger player, the one that has to be targeted. The reason it is able to produce all of these uncomfortable physical symptoms is because it is the boss of our stress system and also its gunslinger.

- More chronic forms of anxiety are a mixture of the PFC giving rise to the symptoms of worry, ruminations, visualisations and catastrophising. It is the secondary activation of the amygdala by the

PFC as a result of this that gives rise to the chronic low- to medium-grade physical symptoms or panicky feelings so common in conditions such as GAD, social anxiety and some phobias.

- Most people who have one of these conditions will be able to relate to the constant low-grade muscle tension, the sighing, the churning stomach, the racing heart, the tension headaches and so on. Once again, it is our old friend the amygdala that is causing these difficulties.

- In chronic anxiety, persistent activation of the amygdala may also lead to the production of higher levels of our chronic-stress hormone, glucocortisol. We have already discussed the physical symptoms – including fatigue, irritable bowels, and sleep difficulties – of this activation. The best example here is general anxiety disorder.

Bidirectional Pathways from the PFC to the Amygdala in Anxiety

As well as understanding the role of the amygdala and different sections of the PFC, it is really important for our understanding of anxiety to briefly examine the pathways between the two structures. Increasingly, we are examining bidirectional anatomical and functional connections between certain parts of the VMPFC, the OFC and various sections of the amygdala – which are critical to anxiety.

There is increasing evidence that anxiety conditions – GAD, social anxiety, some phobias and PTSD, for example – demonstrate a 'functional disruption' in these critical pathways. In general, there is a reduction in the VMPFC-to-amygdala circuits with a concomitant increase in amygdala activity in all of these conditions. It is also increasingly accepted that the stronger the connections between these two brain organs, the better the outcomes in such anxiety disorders.

Some suggest that a functional reduction in activity in this pathway from the VMPFC to the amygdala is inherently present in some who suffer from GAD and social anxiety. This is most likely created by a mixture of genetic predispositions and key environmental influences when we are children, adolescents or young adults. The usual accompanying factor in these anxiety conditions is an overactive amygdala. In general, successful management of these conditions will involve calming down the amygdala by using one set of techniques, and using another set to strengthen the amygdala-VMPFC functional connections by reshaping the PFC.

For those who would like to review these concepts further please see the relevant articles in the bibliography.

Neuroplasticity

When you have finished reading this book, your brain will not be exactly the same as it was before you started. This is because your brain has an extraordinary capacity to change. We call this adaptability neuroplasticity. This is a subject I dealt with in great depth in earlier books, but we will discuss it here in relation to anxiety.

Until recently, it was assumed that when adult circuits in the brain were formed, they were set for life. If our pathways predisposed us to anxiety, depression, anger or hurt, we were doomed to follow where they led, for better or worse. We now know that this is not the case, as the same mechanisms that helped form these paths can – through various therapies – reshape them. The key to reforming and reshaping tracks lies in the neuroplasticity of the brain. This describes the ability of individual neurons to increase or decrease the number of connections they have with other neurons, and through this mechanism to strengthen or weaken various brain pathways.

It's worth examining this concept in more detail. The average neuron is like a little factory, with a central body shape, loads of little spike-like projections at one end and a single tail at the other (see Figure 12). The body contains both our genes and the molecular machinery required to run the factory. The spikes, called dendrites, receive all the information being sent down the line from other neurons. The tail is called the axon, and it passes the relevant information on to the next cell. The real product of the factory is information.

Each dendrite is receiving information from the axon of another neuron, and each neuron has thousands of dendrites, so information pours in (see Figure 13). The plasticity of the brain is based on the number of dendrite connections each neuron chooses to have. Increase the number of connections and pathways get stronger, decrease it and they get weaker.

The boss of the factory is the gene pool in the central nucleus of the cell. This sends out messengers to increase or decrease dendrite connections. It is greatly influenced by outside environmental factors, so it is adaptable to change. Within the brain, thought pathways strongly influence emotional – and, in turn, behavioural – paths. This is all simply organised by increasing or decreasing the number of neuron-dendrite connections within them. Outside the brain, other factors can have the same effect. Take, for example, the effect of interactions between a mother and her child. Love and affection powerfully affect the empathy pathway of the child in a positive way; rejection and lack of affection, in a negative manner. All of this, processed through dendrite-connection increases or decreases in this pathway, shapes how the child will emotionally grow and develop.

The brain has three fairly brutal rules in order to keep order on the one billion neurons, the different sections of the brain and the multiple tracks and pathways between them:

1. Neurons that fire together wire together.

2. Neurons that fire apart wire apart.

3. Use it or lose it.

If a particular set of pathways or tracks through the brain are being used, then the neurons create more dendrite connections and strengthen. If particular pathways are not being used, the brain begins to sideline them. So if my amygdala has stored up strong emotional memories of fear and panic, as in panic attacks or phobias, then the more they happen, the stronger these memories will become and the easier it will be to trigger them the next time.

The amygdala has a long memory and is quite stubborn about changing such memories.

This is why some form of experiential exposure is essential to tackle the amygdala's negative emotional fear memories. This exposure is of great importance, as it is during this process that retraining the amygdala's response   to situations is possible. Without it, nothing will change this organ's instinctive tendency to fire when exposed to situations that it perceives as dangerous.

When the amygdala is exposed to a situation or experience that it regards as dangerous, but finds that this perceived danger is actually false, it has the potential to change. The memory of that change is stored in the VMPFC. From then on, it can modulate the activity of the amygdala when it is exposed to such experiences. So when we are exposed to the same situation, we will no longer ascribe a danger to it. In such cases, the amygdala is modulated by the pathways between it and the VMPFC. Earlier we saw this process in action, when dealing with the world of panic attacks and in managing phobias. Dr Jim used such experiential-flooding-exposure techniques to reshape the amygdala's memory at those key moments.

In other cases, the PFC and amygdala will store up irrational beliefs and negative emotional memories. Social anxiety and general anxiety are good examples. The stronger these pathways become, the more often they will end up being triggered. The good news is that the opposite is also true. If, through CBT or mindfulness, we assist the amygdala and PFC to challenge or disem-power irrational beliefs and emotional memories, negative pathways weaken as more positive ones take over.

For those who suffer from anxiety, this is an important message. If we can reshape our thinking and learn how to challenge our behaviour, we can reshape our amygdala, our PFC and the pathways or circuits in between them. It is fascinating that we can use our brain to change our mind and our mind to reshape our brain, in a never-ending loop which can be positive or negative.

Why Is Anxiety so Poorly Understood and Managed?

We tend to ignore the importance of what is happening in the brain of the person with anxiety. So there is a significant risk of misunderstanding and even dismissing it.

We can fail to understand just how powerful the amygdala really is, and how, on occasion, it can operate almost independently of the PFC. If you try to simply think your way out of a panic attack or a phobia, you are doomed to failure. This is because you are trying to address the PFC's role, when it is often a partial or complete bystander.

Therapy might tend to focus on a person's past, looking for the cause of the anxiety. This does little to help the person deal with their anxiety difficulties in the present.

Anxiety conditions triggered primarily by the PFC must be dealt with differently than those triggered primarily by the amygdala. Panic attacks and phobias, for example, will be treated differently than general anxiety disorder – or even social anxiety or PTSD.

Because the amygdala is always involved – in either a primary or secondary role – we must develop separate strategies to deal with it. Such approaches to dealing with the amygdala may not be sufficient to deal with PFC-driven forms of anxiety.

The amygdala has its own emotional memory, independent of the PFC or other parts of the brain. This memory is strengthened every time something it perceives as unpleasant or dangerous happens.

This is why acute anxiety conditions such as panic attacks and phobias get progressively more entrenched if we don't learn to deal with them early. It is a waste of time trying to think or even talk our way out of such emotional fear memories. The amygdala does not do routine talk therapy, so other approaches have to be tried to settle down this unruly organ.

But we do know that all the parts of our brain that are involved in anxiety – our PFC, our amygdala and the pathways between them – are completely neuroplastic, and therefore can be reset. This is best done through CBT techniques, with the assistance of some other therapies, such as mindfulness. We will discuss these later.

To deal with your anxiety, we have to reshape your thinking and behaviour. This will help us to achieve the ultimate goal – that of reshaping the parts of your brain causing the problem.

Now let's explain how it is possible to reshape the anxiety pathways in your brain.

How Therapies Can Neuroplastically Reshape Our Brain

It is useful to examine how various forms of therapy mentioned so far can assist us in reshaping our anxiety structures and pathways.

Lifestyle

Exercise

In previous books, I have dealt at length with the multiple positive effects of exercise on the brain in depression. In relation to anxiety, regular exercise has been found to calm the amygdala – and particularly the lateral section – by reducing the activity of serotonin receptors that are felt to be of importance in anxiety. Since the amygdala is involved in almost all forms of anxiety, the message is clear: if you are having significant physical symptoms due to the amygdala firing, then regular, sustained daily exercise can play an important role in reshaping this organ to be calmer. This will, in turn, reduce these often uncomfortable symptoms.

Nutrition

This is important, as high sugar hits and caffeine – in the form of coffee or Coke – will end up increasing activity in our amygdala, the organ we are most interested in calming down.

Sleep

The more our sleep is interfered with, the more our amygdala becomes over-active. This can be a vicious circle. The more anxious we become, the more activated our amygdala becomes. This activates our stress system, and we become more hyped up, which further interferes with our sleep. Worry, so common in anxiety, can also indirectly hype up our amygdala. This, in turn, revs up our stress system, which keeps us awake.

This is why in GAD, we must avoid dependence on alcohol, caffeine and other such substances, as these will only worsen the problem.

Good sleep hygiene is important. Later, in one of our cases, we will look at the effect of anxiety on our amygdala when we are sleeping and dreaming, and how it leads to early morning physical symptoms.

Overall, the message is clear: if we have difficulties with sleep, they will increase our amygdala-based anxiety, and if we are very anxious, this will interfere with our sleep. So trying to break this cycle is important in assisting our brain reshape anxiety pathways.

Challenging Technology

If ever there were devices created to keep our amygdala constantly wired, they are the mobile phone and similar devices. Many of us are spending large parts of the day and night checking and rechecking these devices, minute by minute in some cases. This leads to our amygdala and SNS being on constant, vigilant standby. And then we struggle to understand why we are experiencing so many physical symptoms of anxiety. This is particularly relevant to our adolescents, who live and breathe their mobile phones.

We are allowing these devices into our bedrooms, and our children's bedrooms. This not only increases such amygdala and SNS hypervigilance, it disrupts our sleep. All of this behaviour has a detrimental effect on the well-being of our amygdala. Is it any wonder that self-harm is present in almost one in every ten of our school-going adolescents? We are not only assisting them through the world of technology to become more anxious, but also not giving them the skills to know what to do when this anxiety inevitably arrives.

These devices are also giving our PFCs continuous opportunities to worry, ruminate and visually catastrophise, often about seemingly 'critically important' issues. (These are often of little real consequence to our lives.) This leads to further indirect stimulation of our already harassed amygdala. This particularly affects our adolescents but, if we are honest, it affects us adults as well. We are flooding our brains with too much information. We are not getting enough down time with this relentless barrage.

If we suffer from anxiety and want to start reshaping our brains and minds, we need to put this monster back in its box by introducing some technology hygiene into our lives. Learning where the off or mute button is situated is not a bad start, as is reviewing our addiction to social media such as Facebook and Twitter.

Realistically, we just need to retrain ourselves as to how, when and where we use these devices. This requires being honest with ourselves and making the real behavioural changes. All families would benefit from technology being placed in a central location at night, out of the bedroom – and switching off Internet access. Remember that a lack of sleep is a major cause of our amygdala being twitchy and irritable. So, mind your amygdala and turn off these devices at night.

Breathing Exercises

We know that regular breathing exercises calm down the amygdala. They also activate our PNS, which can counteract the SNS-driven physical symptoms prompted by the amygdala. This can be very helpful, although not in panic attacks.

Muscle-relaxation Exercises

These have an effect similar to that of breathing exercises. If taught by appropriately trained therapists, they can have a calming effect on the amygdala through the same mechanisms.

Mindfulness

Let's take a moment to look at the neuroscience of mindfulness. In previous books, I have dealt with the practice and neuroscience of mindfulness, and the work of Richard J. Davidson and Jon Kabat-Zinn, in particular. In this section, I will confine myself to the role of mindfulness in anxiety.

Mindfulness and meditation that focuses on breathing, in particular, directly calms down the amygdala, with an associated increase in our PNS, whose job it is to counteract the amygdala's constant stimulation of the SNS. So if our amygdala is buzzing too much, and we are having a lot of SNS-driven secondary physical symptoms, then mindfulness can soothe this unruly organ. We need to be doing regular, short daily mindfulness exercises.

The more significant effects on the brain are probably more indirect and focus on the effects of mindfulness on particular sections of the PFC, particularly the anterior cingulate cortex or ACC (Attention Box) and the VMPFC. Both – particularly the latter – have important neurocircuitry links to the amygdala. In many cases of anxiety, the VMPFC is overstimulating the amygdala through these connections. Mindfulness, through its effects on the above PFC sections, when practised regularly, ends up disengaging these links. This is why it should be part of the total package when dealing with anxiety, as it is teaching the brain to disengage from the amygdala, which, after all, is the major source of physical symptoms with this condition.

Mindfulness also comes into its own when we are unable to let go, despite all CBT assistance, of irrational obsessive thoughts, as in OCD and some forms of GAD that have to do with control.

Drug Therapy

It is worthwhile to briefly examine the effects of certain drugs on our amygdala and PFC.

Often, minor tranquillisers like diazepam (Valium) and Xanax are used to try to calm down acute and chronic anxiety. But they can end up inhibiting attempts to reset our amygdala. Apart from obvious risks, such as addiction, the use of these drugs, we now know, will inhibit more appropriate therapies such as CBT, which may assist us in banishing some of these conditions altogether. This is because most of the neuroplastic changes to reshape our amygdala take place in the lateral amygdala, and these drugs block this from happening.

The use of SSRIs, which act on our serotonin system and are more commonly associated with the treatment of depression, has been shown to be of assistance in more serious forms of anxiety, particularly OCD and severe forms of PTSD and GAD. In such situations, SSRIs can predispose the amygdala to be more sensitive to talk therapies. In this, their effect has some similarity to their role in depression. But they do have side effects, and, in the majority of cases, are neither necessary nor even particularly useful in the management of most anxiety conditions. The better long-term approach to anxiety disorders – apart from severe PTSD, OCD or GAD with depression – is to use talk therapies.

Talk Therapy

Any successful form of talk therapy in the management of most anxiety disorders must involve some form of exposure or behavioural challenging of our amygdala, the driver of the physical symptoms so prevalent in them.

Treatment, involving exposure of this form, is essential in panic attacks, phobias, social anxiety and OCD. Here, the person is exposed to the trigger and the associated amygdala-driven emotions of fear and panic plus the associated physical symptoms. This can be done gradually or 'full-on'. Current evidence suggests that the amygdala handles the latter approach better.

This is because it is the lateral amygdala that is most capable of changing its emotional memory of fear. It is best reshaped by exposing it to the danger-associated emotion and physical symptoms. Doing this experientially helps it to learn that the trigger and danger are not actually real. It then learns to downplay its previous emotional memory of the trigger. It can be more uncomfortable, but is much more effective and often significantly shortens the time it takes to deal with these conditions.

All CBT techniques, to be successful in the treatment of anxiety disorders, will involve some elements of exposure behavioural techniques.

Apart from applying these behavioural changes to the amygdala, CBT also has the power to challenge and change the PFC, and thus reshape the brain itself. It does so by challenging many of the irrational beliefs and catastrophic visualisations which drive the cognitive side of anxiety disorders such as GAD, social anxiety, PTSD and OCD and some phobias. Many of these cognitive techniques aimed at the PFC will, if successful, be subsequently 'remembered' by the hippocampus. We know that pathways from the VMPFC to the amygdala are also reshaped if these techniques are effective.

How Does CBT Work in Our Brain?

To understand CBT, it is helpful to realise that all of us develop and consolidate particular mind/brain pathways, which, as we age, become more fixed. Under pressure, these pathways are triggered, and we will think, feel and behave in certain constant patterns, some of which may lead to distressing consequences.

Some may become anxious and develop panic attacks. Others may find themselves sinking into the world of negative thinking and depression. CBT offers a structured method of reshaping these pathways, breaking the unhelpful cycle leading to the above. This cannot be done instantly, but, with persistence, it can transform lives. I like the following allegory (see Figure 14).

Frank, a farmer for twenty years, uses a particular track through a field to reach his cattle. The field is full of high grass and the path is a disaster – full of ruts and water-filled potholes. He regularly falls, arriving at his destination with cuts and bruises, sometimes wet, usually cursing and swearing. He has become resigned to his fate, and knows that the worse the weather, the more inconvenienced he will be.

One day, a wise neighbour brings Frank over to another part of the field and suggests creating a new route. Frank, although bothered at having to wade his way through the long grass, decides to give it a go. It is difficult the first time, but he arrives unscathed. Day by day, with the help of his friend, he takes this new path. After ten days, the grass is beginning to lie down; by day fifty, a track is appearing; by day one hundred, a new pathway has been formed. The old path becomes overgrown, and Frank no longer arrives at his destination bleeding, wet and bruised. He has made a useful new pathway.

The story doesn't end there either, for the new path Frank has formed will in time become, like an old coat, worn and tattered, to be discarded. It will become the old path, and he will have to reshape new ones in the future. Life is a journey, and it is all about finding new pathways, as the one track is rarely sufficient. Pathway changes will often be necessary, and we have to develop the ability to adapt.

These are the skills we learn in CBT. Sometimes we develop unhelpful and unhealthy mind/brain pathways, which lead to mental distress, but we can see no other way forward. With the help of a therapist, we, like Frank, can take those first tentative steps towards making new pathways, gradually breaking down resistance to their formation, ending up with new, healthy tracks, and letting the old ones fade away. Although the new tracks will greatly improve our lives, there may come a time when have to make further pathway changes. If we learn the appropriate skills, this should not be a problem.

We now know that CBT uses the more logical, cognitive sections in our brain. It should therefore be no surprise that the DPFC (the logic box) – which is the cold, logical and analytical part of the brain – is shown, on scanning, to be particularly active in CBT. This makes sense, as we are attempting to rationalise our emotions by examining the thinking behind them, and their behavioural consequences. The DPFC works closely with the hippocampus (the memory box), as we have to be able to memorise the changes made when applying CBT to conditions such as anxiety and depression. One other key player is the anterior cingulate cortex or ACC (attention box), another section of our PFC. This is the area of the brain where we learn to reappraise emotions.

When analysing and challenging the visualisations, ruminations and catastrophising behind anxiety, for example, we will be recruiting these three areas of the brain to carry out these tasks. If successful, there will be neuroplastic changes in these areas and the pathways between them. There will also be slower secondary changes to the amygdala.

We must remember that the DPFC is theoretically the boss in the brain, but generally leaves most of the emotional monitoring of the amygdala to its two vice chairmen, the VMPFC and OFC. But it does have close links with them and through these connections exerts, more indirectly, an effect on the amygdala. This is often called by neuroscientists a top-down approach to calming the emotional maelstroms created by the amygdala in anxiety and depression.

★

The power of these approaches to reshape anxiety pathways cannot be over-estimated. (Although they must be combined with the lifestyle changes already detailed.) It therefore should not be surprising that in this book I have been promoting CBT techniques – and where appropriate, mindfulness – to help reshape our minds and our brains.

We truly are extraordinary beings. We not only create in our own brains pathways that can generate anxiety, but we can also use the same brain to reshape our mind. And this, in turn, allows us to reshape the very brain which created the problems to start with.

15.
A Final Message

There will be many who will read through this book and think to themselves, *It can't be this easy.* But we have overcomplicated the world of anxiety.

- Anxiety is, in general, created by functional overactivity of the amygdala or the PFC or malfunctioning neurocircuitry between the two.

- These malfunctions occur due to a combination of genetic and environmental factors in our childhood, adolescence and young-adult life, but may manifest themselves at different ages and phases of our lives.

- These circuits are all neuroplastic, and therefore capable of change and adaptability. This concept lies at the heart of this book.

- The brain and the mind are in a constant feedback loop, so we can use our mind to reshape our brain's pathways. We can also use our logical brain to examine and challenge what is going on in our mind.

- It is this powerful interactive capacity that allows us to really change the above structures and circuits.

- The amygdala must be seen as the most important player, either directly or indirectly, in anxiety conditions – particularly in panic attacks.

- The amygdala is also the main source of the uncomfortable physical symptoms that we experience in anxiety and panic.

- The amygdala has to be seen as an organ that does not play by the usual rules. So talk therapy, in its customary forms, will not be effective in reshaping it.

- The modern neuroscientific and clinical approach is to challenge the amygdala – with flooding techniques, in particular. Exercise and mindfulness are also felt to be of benefit.

- The PFC has the job of trying to modulate or calm down the amygdala, but, in most anxiety conditions, it is struggling to keep this headstrong organ in place.

- The PFC is also the source of much of the catastrophising, ruminating and worrying so prevalent in anxiety conditions such as GAD and social anxiety.

- Because it is in regular contact with the amygdala, the PFC, when misbehaving in anxiety conditions, sets off the amygdala, which explains why we have so many physical symptoms associated with these conditions.

- The modern approach to the PFC's role in anxiety conditions is to use talk therapies such as CBT to try to challenge the PFC's misinterpretations of what is happening to us in our lives, which lead to such conditions. In a small number of cases, drug therapy can be of assistance in this process.

- If you can use the various approaches given in this book and apply them to your life, you have the power to reshape, through your mind, the amygdala, the PFC and the pathways between them.

- This can reshape your brain and lead to a significant reduction in the physical symptoms so dominant in anxiety.

- If you can reshape your mind and your brain in anxiety and panic, you will enter a new world.

- My final message is to be kind to yourself. Learn to unconditionally love and accept yourself for who you are. Become a true Raggy Doll, which is the real secret to good mental health.

Appendix:
Self-Help Groups

Aware

Aware is a voluntary organisation established in 1985 to support those experiencing depression and their families. Aware endeavours to create a society where people with mood disorders and their families are understood and supported, and to obtain the resources to enable them to defeat depression. Weekly support group meetings at approximately fifty locations nationwide, including Northern Ireland, offer peer support and provide factual information, and enable people to gain the skills they need to help them cope with depression. Aware's 'Beat the Blues' educational programme is run in secondary schools.

Helpline: 1890 303 302

support@aware.ie | www.aware.ie | 01 661 7211

72 Lower Leeson Street, Dublin 2

Samaritans

Samaritans was started in 1953 in London by a young vicar called Chad Varah; the first branch in the Republic of Ireland opened in Dublin in 1970.

Samaritans provides a twenty-four-hour-a-day confidential service offering emotional support for people who are experiencing feelings of distress or despair, including those which may lead to suicide.

Helpline: 116 123

jo@samaritans.org | www.samaritans.org

Grow

Established in Ireland in 1969, GROW is Ireland's largest mutual-help organisation in the area of mental health. It is anonymous, nondenominational, confidential and free. No referrals are necessary. GROW aims to achieve self-activation through mutual help. Its members are enabled, over time, to craft a step-by-step recovery or personal-growth plan, and to develop leadership skills that will help others.

Helpline: 1 890 474 474

info@grow.ie | www.grow.ie

Barrack Street, Kilkenny

Irish Association of Suicidology

The Irish Association of Suicidology aims to facilitate communication between clinicians, volunteers, survivors and researchers in all matters relating to suicide and suicidal behaviour; to promote awareness of the problems of suicide and suicidal behaviour in the general public by holding conferences and workshops and through the communication of relevant materials through the media; to ensure that the public is better informed about suicide prevention; to support and encourage relevant research; and to encourage and support the formation of groups to help those bereaved by suicide.

01 667 4900 | office@ias.ie | www.ias.ie

16 New Antrim Street, Castlebar, County Mayo

Console

Console is a registered charity supporting and helping people bereaved through suicide. They respect each individual's unique journey through the grieving process following their tragic loss. Console promotes positive mental health within the community in an effort to reduce the high number of attempted suicides and deaths through suicide.

Helpline: 1800 247 247

info@console.ie | www.console.ie | 01 610 2638

Console House, 4 Whitethorn Grove, Celbridge, County Kildare

Rainbows Ireland

Rainbows was founded in America by Suzy Yehl Marta to help children and adults who have been bereaved through parental death, separation or divorce to work through the grieving process which follows any significant loss. The charity provides a safe setting in which children can talk through their feelings with other children who are experiencing similar situations.

ask@ www.rainbowsireland.ie | www.rainbowsireland.ie | 01 473 4175

Loreto Centre, Crumlin Road, Dublin 12

ChildLine

ChildLine, a service run by the ISPCC, seeks to empower and support children using the medium of telecommunications and information technology. The service is designed for all children and young people up to the age of eighteen in Ireland.

Helpline: 1800 66 66 66

Cuan Mhuire

Cuan Mhuire is a charitable organisation founded by Sister Consilio Fitzgerald in 1965. It provides a comprehensive structured, abstinence-based residential programme dealing with alcohol, gambling and drug addiction in the north and south of Ireland, with centres in Athy, Bruree, Coolarne, Farnanes and Newry.

cuanmhuire@gmail.com | www.cuanmhuire.ie

Gamblers Anonymous Ireland

Holds self-help meetings for gamblers and those close to them.

Dublin 01 872 1133

Cork 087 285 9522

Galway 086 349 4450

Tipperary 085 783 1045

Waterford 087 185 0294

info@gamblersanonymous.ie | gamblersanonymous.ie

Al-Anon/Alateen

Self-help meetings for spouses and teenagers (aged twelve to seventeen) affected by those addicted to alcohol.

Helpline: 01 873 2699

info@al-anon-ireland.org | www.alanon.ie | 01 8783624

5 Capel Street, Dublin 1

Narcotics Anonymous

Self-help groups for those addicted to drugs.

na@ireland.org | na-ireland.org | 01 672 8000

20 Bride Street, Dublin 8

The Irish Council for Psychotherapy

Produces a directory of psychotherapists working in Ireland.
psychotherapy-ireland.com | 01 902 3819
13 Upper Leeson Street, Dublin 4

No Panic

No Panic is a charity which aims to facilitate the relief and rehabilitation of people suffering from panic attacks, phobias, obsessive compulsive disorders and other related anxiety disorders, including tranquilliser withdrawal, and to provide support to sufferers and their families and carers. Founded by Colin M. Hammond in the UK, this group has extended its activities to Ireland, where it is organised by therapist Caroline McGuigan.

Helpline: +44 844 967 4848
Youth Helpline: +44 175 384 0393
admin@nopanic.org.uk | nopanic.org.uk | +44 195 268 0460

Headstrong

Headstrong is an initiative spearheaded by psychologist Dr Tony Bates, working with communities in Ireland to ensure that young people aged twelve to twenty-five are better supported to achieve mental health and well-being. Headstrong was set up in response to an identified need to address the issue of youth mental health in Ireland. It is an independent, non-profit NGO. It acts as an expert partner to the Health Services Executive and other people and services concerned with providing mental health and well-being support to young people in Ireland. Headstrong views mental health as existing along a continuum spanning general well-being to distress to mental-health disorders that require specialised care. Headstrong's Jigsaw Programme aims to change the way communities in Ireland think about mental health and support young people in the process.

info@headstrong.ie | www.headstrong.ie | 01 472 7010

Bibliography

Allman, J. M., A. Hakeem, J. M. Erwin, E. Nimchinsky and P. Hof (2001), 'The anterior cingulate cortex. The evolution of an interface between emotion and cognition', *Annals of the New York Academy of Sciences*, 935 (1), 107-17.

Anderson, E. and G. Shivakumar (2013), 'Effects of exercise and physical activity on anxiety', *Frontiers in Psychiatry*, 4: 1-4.

Anderson, M. C., K. N. Ochsner, B. Kuhl, J. Cooper, E. Robertson, S. W. Gabrieli, G. H. Glover, J. D. E. Gabrieli (2004), 'Neural systems underlying the suppression of unwanted memories', *Science*, 303, 232-35.

Arnsten, F. T. and R. M. Shansky (2004), 'Adolescence: Vulnerable period for stress-induced prefrontal cortical function?', *Annals of the New York Academy of Sciences*, 1021 (1), 143-47.

Asbahr, F. R. (2004), 'Anxiety disorders in childhood and adolescence: clinical and neurobiological aspects', *Jornal de Pediatria*, 80 (2), 28-34.

Barry, H. P. (2007). *Flagging the Problem: A New Approach to Mental Health*. Dublin: Liberties Press.

Barry, H. P. (2010). *Flagging Stress: Toxic Stress and How to Avoid It*. Dublin: Liberties Press.

Barry, H. P. (2013a). *Flagging Depression: A Practical Guide*. Dublin: Liberties Press.

Barry, H. P. (2013b). *Flagging the Therapy: Pathways Out of Depression and Anxiety*. Dublin: Liberties Press.

Barry, H. P. and E. Murphy. (2015). *Flagging the Screenager: Guiding your Child*

Through Adolescence and Young Adulthood. Dublin: Liberties Press.

Bandelow, B., D. Wedekind and T. Leon (2007), 'Pregabalin for the treatment of general anxiety disorder: a novel pharmacologic intervention', *Expert Review of Neurotherapeutics*, 7 (7), 769-81.

Banks, S.J, K.T. Eddy, M. Angstadt, N.J, Pradeep and K. L. Phan (2007), 'Amygdala frontal connectivity during emotion regulation', *Social Cognitive and Affective Neuroscience* Advance Access published 21 July 2007.

Bender, E. (2004), 'Brain data reveal why psychotherapy works', Psychiatric-*News*, 39 (9), 34-76.

Bukalo, O., R. P. Courtney, S. Silverstein, C. Brehm, N. D. Hartley and N. Whittle et al (2015), 'Prefrontal inputs to the amygdala instruct fear extinction memory formation', Sci. Adv. 1, e1500251.

Canli, T. and K. P. Lesch (2007), 'Long story short: the serotonin transporter in emotion regulation and social cognition', *Nature Neuroscience*, 10 (9), 1103-9.

Canli, T., M. Qui, K. Omura, E. Congdon, B. W. Haas, Z. Amin, M. J. Herrman, R. T. Constable and K. P. Lesch (2006), 'Neural correlates of epigenesis', *Proceedings of the National Academy of Sciences of the USA*, 103 (43), 16033-38.

Charney, D. and W.C. Drevets, (2002) 'Neurobiological basis of anxiety disorders', *Neuropsychopharmacology: The Fifth Generation of Progress* (901-930). Edited by Kenneth L. Davis, Dennis Charney, Joseph T. Coyle, and Charles Nemeroff. American College of Neuropsychopharmacology.

Crane, R. and D. Elias (2006), 'Being with what is – mindfulness practice for counsellors and psychotherapists', *Therapy Today*, 17 (10), 31.

David, L. (2006), *Using CBT in general practice*, Bloxham: Scion.

Davidson, R. J. (2004), 'What does the prefrontal cortex 'do' in affect: perspectives on frontal EEG asymmetry research', *Biological Psychology*, 67, 219-233.

Davidson, R. J. (2001), 'Toward a biology of personality and emotion', *Annals of the New York Academy of Sciences*, 935 (1), 191-207.

Delgado, M, R., K. I. Nearing, J. E. LeDoux and E. A. Phelps (2008), 'Neural circuitry underlying the regulation of conditioned fear and its relation to extinction' *Neuron* Vol. 59, 829 –838.

Diego, C., A. Siracusano, P. Calabresi and G. Bernardi (2005), 'Removing pathogenic memories: a neurobiology of psychotherapy', *Molecular*.

Doidge, N. (2008), *The brain that changes itself*, London: Penguin Books.

Etkin, A. and T. D. Wager (2007), 'Functional neuroimaging of anxiety: a meta-analysis of emotional processing in PTSD, social anxiety disorder, and specific phobia', *American Journal of Psychiatry*, 164, 1476-88.

Etkin, A., C. Pittenger, J. Polan and R. Kandal (2005), 'Towards a neurobiology of psychotherapy: basic science and clinical applications', *Journal of Neuropsychiatry-Clinical Neuroscience*, 17, 145-58

Farb, N. A. S., Z. V. Segal, H. Mayberg, J. Bean, D. McKeon, Z. Fatima and A. K. Anderson (2007), 'Attending to the present: mindfulness meditation reveals distinct neural modes of self-reference', *Social, Cognitive and Affective Neuroscience*, 2 (4), 313-22.

Fuchs, T. (2004), 'Neurobiology and psychotherapy: an emerging dialogue', *Current Opinion in Psychiatry*, 17, 479-485.

Fyer, A. J. (1998), 'Current approaches to etiology and pathophysiology of specific phobia', *Biological Psychiatry*, 44 (12), 1295-1304.

Gabbard, G. (2000), 'A neurobiologically informed perspective on psychotherapy', *British Journal of Psychiatry*, 177, 117-122.

Gage, F. H. (2003), 'Brain repair yourself', *Scientific American*.

Goldapple, K. (2004), 'Modulation of cortical-limbic pathways in major depression: treatment-specific effects of cognitive behaviour therapy', *Archives of General Psychiatry*, 61, 34-41.

Goleman, D. (2006), *Social intelligence*, London: Arrow Books.

Goossens, L., S. Sunaert, R. Peeters, E. J. L. Griez and K. R. J. Schruers (2007), 'Amygdala hyperfunction in phobic fear normalises after exposure', *Biological Psychiatry*, 62, 1119-25.

Graeff, F. G. and C. M. Del-Ben (2008), 'Neurobiology of panic disorder: from animal models to brain neuroimaging', *Neuroscience and Behavioural Reviews*, 32 (7), 1326-35.

Graybiel, A. M. and S. L. Rauch (2000), 'Toward a neurobiology review of obsessive-compulsive disorder', *Neuron*, 28, 343-7.

Greenwood, B. N., P.V. Strong, A.B. Loughridge, H.E. Day, P.J. Clark, A. Mika, et al (2012), '5HT2C receptors in the basolateral amygdala and dorsal striatum are a novel target for the anxiolytic and antidepressant effects of exercise', *Plos One*, 7:e46118.

Guoshi, L. and T. Amano, D. Pare and S. N Satish (2011) 'Impact of infralimbic inputs on intercalated amygdala neurons: a biophysical modeling study' *Learn. Mem.*, 18: 226-240.

Harrison, E. (2003), *The 5-minute meditator*, London: Piatkus Books.

Holzela, B. K, E. A. Hogea, D. N. Grevea, T. Garda, J. D. Creswellc, K. W. Brownd, L. F. Barretta, C. Schwartza, D. Vaitlb and S. W. Lazara, (2013), 'Neural mechanisms of symptom improvements in general anxiety disorder following mindfulness training', *NeuroImage*: 2, 448–458.

Hopkins, M. E., Davis, F. C., Vantieghem, M. R., Whalen, P. J., & Bucci, D. J. (2012). 'Differential effects of acute and regular physical exercise on cognition and affect', *Neuroscience*, 215, 59-68.

Jha, A. P., J. Krompinger and M. J. Baime (2007), 'Mindfulness training modifies subsystems', *Cognitive, Affective and Behavioural Neuroscience*, 7 (2), 109-19.

Kabat-Zinn, Jon (2008), *Wherever you go, there you are*, London: Piatkus. (2008), *Full catastrophe living*, London: Piatkus.

Kandel, E. R. and L. R. Squire (2001), 'Neuroscience: breaking down scientific barriers to the study of brain and mind', *Annals of the New York Academy of Sciences*, 935 (1), 118-35.

Kandel, E. R. (1999), 'Biology and the future of psychoanalysis: a new intellectual framework for psychiatry revisited', *American Journal of Psychiatry*, 156, 505-24.

Kim, S. H. and S. Hamann (2007), 'Neural correlates of positive and negative emotion regulation', *Journal of Cognitive Neuroscience*, 19 (5), 776-98.

Kim, M.J and P. J. Whalen (2009), 'The structural integrity of an amygdala – prefrontal pathway predicts trait anxiety', *Journal of Neuroscience*, 29(37):11614-11618.

Kim, M. J., D. G. Gee, R. A. Loucks, F.C. Davis and P. J. Whalen, (2011), 'Anxiety dissociates dorsal and ventral medial prefrontal cortex functional connectivity with the amygdala at rest', *Cerebral Cortex*, 21, 1667 1673.

Krystal, J. H. (2007), 'Neuroplasticity as a target for the pharmacotherapy of psychiatric disorders: New opportunities for synergy with psychotherapy', *Biological Psychiatry*, 62, 833-4.

Kumari, V. (2006), 'Do psychotherapies produce neurobiological effects?', *Acta Neuropsychiatrica*, 18, 61-70.

LeDoux, J. E. (2015). *Anxious: using the brain to understand and treat fear and anxiety*. New York: Viking.

LeDoux, J. E. (2008), 'Amygdala', *Scholarpedia*, 3(4):2698.

LeDoux J. E. (2003), 'The emotional brain, fear, and the amygdala', *Cellular and Molecular Neurobiology*, 23, Nos. 4/5.

Li, D., P. Chokka and P. Tibbo (2001), 'Towards an integrative understanding of social phobia', *Journal of Psychiatry and Neuroscience*, 26 (3), 190-202.

Liggan, D. Y. and J. Jay (1999), 'Some neurobiological aspects of psychotherapy: a review', *Journal of Psychotherapy Practice and Research*, 8 (2), 103-14.

Maron, E. and J. Shlik (2006), 'Serotonin function in panic disorder: important, but why?', *Neuropsychopharmacology*, 31, 1-11.

Martinowich, K., H. Manji and B. Lu (2007), 'New insights into BDNF function in depression and anxiety', *Nature Neuroscience*, 10, 1089-93.

Mathew, S. J., R. B. Price and D. S. Charney (2008), 'Recent advances in the neurobiology of anxiety disorders: implications for novel therapeutics', *American Journal of Medical Genetics*, 148, 89-98.

Mayberg, H. S. (2003), 'Modulating dysfunctional limbic-cortical circuits in depression: towards development of brain-based algorithms for diagnosis and optimised treatment', *British Medical Bulletin*, 65, 193-207.

Mezzasalma, M. A., A. M. Valença, F. L. Lopes, I. Nascimento, W. A. Zinb and A. E. Nardia (2004), 'Neuroanatomy of panic disorder', *Rev Bras Pisquiatr* 2004; 26 (3): 202-6.

McGaugh, J. L. (2002), 'Memory consolidation and the amygdala: a systems perspective', *Trends in Neurosciences*, 25 (9), 456-80.

McMahon E. M. , Reulbach U. Corcoran, P. Keeley , H. S., Perry I. J. and Arensman E. (2010), 'Factors associated with deliberate selfharm among Irish adolescents', *Psychological Medicine*, 40 (11), 1811-1819.

Milad, R. and S. L. Raunch (2007), 'The role of the orbitofrontal cortex in anxiety disorders', *Annals of the New York Academy of Sciences*, 1121 (1), 546-61.

Moffitt, T. E., H. Harrington, A. Caspi, J. Kim-Cohen, D. Goldberg, A. M. Gregory and R. Poulton (2007), 'Depression and generalised anxiety disorder', *Archives of General Psychiatry*, 64 (6), 651-60.

Montgomery, S. A. (2006), 'Pregabalin for the treatment of generalised anxiety disorder', *Expert Opinion on Pharmacotherapy*, 7 (15), 2139-54.

Morgane, P. J., J. R. Galler and D. J. Mokler (2005), 'A review of systems and networks of the limbic forebrain/limbic midbrain', *Progress in Neurobiology*, 75, 143-60.

Moss, H. and A. R. Damasio (2001), 'Emotion, cognition, and the human brain', *New York Academy of Sciences*, 935, 98-100.

Murphy, E. (2009), 'The raggy doll club', *Forum*.

Murphy, E. (2013). *Five steps to happiness*. Dublin: Liberties Press.

Myers-Schulz, B. and M. Koenigs (2012), 'Functional anatomy of ventromedial prefrontal cortex: implications for mood and anxiety disorders', *Molecular Psychiatry*, 17, 132-141.

Nataraja, S. (2008). *The blissful brain*. London: Octopus Publishing Group Ltd.

Newport, D. J. and C. B. Nemeroff (2003), 'Neurobiology of post-traumatic stress disorder', *Focus*, 1 (3), 313-21.

Nutt, D. J. (2001), 'Neurobiological mechanisms in generalised anxiety disorder', *Journal of Clinical Psychiatry*, 62, 22-7.

Ochsner, K. N., R. R. Ray, B. Hughes, K. Mc Rae, J. C. Cooper, J. Weber, J. D. Gabrieli and J. J. Gross, (2009), 'Bottom-up and top-down processes in emotion generation', *Association for Psychological Science*, 20, 1322-1331.

Ochsner, K. N. and J. J. Gross (2005), 'The cognitive control of emotion', *Trends in Cognitive Sciences*, 9 (5), 242-9.

Ochsner, K. N., R. D. Ray, J. C. Cooper, E. R. Robertson, S. Chopra, J. D. Gabrieli and J. J. Gross (2004), 'For better or for worse: neural systems supporting the cognitive down- and up-regulation of negative emotion', *Neuroimage*, 23 (2), 483-99.

Ochsner, K. N., S. A. Bunge, J. J. Gross and J. D. Gabrieli (2002), 'Rethinking feelings: an fMRI study of the cognitive regulation of emotion', *Journal of Cognitive Neuroscience*, 14, 1215.

Martin E. I., K. J. Ressler, E. Binder and C. B. Nemeroff, (2009), 'The neurobiology of anxiety disorders: brain imaging, genetics, and psychoneuroendocrinology', *Psychiatr. Clin. North Am.* 32 (3): 549-575.

Paquette, V., J. Le'vesque, B. Mensour, J. Leroux, G. Beaudoin, P. Bourgouin (2003), 'Change the mind and you change the brain: effects of cognitive-behavioural therapy on the neural correlates of spider phobia', *Neuroimage*, 18, 401-9.

Phelps, E. A., M. R. Delgado, K. I. Nearing and J. E. LeDoux, (2004), 'Extinction learning in humans: role of the amygdala and vmPFC', *Neuron*, 43, 897-

905.

Phelps, E. A. and LeDoux, J. E. (2005), 'Contributions of the amygdala to emotion processing: from animal models to human behaviour', *Neuron*, 48, 175-187.

Phillips, M. L., W. C. Drevets, S. L. Rauch and R. Lame (2003), 'Neurobiology of emotion perception I: the neural basis of normal emotion perception', *Biological Psychiatry*, 54, 504-14.

Pilkington, K., G. Kirkwood, H. Rampes, M. Cummings and J. Richardson (2007), 'Acupuncture for anxiety and anxiety disorders – a systematic literature review', *Acupuncture in Medicine*, 25 (1-2), 1-10.

Pittman, C. M and Karle, E. M. (2015). *Rewire your anxious brain*. California: New Harbinger Publications Inc.

Rempel-Clower, N. L. (2007), 'Role of orbitofrontal cortex connections in emotion', *Annals of the New York Academy of Sciences*, 1121 (1), 72-86.

Reinecke, A., K. Thilo , N. Filippini, A. Croft and C. J. Harmer (2014), 'Predicting rapid response to cognitive-behavioural treatment for panic disorder: the role of hippocampus, insula, and dorsolateral prefrontal cortex', *Behav. Res. Ther.* 62: 120-8.

Reinecke, A., L. Waldenmaier, M. J. Cooper and C. J. Harmer, (2014), 'Changes in automatic threat processing precede and predict clinical changes with exposure-based cognitive-behaviour therapy for panic disorder', *Biol. Psychiatry*, 73 (11): 1064-70.

Ressler, K. J. and H. S. Mayberg (2007), 'Targeting abnormal neural circuits in mood and anxiety disorders: from the laboratory to the clinic', *Nature Neuroscience*, 10, 1116-24.

Roffman, J. L., C. D. Marci, D. M. Glick, D. D. Dougherty and S. L. Rauch (2005), 'Neuroimaging and the functional neuroanatomy of psychotherapy', *Psychological Medicine*, 35, 1385-98.

Roy, A. K., J. L. Fudge, C. Kelly, J. S.A. Perry, T. Daniele, C. Carlisi, B. Benson, F. X. Castellanos, M. P. Milham, D. S. Pine and M. Ernst, (2013) 'Intrinsic functional connectivity of amygdala-based networks in adolescent general anxiety disorder', *J. Am. Acad. Child Adolesc. Psychiatry*, 52(3): 290–299.

Rozeske, R. R., S. Valerio, F. Chaudun and C. Herry, (2015), 'Prefrontal neuronal circuits of contextual fear conditioning', *Genes, brain and behaviour*, 14 (1) 22-36.

Sapolsky, R. (2003), 'Taming stress', *Scientific American*.

Shin, L. M. and I. Liberzon (2010), 'The neurocircuitry of fear, stress, and anxiety disorders', *Neuropsychopharmacology*, 35(1): 169-191.

Somerville, L. H., H. Kim, T. Johnstone, A. L. Alexander and P. J. Whalen (2004), 'Human amygdala responses during presentation of happy and neutral faces: correlations with state anxiety', *Biological Psychiatry*, 55, 897-903.

Sotres-Bayon, F., C. K. Cain and J. E. LeDoux (2006), 'Brain mechanisms of fear extinction: historical perspectives on the contribution of prefrontal cortex', *Biological Psychiatry*, 60, 329-36.

Stein, D. J., H. G. Westenberg and M. R. Liebowitz (2002), 'Social anxiety disorder and general anxiety disorder: serotonergic and dopaminergic neurocircuitry', *Journal of Clinical Psychiatry*, 63 (6), 12-9.

Straube, T., M. Glauer, S. Dilger, H. Mentzel and W. H. R. Miltner (2006), 'Effects of cognitive-behavioural therapy on brain activation in specific phobia', *Neuroimage*, 29, 125-35.

Sussman, N. (2007), 'Functional neuroimaging of anxiety disorders: focus on the amygdala and insula', *Psychiatry Weekly*, 2 (40).

Tromp, Do. P. M., D. W. Grupe, D. J. Oathes, D. R. McFarlin, P. J. Hernandez, T. R. A. Kral et al. (2013), 'Reduced structural connectivity of a major frontolimbic pathway in general anxiety disorder', *Arch. Gen. Psychiatry*. 69(9): 925-934.

Van der Helm, E., J. Yao, S. Dutt, V. Rao, J. M. Salentin and M. P. Walker (2011), 'REM sleep depotentiates amygdala activity to previous emotional experiences', *Current Biology* 21, 2029-2032.

Van der Watt, G., J. Laugharne and A. Janca (2008), 'Complementary and alternative medicine in the treatment of anxiety and depression', *Current Opinion in Psychiatry*, 21 (1), 37-42.

Wykes, T., M. Brammer, J. Mellers, P. Bray, C. Reeder, C. Williams and J. Corner (2002), 'Effects on the brain of a psychological treatment: cognitive remediation therapy', *British Journal of Psychiatry*, 181, 144-52.

Williams, M., J. Teasdale, Z. Segal and J. Kabat-Zinn (2007). *The mindful way through depression*. New York: The Guildford Press.

Zeidan, F., K. T. Martucci, R.A. Kraft, J.G. Mc Haffie and R.C. Coghill (2014), 'Neural correlates of mindfulness meditation-related anxiety relief', *Soc. Cogn. Affect Neurosci.* 9 (6): 751-759.

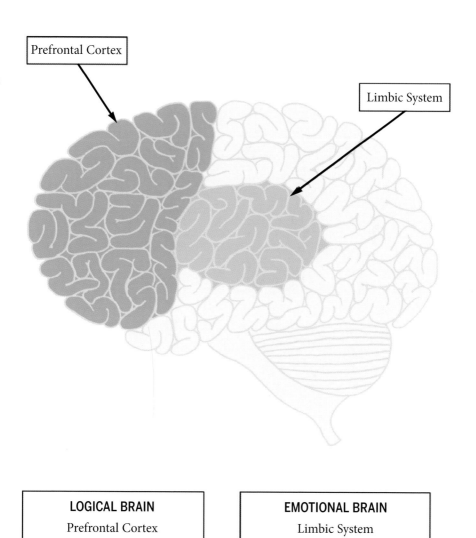

Figure 1: The Logical Brain and the Emotional Brain

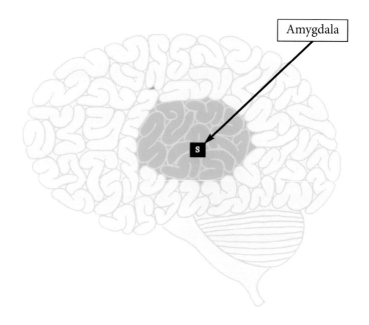

Figure 2: The Stress Box

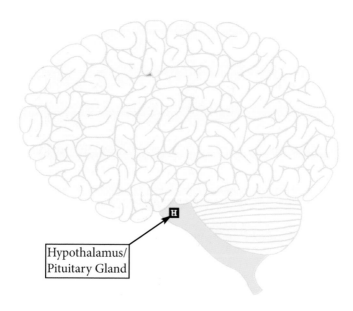

Figure 3: Hormone Control Box

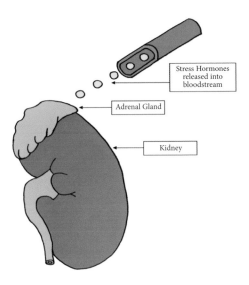

Figure 4: The Adrenal Gland

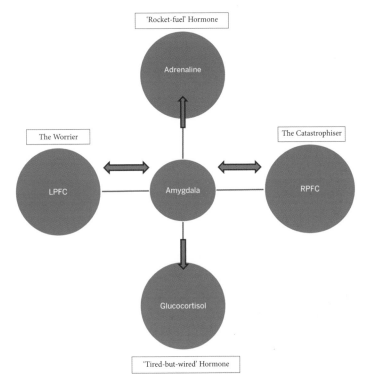

Figure 5: Key Players in Anxiety

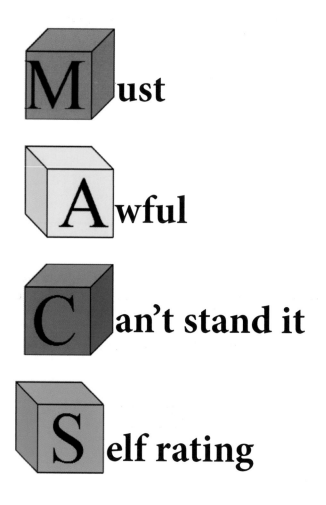

Must

Awful

Can't stand it

Self rating

Figure 6: The Big MACS

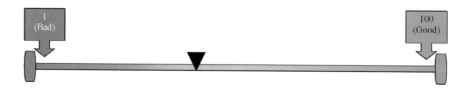

Figure 7: The Rating Scale

Based on the 1980s cartoon series *The Raggy Dolls*, created by
Melvyn Jacobson and produced for Yorkshire TV. Adapted for
therapeutic use by CBT therapist Enda Murphy

Figure 8: The Raggy Doll Club

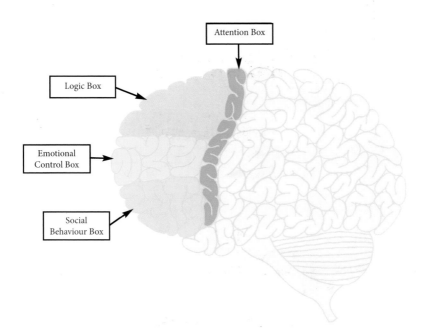

Figure 9: The Four Main Divisions of the Prefrontal Cortex

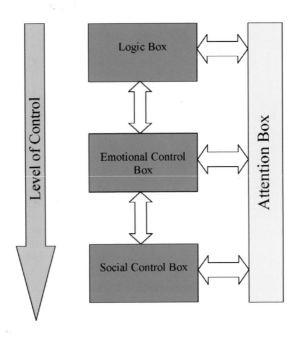

Figure 10: The Prefrontal Cortex's Hierarchical Structure

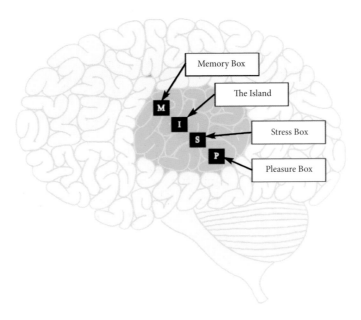

Figure 11: The Four Divisions of the Limbic System

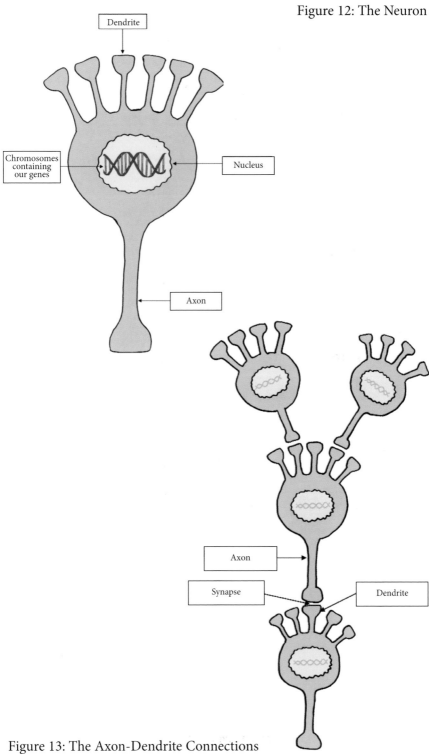

Figure 12: The Neuron

Figure 13: The Axon-Dendrite Connections

Figure 14: Frank's Path